IMAGINARY
INTERVIEWS

BY
W. D. HOWELLS

ILLUSTRATED

HARPER & BROTHERS PUBLISHERS
NEW YORK AND LONDON
1910

CONTENTS

IMAGINARY INTERVIEWS

iii

CONTENTS

OTHER ESSAYS

ILLUSTRATIONS

IMAGINARY INTERVIEWS

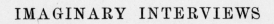

IMAGINARY INTERVIEWS

I

THE RESTORATION OF THE EASY CHAIR BY WAY OF INTRODUCTION

IT is not generally known that after forty-two years
of constant use the aged and honored movable which
now again finds itself put back in its old place in the
rear of *Harper's Magazine* was stored in the warehouse of a certain safety-deposit company, in the winter of 1892. The event which had then vacated the
chair is still so near as to be full of a pathos tenderly
personal to all readers of that magazine, and may not
be lightly mentioned in any travesty of the facts by
one who was thought of for the empty place. He,
before putting on the mask and mimic editorial robes
—for it was never the real editor who sat in the Easy
Chair, except for that brief hour when he took it to
pay his deep-thought and deep-felt tribute to its last
occupant—stood with bowed face and uncovered head
in that bravest and gentlest presence which, while it
abode with us here, men knew as George William
Curtis.

It was, of course, in one of the best of the fireproof
warehouses that the real editor had the Easy Chair
stored, and when the unreal editor went to take it

out of storage he found it without trouble in one of those vast rooms where the more valuable furniture and bric-à-brac are guarded in a special tutelage. If instinct had not taught him, he would have known it by its homely fashion, which the first unreal editor had suggested when he described it as an " old redbacked Easy Chair that has long been an ornament of our dingy office." That unreality was Mr. Donald G. Mitchell, the graceful and gracious Ik Marvel, dear to the old hearts that are still young for his *Dream Life* and his *Reveries of a Bachelor,* and never unreal in anything but his pretence of being the real editor of the magazine. In this disguise he feigned that he had " a way of throwing " himself back in the Easy Chair, " and indulging in an easy and careless overlook of the gossiping papers of the day, and in such chit-chat with chance visitors as kept him informed of the drift of the town talk, while it relieved greatly the monotony of his office hours." Not " bent on choosing mere gossip," he promised to be " on the watch for such topics or incidents as " seemed really important and suggestive, and to set them " down with all that gloss, and that happy lack of sequence, which make every - day talk so much better than every - day writing."

While the actual unreality stood thinking how perfectly the theory and practice of the Easy Chair for hard upon fifty years had been forecast in these words, and while the warehouse agent stood waiting his pleasure, the Easy Chair fetched a long, deep sigh. Sigh one must call the sound, but it was rather like that soft complaint of the woody fibres in a table which disembodied spirits are about to visit, and which continues to exhale from it till their peculiar vocabulary utters itself in a staccato of muffled taps. No one who has

2

heard that sound can mistake it for another, and the unreal editor knew at once that he confronted in the Easy Chair an animate presence.

"How long have I been here?" it asked, like one wakened from a deep sleep.

"About eight years," said the unreal editor.

"Ah, I remember," the Easy Chair murmured, and, as the unreal editor bent forward to pluck away certain sprays of foliage that clung to its old red back, it demanded, "What is that?"

"Some bits of holly and mistletoe."

"Yes," the Easy Chair softly murmured again. "The last essay he wrote in me was about Christmas. I have not forgotten one word of it all: how it began, how it went on, and how it ended! ' In the very promise of the year appears the hectic of its decay. . . . The question that we have to ask, forecasting in these summer days the coming of Christmas which already shines afar off, is this: whether while we praise Christmas as a day of general joy we take care to keep it so. . . . Thackeray describes a little dinner at the Timminses'. A modest couple make themselves miserable and spend all their little earnings in order to give a dinner to people for whom they do not care, and who do not care for them. . . . Christmas is made miserable to the Timminses because they feel that they must spend lavishly and buy gifts like their richer neighbors. . . . You cannot buy Christmas at the shops, and a sign of friendly sympathy costs little. . . . Should not the extravagance of Christmas cause every honest man and woman practically to protest by refusing to yield to the extravagance?' There!" the Easy Chair broke off from quoting, "that was Curtis! The kind and reasonable mood, the righteous conscience incarnate in the studied art, the charming literary allusion for the sake of the unliterary lesson, the genial philosophy—

> 'not too good
> For human nature's daily food'—

the wisdom alike of the closet and the public square, the large patience and the undying hopefulness! Do you think," the Easy Chair said, with a searching severity one would not have expected of it, " that you are fit to take his place?"

In evasion of this hard question the unreal editor temporized with the effect of not having heard it. " I believe that he and Mr. Mitchell were the only writers of your papers till Mr. Alden wrote the last?"

The Easy Chair responded, dryly, " You forget Aldrich."

" If I do, I am the only pebble on the shore of time that does or will," retorted the unreal editor. " But he wrote you for only two months. I well remember what a pleasure he had in it. And he knew how to make his readers share his pleasure! Still, it was Mr. Mitchell who invented you, and it was Curtis who characterized you beyond all the rest."

" For a while," said the Easy Chair, with autobiographical relish, " they wrote me together, but it was not long before Mr. Mitchell left off, and Curtis kept on alone, and, as you say, he incomparably characterized me. He had his millennial hopes as well as you. In his youth he trusted in a time

> 'When the common sense of most shall hold a fretful realm
>   in awe,
> And the kindly earth shall slumber, lapt in universal law,'

and he never lost that faith. As he wrote in one of my best papers, the famous paper on Brook Farm,

4

'Bound fast by the brazen age, we can see that the way back to the age of gold lies through justice, which will substitute co-operation for competition.' He expected the world to be made over in the image of heaven some time, but meanwhile he was glad to help make it even a little better and pleasanter than he found it. He was ready to tighten a loose screw here and there, to pour a drop of oil on the rusty machinery, to mend a broken wheel. He was not above putting a patch on a rift where a whiff of infernal air came up from the Bottomless Pit—"

"And I also believe in alleviations," the unreal editor interrupted. "I love justice, but charity is far better than nothing; and it would be abominable not to do all we can because we cannot at once do everything. Let us have the expedients, the ameliorations, even the compromises, *en attendant* the millennium. Let us accept the provisional, the makeshift. He who came on Christmas Day, and whose mission, as every Christmas Day comes to remind us, was the brotherhood, the freedom, the equality of men, did not He warn us against hastily putting new wine into old bottles? To get the new bottles ready is slow work: that kind of bottle must grow; it cannot be made; and in the mean time let us keep our latest vintages in the vat till we have some vessel proof against their fermentation. I know that the hope of any such vessel is usually mocked as mere optimism, but I think optimism is as wise and true as pessimism, or is at least as well founded; and since the one can no more establish itself as final truth than the other, it is better to have optimism. That was always the philosophy of the Easy Chair, and I do not know why that should be changed. The conditions are not changed."

There was a silence which neither the Easy Chair

nor the unreal editor broke for a while. Then the Chair suggested, " I suppose that there is not much change in Christmas, at any rate ?"

" No," said the unreal editor; " it goes on pretty much as it used. The Timminses, who give tiresome little dinners which they cannot afford to dull people who don't want them, are still alive and miserably bent on heaping reluctant beneficiaries with undesired favors, and spoiling the simple ' pleasure of the time ' with the activities of their fatuous vanity. Or perhaps you think I ought to bring a hopeful mind even to the Timminses ?"

" I don't see why not," said the Easy Chair. " They are not the architects of their own personalities."

" Ah, take care, take care!" cried the unreal editor. " You will be saying next that we are the creatures of our environment; that the Timminses would be wiser and better if the conditions were not idiotic and pernicious; and you know what *that* comes to!"

" No, I am in no danger of that," the Easy Chair retorted. " The Timminses are no such victims of the conditions. They are of that vast moderately moneyed class who can perfectly well behave with sense if they will. Nobody above them or below them asks them to be foolish and wasteful."

" And just now you were making excuses for them!"

" I said they were not the architects of their own personalities; but, nevertheless, they are masters of themselves. They are really free to leave off giving little dinners any day they think so. It should be the moralist's business to teach them to think so."

" And that was what Curtis gladly made his business," the unreal editor somewhat sadly confessed, with an unspoken regret for his own difference. More than

6

once it had seemed to him in considering that rare nature that he differed from most reformers chiefly in loving the right rather than in hating the wrong; in fact, in not hating at all, but in pitying and accounting for the wrong as an ancient use corrupted into an abuse. Involuntarily the words of the real editor in that beautiful tribute to the high soul they were praising came to the unreal editor's lips, and he quoted aloud to the Easy Chair: "'His love of goodness was a passion. He would fain have seen all that was fair and good, and he strove to find it so; and, finding it otherwise, he strove to make it so. . . . With no heart for satire, the discord that fell upon his sensitive ear made itself felt in his dauntless comment upon social shams and falsehoods. . . . But he was a lover of peace, and, . . . as he was the ideal gentleman, the ideal citizen, he was also the ideal reformer, without eccentricity or exaggeration. However high his ideal, it never parted company with good sense. He never wanted better bread than could be made of wheat, but the wheat must be kept good and sound,' and I may add," the unreal editor broke off, "that he did not hurry the unripe grain to the hopper. He would not have sent all the horses at once to the abattoir because they made the city noisy and noisome, but would first have waited till there were automobiles enough to supply their place."

The Easy Chair caught at the word. "Automobiles?" it echoed.

"Ah, I forgot how long you have been stored," said the unreal editor, and he explained as well as he could the new mode of motion, and how already, with its soft rubber galoshes, the automobile had everywhere stolen a march upon the iron heels of the horses in the city avenues.

7

He fancied the Easy Chair did not understand, quite, from the intelligent air with which it eagerly quitted the subject.

"Well," it said at last, "this isn't such a bad time to live in, after all, it appears. But for a supreme test of your optimism, now, what good can you find to say of Christmas? What sermon could you preach on that hackneyed theme which would please the fancy and gladden the heart of the readers of a Christmas number, where you should make your first appearance in the Easy Chair?"

To himself the unreal editor had to own that this was a poser. In his heart he was sick of Christmas: not of the dear and high event, the greatest in the memory of the world, which it records and embodies, but the stale and wearisome Christmas of the Christmas presents, purchased in rage and bestowed in despair; the Christmas of Christmas fiction; the Christmas of heavy Christmas dinners and indigestions; the Christmas of all superfluity and surfeit and sentimentality; the Christmas of the Timminses and the Tiny Tims. But while he thought of these, by operation of the divine law which renders all things sensible by their opposites, he thought of the other kinds of Christmas which can never weary or disgust: the Christmas of the little children and the simple-hearted and the poor; and suddenly he addressed himself to the Easy Chair with unexpected and surprising courage.

"Why should that be so very difficult?" he demanded. "If you look at it rightly, Christmas is always full of inspiration; and songs as well as sermons will flow from it till time shall be no more. The trouble with us is that we think it is for the pleasure of opulent and elderly people, for whom there can be no pleasures, but only habits. They are used to having everything, and as joy dwells in novelty it has ceased to be for them in Christmas gifts and giving and all manner of Christmas conventions. But for the young to whom these things are new, and for the poor to whom they are rare, Christmas and Christmasing are sources of perennial happiness. All that you have to do is to guard yourself from growing rich and from growing old, and then the delight of Christmas is yours forever. It is not difficult; it is very simple; for even if years and riches come upon you in a literal way, you can by a little trying keep yourself young and poor in spirit. Then you can always rejoice with the innocent and riot with the destitute.

" I once knew a father," the unreal editor continued, " a most doting and devoted father, who, when he bent over the beds of his children to bid them good-night, and found them ' high sorrowful and cloyed,' as the little ones are apt to be after a hard day's pleasure, used to bid them ' Think about Christmas.' If he offered this counsel on the night, say, of the 26th of December, and they had to look forward to a whole year before their hopes of consolation could possibly find fruition, they had (as they afterward confessed to him) a sense of fatuity if not of mocking in it. Even on the Fourth of July, after the last cracker had been fired and the last roman candle spent, they owned that they had never been able to think about Christmas to an extent that greatly assuaged their vague regrets. It was not till the following Thanksgiving that they succeeded in thinking about Christmas with anything like the entire cheerfulness expected of them."

" I don't see any application in this homily," said the Easy Chair, " or only an application disastrous to

2 9

your imaginable postulate that Christmas is a beneficent and consolatory factor in our lives."

"That is because you have not allowed me to con-
clude," the unreal editor protested, when the Easy
Chair cut in with,

"There is nothing I would so willingly allow you
to do," and "laughed and shook" as if it had been
"Rabelais's easy chair."

The unreal editor thought it best to ignore the un-
timely attempt at wit. "The difficulty in this case
with both the father and the children was largely temperamental; but it was chiefly because of a defect in
their way of thinking about Christmas. It was a very
ancient error, by no means peculiar to this amiable
family, and it consisted in thinking about Christmas
with reference to one's self instead of others."

"Isn't that rather banal?" the Easy Chair asked.

"Not at all banal," said the unreal editor, resisting
an impulse to do the Easy Chair some sort of violence.
At the same time he made his reflection that if preachers were criticised in that way to their faces there
would shortly be very few saints left in the pulpit.
He gave himself a few moments to recover his temper,
and then he went on: "If Christmas means anything
at all, it means anything but one's own pleasure. Up
to the first Christmas Day the whole world had supposed that it could be happy selfishly, and its children
still suppose so. But there is really no such thing as
selfish, as personal happiness."

"Tolstoy," the Easy Chair noted.

"Yes, Tolstoy," the unreal editor retorted. "He
more than any other has brought us back to the knowledge of this truth which came into the world with
Christmas, perhaps because he, more than any other,
has tried to think and to live Christianity. When

once you have got this vital truth into your mind, the whole universe is luminously filled with the possibilities of impersonal, unselfish happiness. The joy of living is suddenly expanded to the dimensions of humanity, and you can go on taking your pleasure as long as there is one unfriended soul and body in the world.

"It is well to realize this at all times, but it is peculiarly fit to do so at Christmas-time, for it is in this truth that the worship of Christ begins. Now, too, is the best time to give the Divine Word form in deed, to translate love into charity. I do not mean only the material charity that expresses itself in turkeys and plum - puddings for the poor, but also that spiritual charity which takes thought how so to amend the sorrowful conditions of civilization that poverty, which is the antithesis of fraternity, shall abound less and less.

'Now is the time, now is the time,
Now is the hour of golden prime'

for asking one's self, not how much one has given in goods or moneys during the past year, but how much one has given in thought and will to remove forever the wrong and shame of hopeless need; and to consider what one may do in the coming year to help put the poor lastingly beyond the need of help.

"To despair of somehow, sometime doing this is to sin against the light of Christmas Day, to confess its ideal a delusion, its practice a failure. If on no other day of all the three hundred and sixty-five, we must on this day renew our faith in justice, which is the highest mercy."

The Easy Chair no longer interrupted, and the unreal editor, having made his point, went on after the manner of preachers, when they are also editors, to

11

make it over again, and to repeat himself pitilessly, unsparingly. He did not observe that the Easy Chair had shrunk forward until all its leathern seat was wrinkled and its carven top was bent over its old red back. When he stopped at last, the warehouse agent asked in whisper,

"What do you want done with it, sir?"

"Oh," said the unreal editor, "send it back to Franklin Square"; and then, with a sudden realization of the fact, he softly added, "Don't wake it."

There in Franklin Square, still dreaming, it was set up in the rear of the magazine, where it has become not only the place, but the stuff of dreams such as men are made of. From month to month, ever since, its reveries, its illusions, which some may call deliverances, have gone on with more and more a disposition to dramatize themselves. It has seemed to the occupant of the Easy Chair, at times, as if he had suffered with it some sort of land-change from a sole entity to a multiple personality in which his several selves conversed with one another, and came and went unbidden. At first, after a moment of question whether his imagination was not frequented by the phantoms of delight which in the flesh had formerly filled his place, whether the spirits which haunted him in it were not those of Mitchell, of Curtis, of Aldrich, he became satisfied from their multitude and nature that they were the subdivisions of his own ego, and as such he has more and more frankly treated them.

II

A YEAR OF SPRING AND A LIFE OF YOUTH

On one of those fine days which the April of the
other year meanly grudged us, a poet, flown with the
acceptance of a quarter-page lyric by the real editor in
the Study next door, came into the place where the Easy
Chair sat rapt in the music of the elevated trains and
the vision of the Brooklyn Bridge towers. "Era la
stagione nella quale la rivestita terra, più che tutto
l' altro anno, si mostra bella," he said, without other
salutation, throwing his soft gray hat on a heap of
magazines and newspapers in the corner, and finding
what perch he could for himself on the window-sill.

"What is that?" he of the Easy Chair gruffly demanded; he knew perfectly well, but he liked marring
the bloom on a fellow-creature's joy by a show of savage
ignorance.

"It's the divine beginning of Boccaccio's 'Fiam-
metta,' it is the very soul of spring; and it is so in-
alienably of Boccaccio's own time and tongue and sun
and air that there is no turning it into the language of another period or climate. What would you
find to thrill you in, 'It was the season in which the
reapparelled earth, more than in all the other year,
shows herself fair'? The rhythm is lost; the flow,
sweet as the first runnings of the maple where the wood-
pecker has tapped it, stiffens into sugar, the liquid form

13

is solidified into the cake adulterated with glucose, and sold for a cent as the pure Vermont product."

As he of the Easy Chair could not deny this, he laughed recklessly. " I understood what your passage from Boccaccio meant, and why you came in here praising spring in its words. You are happy because you have sold a poem, probably for more than it is worth. But why do you praise spring ? What do you fellows do it for ? You know perfectly well that it is the most capricious, the most treacherous, the most delusive, deadly, slatternly, down - at - heels, milkmaid-handed season of the year, without decision of character or fixed principles, and with only the vaguest raw-girlish ideals, a red nose between crazy smiles and streaming eyes. If it did not come at the end of winter, when people are glad of any change, nobody could endure it, and it would be cast neck and crop out of the calendar. Fancy spring coming at the end of summer ! It would not be tolerated for a moment, with the contrast of its crude, formless beauty and the ripe loveliness of August. Every satisfied sense of happiness, secure and established, would be insulted by its haphazard promises made only to be broken. ' Rather,' the outraged mortal would say, ' the last tender hours of autumn, the first deathful - thrilling snowfall, with all the thoughts of life wandering flake-like through the dim air — rather these than the recurrence of those impulses and pauses, those kisses frozen on the lips, those tender rays turning to the lash of sleet across the face of nature. No, the only advantage spring can claim over her sister seasons is her novelty, the only reason she can offer for being the spoiled child of the poets is that nobody but the poets could keep on fancying that there was any longer the least originality in her novelty."

14

The poet attempted to speak, in the little stop he of the Easy Chair made for taking breath, but he was not suffered to do so.

"Every atom of originality has been drained from the novelty of spring ' in the process of the suns,' and science is rapidly depriving her even of novelty. What was once supposed to be the spring grass has been found to be nothing but the fall grass, with the green stealing back into the withered blades. As for the spring lamb which used to crop the spring grass, it is now out of the cold-storage where the spring chicken and the new-laid eggs of yesteryear come from. It is said that there are no birds in last year's nests, but probably a careful examination would discover a plentiful hatch of nestlings which have hibernated in the habitations popularly supposed to be deserted the June before this. Early spring vegetables are in market throughout the twelvemonth, and spring flowers abound at the florists' in December and January. There is no reason why spring should not be absorbed into winter and summer by some such partition as took place politically in the case of Poland. Like that unhappy kingdom, she has abused her independence and become a molestation and discomfort to the annual meteorology. As a season she is distinctly a failure, being neither one thing nor the other, neither hot nor cold, a very Laodicean. Her winds were once supposed to be very siccative, and peculiarly useful in drying the plaster in new houses; but now the contractors put in radiators as soon as the walls are up, and the work is done much better. As for the germinative force of her suns, in these days of intensive farming, when electricity is applied to the work once done by them, they can claim to have no virtue beyond the suns of July or August, which most seeds find effective enough. If spring were absorbed into summer, the heat of that season would be qualified, and its gentler warmth would be extended to autumn, which would be prolonged into the winter. The rigors of winter would be much abated, and the partition of spring among the other seasons would perform the mystic office of the Gulf Stream in ameliorating our climate, besides ridding us of a time of most tedious and annoying suspense. And what should we lose by it?"

The poet seemed not to be answering the Easy Chair directly, but only to be murmuring to himself, "Youth."

"Youth! Youth!" the Easy Chair repeated in exasperation. "And what is youth?"

"The best thing in the world."

"For whom is it the best thing?"

This question seemed to give the poet pause. "Well," he said, finally, with a not very forcible smile, "for itself."

"Ah, there you are!" he of the Easy Chair exclaimed; but he could not help a forgiving laugh. "In a way you are right. The world belongs to youth, and so it ought to be the best thing for itself in it. Youth is a very curious thing, and in that it is like spring, especially like the spring we have just been having, to our cost. It is the only period of life, as spring is the only season of the year, that has too much time on its hands. Yet it does not seem to waste time, as age does, as winter does; it keeps doing something all the while. The things it does are apparently very futile and superfluous, some of them, but in the end something has been accomplished. After a March of whimsical suns and snows, an April of quite fantastical frosts and thaws, and a May, at least partially, of cold mists and parching winds, the flowers, which the florists have been forcing for the purpose, are blooming in the park; the grass is green wherever it has not had the roots trodden out of it, and a filmy foliage, like the soft foulard tissues which the young girls are wearing, drips from the trees. You can say it is all very painty, the verdure; too painty; but you cannot reject the picture because of this little mannerism of the painter. To be sure, you miss the sheeted snows and the dreamy weft of leafless twigs against the hard, blue sky. Still, now it has come, you cannot deny that the spring is pretty, or that the fashionable colors which it has introduced are charming. It is said that these are so charming that a woman of the worst taste cannot choose amiss among them. In spite of her taste, her hat comes out a harmonic miracle; her gown, against all her endeavors, flows in an exquisite symphony of the tender audacities of tint with which nature mixes her palette; little notes of chiffon, of tulle, of feather, blow all about her. This is rather a medley of metaphors, to which several arts contribute, but you get my meaning?" In making this appeal, he of the Easy Chair saw in the fixed eye of the poet that remoteness of regard which denotes that your listener has been hearing very little of what you have been saying.

"Yes," the poet replied with a long breath, "you are right about that dreamy weft of leafless twigs against the hard, blue sky; and I wonder if we quite do justice to the beauty of winter, of age, we poets, when we are so glad to have the spring come."

"I don't know about winter," he of the Easy Chair said, "but in an opera which the English Lord Chamberlain provisionally suppressed, out of tenderness for an alliance not eventually or potentially to the advantage of these States, Mr. William Gilbert has done his duty to the decline of life, where he sings,

> ' There is beauty in extreme old age;
> There's a fascination frantic
> In a ruin that's romantic.'

Or, at least no one else has said so much for ' that time of life,' which another librettist has stigmatized as

' Bare, ruined choirs, where late the sweet birds sang.' "

" Yes, I know," the poet returned, clinging to the thread of thought on which he had cast himself loose. " But I believe a great deal more could be said for age by the poets if they really tried. I am not satisfied of Mr. Gilbert's earnestness in the passage you quote from the ' Mikado,' and I prefer Shakespeare's ' bare, ruined choirs.' I don't know but I prefer the hard, unflattering portrait which Hamlet mockingly draws for Polonius, and there is something almost caressing in the notion of ' the lean and slippered pantaloon.' The worst of it is that we old fellows look so plain to one another; I dare say young people don't find us so bad. I can remember from my own youth that I thought old men, and especially old women, rather attractive. I am not sure that we elders realize the charm of a perfectly bald head as it presents itself to the eye of youth. Yet, an infant's head is often quite bald."

" Yes, and so is an egg," the Easy Chair retorted, " but there is not the same winning appeal in the baldness of the superannuated bird which has evolved from it—eagle or nightingale, parrot or

Many-wintered crow that leads the clanging rookery home.

Tennyson has done his best in showing us venerable in his picture of

18

'the Ionian father of the rest:
A million wrinkles carved his silver skin,
A hundred winters snowed upon his breast.'

But who would not rather be Helen than Homer, her
face launching a thousand ships and burning the top-
less tower of Ilion—fairer than the evening air and
simply but effectively attired in the beauty of a thousand stars? What poet has ever said things like that
of an old man, even of Methuselah?"

"Yes," the poet sighed. "I suppose you are partly
right. Meteorology certainly has the advantage of humanity in some things. We cannot make much of age
here, and hereafter we can only conceive of its being
turned into youth. Fancy an eternity of sensibility!"

"No, I would rather not!" he of the Easy Chair
returned, sharply. "Besides, it is you who are trying
to make age out a tolerable, even a desirable thing."

"But I have given it up," the poet meekly replied.
"The great thing would be some rearrangement of our
mortal conditions so that once a year we could wake
from our dream of winter and find ourselves young.
Not merely younger, but *young*—the genuine article.
A tree can do that, and does it every year, until after
a hundred years, or three hundred, or a thousand, it
dies. Why should not a man, or, much more impor-
tantly, a woman, do it? I think we are very much
scanted in that respect."

"My dear fellow, if you begin fault-finding with
creation, there will be no end to it. It might be answered that, in this case, you can walk about and a
tree cannot; you can call upon me and a tree cannot.
And other things. Come! the trees have not got it all
their own way. Besides, imagine the discomforts of
a human springtime, blowing hot and blowing cold,

freezing, thawing, raining, and drouthing, and never being sure whether we are young or old, May or December. We should be such nuisances to one another that we should ask the gods to take back their gift, and you know very well they cannot."

"Our rejuvenescence would be a matter of temperament, not temperature," the poet said, searching the air hopefully for an idea. "I have noticed this spring that the isothermal line is as crooked as a railroad on the map of a rival. I have been down in New Hampshire since I saw you, and I found the spring temperamentally as far advanced there as here in New York. Of course not as far advanced as in Union Square, but quite as far as in Central Park. Between Boston and Portsmouth there were bits of railroad bank that were as green as the sward beside the Mall, and every now and then there was an enthusiastic maple in the wet lowlands that hung the air as full of color as any maple that reddened the flying landscape when I first got beyond the New York suburbs on my way north. At Portsmouth the birds were singing the same songs as in the Park. I could not make out the slightest difference."

"With the same note of nervous apprehension in them?"

"I did not observe that. But they were spring songs, certainly."

"Then," the Easy Chair said, "I would rather my winter were turned into summer, or early autumn, than spring, if there is going to be any change of the mortal conditions. I like settled weather, the calm of that time of life when the sins and follies have been committed, the passions burned themselves out, and the ambitions frustrated so that they do not bother, the aspirations defeated, the hopes brought low. Then you have some comfort. This turmoil of vernal striving makes me tired."

"Yes, I see what you mean," the poet assented. "But you cannot have the seasons out of their order in the rearrangement of the mortal conditions. You must have spring and you must have summer before you can have autumn."

"Are those the terms? Then I say, Winter at once! Winter is bad enough, but I would not go through spring again for any— In winter you can get away from the cold, with a good, warm book, or a sunny picture, or a cozy old song, or a new play; but in spring how will you escape the rawness if you have left off your flannels and let out the furnace? No, my dear friend, we could not stand going back to youth every year. The trees can, because they have been used to it from the beginning of time, but the men could not. Even the women—"

At this moment a beatific presence made itself sensible, and the Easy Chair recognized the poet's Muse, who had come for him. The poet put the question to her. "Young?" she said. "Why, you and I are *always* young, silly boy! Get your hat, and come over to Long Island City with me, and see the pussy-willows along the railroad-banks. The mosquitoes are beginning to sing in the ditches already."

III

SCLEROSIS OF THE TASTES

THE other day one of those convertible familiars of the Easy Chair, who

"Change and pass and come again,"

looked in upon it, after some months' absence, with the effect of having aged considerably in the interval. But this was only his latest avatar; he was no older, as he was no younger, than before; to support a fresh character, he had to put on an appropriate aspect, and having, at former interviews, been a poet, a novelist, a philosopher, a reformer, a moralist, he was now merely looking the part of a veteran observer, of a psychologist grown gray in divining the character of others from his own consciousness.

"Have you ever noticed," he began, "that the first things we get stiff in, as we advance in life, are our tastes? We suppose that it is our joints which feel the premonitions of age; and that because we no longer wish to dance or play ball or sprint in college races we are in the earliest stage of that sapless condition when the hinges of the body grind dryly upon one another, and we lose a good inch of our stature, through shrinkage, though the spine still holds us steadfastly upright."

"Well, isn't that so?" the Easy Chair asked, tranquilly.

"It may be so, or it may not be so," the veteran observer replied. "Ultimately, I dare say, it *is* so. But what I wish to enforce is the fact that before you begin to feel the faintest sense of stiffening joints you are allowing yourself to fall into that voluntary senescence which I call getting stiff in the tastes. It is something that I think we ought to guard ourselves against as a sort of mental sclerosis which must end fatally long before we have reached the patriarchal age which that unbelieving believer Metchnikoff says we can attain if we fight off physical sclerosis. He can only negatively teach us how to do this, but I maintain we can have each of us in our power the remedy against stiffening tastes."

"I don't see how," the Easy Chair said, more to provoke the sage to explanation than to express dissent.

"I will teach you how," he said, "if you will allow me to make it a personal matter, and use you in illustration."

"Why not use yourself?"

"Because that would be egotistical, and the prime ingredient of my specific against getting stiff in the tastes is that spiritual grace which is the very antidote, the very antithesis of egotism. Up to a certain point, a certain time, we are usefully employed in cultivating our tastes, in refining them, and in defining them. We cannot be too strenuous in defining them; and, as long as we are young, the catholicity of youth will preserve us from a bigoted narrowness. In æsthetic matters—and I imagine we both understand that we are dealing with these—the youngest youth has no tastes; it has merely appetites. All is fish that comes to its net; if anything, it prefers the gaudier of the

23

finny tribes; it is only when it becomes sophisticated that its appetites turn into tastes, and it begins to appreciate the flavor of that diseased but pearl-bearing species of oyster which we call genius, because we have no accurate name for it. With the appreciation of this flavor comes the overpowering desire for it, the incessant and limitless search for it. To the desire for it whole literatures owe their continued existence, since, except for the universal genius-hunger of youth, the classics of almost all languages would have perished long ago. When indiscriminate and omnivorous youth has explored those vast and mostly lifeless seas, it has found that the diseased oyster which bears the pearls is the rarest object in nature. But having once formed the taste for it, youth will have no other flavor, and it is at this moment that its danger of hardening into premature age begins. The conceit of having recognized genius takes the form of a bigoted denial of its existence save in the instances recognized. This conceit does not admit the possibility of error or omission in the search, and it does not allow that the diseased oyster can transmit its pearl-bearing qualities and its peculiar flavors; so that the attitude of aging youth, in the stiffening of its tastes, is one of rejection toward all new bivalves, or, not to be tediously metaphorical, books."

The veteran observer fell silent at this point, and the Easy Chair seized the occasion to remark: "Yes, there is something in what you say. But this stiffening of the tastes, this sclerosis of the mind, is hardly an infectious disease—"

"Ah, but it *is* infectious," the veteran observer exclaimed, rousing himself, "infectious as far as the victim can possibly make it so. He wishes nothing so much as to impart his opinions in all their rigid-

ity to everybody else. Take your own case, for instance—"

" No, we would rather not," the Easy Chair interposed.

" But you must make the sacrifice," the veteran observer persisted. " You will allow that you are extremely opinionated?"

" Not at all."

" Well, then, that you are devoutly conscientious in
the tenure of your æsthetic beliefs?"

" Something like that, yes."

" And you cannot deny that in times past you have
tried your best to make others think with you?"

" It was our duty."

" Well, let it pass for that. It amounted to an effort to make your mental sclerosis infectious, and it
was all the worse because, in you, the stiffening of the
tastes had taken the form of aversions rather than
preferences. You did not so much wish your readers
to like your favorite authors as to hate all the others.
At the time when there was a fad for making lists of
The Hundred Best Authors, I always wondered that
you didn't put forth some such schedule."

" We had the notion of doing something of the kind,"
the Easy Chair confessed, " but we could not think of
more than ten or a dozen really first-rate authors, and
if we had begun to compile a list of the best authors
we should have had to leave out most of their works.
Nearly all the classics would have gone by the board.
What havoc we should have made with the British
poets! The Elizabethan dramatists would mostly have
fallen under the ban of our negation, to a play, if not
to a man. Chaucer, but for a few poems, is impossible;
Spenser's poetry is generally duller than the Presidents' messages before Mr. Roosevelt's time; Milton

is a trial of the spirit in three-fourths of his verse; Wordsworth is only not so bad as Byron, who thought him so much worse; Shakespeare himself, when he is reverently supposed not to be Shakespeare, is reading for martyrs; Dante's science and politics outweigh his poetry a thousandfold, and so on through the whole catalogue. Among the novelists—"

"No, don't begin on the novelists! Every one knows your heresies there, and would like to burn you along with the romances which I've no doubt you would still commit to the flames. I see you are the Bourbon of criticism; you have learned nothing and forgotten nothing. But why don't you turn your adamantine immutability to some practical account, and give the world a list of The Hundred Worst Books?"

"Because a hundred books out of the worst would be a drop out of the sea; there would remain an immeasurable welter of badness, of which we are now happily ignorant, and from which we are safe, as long as our minds are not turned to it by examples."

"Ah," our visitor said, "I see that you are afraid to confess yourself the popular failure as a critic which you are. You are afraid that if you made a list of The Hundred Worst Books you would send the classes to buying them in the most expensive binding, and the masses to taking them out of all the public libraries."

"There is something in what you say," the Easy Chair confessed. "Our popular failure as a critic is notorious; it cannot be denied. The stamp of our disapproval at one time gave a whole order of fiction a currency that was not less than torrential. The flood of romantic novels which passed over the land, and which is still to be traced in the tatters of the rag-doll heroes and heroines caught in the memories of readers along its course, was undoubtedly the effect of our adverse criticism. No, we could not in conscience compile and publish a list of The Hundred Worst Books; it would be contrary, for the reasons you give, to public morals."

"And don't you think," the observer said, with a Socratic subtlety that betrayed itself in his gleaming eye, in the joyous hope of seeing his victim fall into the pit that his own admissions had digged for him, "and don't you think that it would also bring to you the unpleasant consciousness of having stiffened in your tastes?"

"It might up to a certain point," we consented. "But we should prefer to call it confirmed in our convictions. Wherever we have liked or disliked in literature it has been upon grounds hardly distinguishable from moral grounds. Bad art is a vice; untruth to nature is the eighth of the seven deadly sins; a false school in literature is a seminary of crime. We are speaking largely, of course—"

"It certainly sounds rather tall," our friend sarcastically noted, "and it sounds very familiar."

"Yes," we went on, "all the ascertained veracities are immutable. One holds to them, or, rather, they hold to one, with an indissoluble tenacity. But convictions are in the region of character and are of remote origin. In their safety one indulges one's self in expectations, in tolerances, and these rather increase with the lapse of time. We should say that your theory of the stiffening tastes is applicable to the earlier rather than the later middle life. We should say that the tastes if they stiffen at the one period limber at the other; their forbidding rigidity is succeeded by an acquiescent suppleness. One is aware of an involuntary hospitality toward a good many authors whom one would once have turned destitute from the door, or with a dole of Or-

27

ganized Charity meal-tickets at the best. But in that
maturer time one hesitates, and possibly ends by asking the stranger in, especially if he is young, or even
if he is merely new, and setting before him the cold
potato of a qualified approval. One says to him: ' You
know I don't think you are the real thing quite, but
taking you on your own ground you are not so bad.
Come, you shall have a night's lodging at least, and if
you improve, if you show a tendency to change in the
right direction, there is no telling but you may be allowed to stay the week. But you must not presume;
you must not take this frosty welcome for an effect of
fire from the hearth where we sit with our chosen
friends.' Ten to one the stranger does not like this
sort of talk, and goes his way—the wrong way. But,
at any rate, one has shown an open mind, a liberal
spirit; one has proved that one has not stiffened in
one's tastes; that one can make hopeful allowances in
hopeful cases."

" Such as ?" the observer insinuated.

" Such as do not fit the point exactly. Very likely
the case may be that of an old or elderly author. It
has been only within a year or two that we have formed
the taste for an English writer, no longer living, save
in his charming books. James Payn was a favorite
with many in the middle Victorian period, but it is
proof of the flexibility of our tastes that we have only
just come to him. After shunning Anthony Trollope
for fifty years, we came to him, almost as with a rush,
long after our half-century was past. Now, James
Payn is the solace of our autumnal equinox, and
Anthony Trollope we read with a constancy and a recurrence surpassed only by our devotion to the truth
as it is in the fiction of the Divine Jane; and Jane
Austen herself was not an idol of our first or even our

second youth, but became the cult of a time when if our tastes had stiffened we could have cared only for the most modern of the naturalists, and those preferably of the Russian and Spanish schools. A signal proof of their continued suppleness came but the other day when we acquainted ourselves with the work of the English novelist, Mr. Percy White, and it was the more signal because we perceived that he had formed himself upon a method of Thackeray's, which recalled that master, as the occasional aberrations of Payn and Trollope recall a manner of him. But it is Thackeray's most artistic method which Mr. White recalls in his studies of scamps and snobs; he allows them, as Thackeray allows Barry Lyndon and the rest, to tell their own stories, and in their unconsciousness of their own natures he finds play for an irony as keen and graphic as anything in fiction. He deals with the actual English world, and the pleasure he gave us was such as to make us resolve to return to Thackeray's vision of his own contemporaneous English world at the first opportunity. We have not done so yet; but after we have fortified ourselves with a course of Scott and Dickens, we are confident of being able to bear up under the heaviest-handed satire of *Vanity Fair.* As for *The Luck of Barry Lyndon* and *The Yellowplush Papers,* and such like, they have never ceased to have their prime delight for us. But their proportion is quite large enough to survive from any author for any reader; as we are often saying, it is only in bits that authors survive; their resurrection is not by the whole body, but here and there a perfecter fragment. Most of our present likes and dislikes are of the period when you say people begin to stiffen in their tastes. We could count the authors by the score who have become our favorites in that period, and those we have dropped are almost as many. It is not necessary to say who they all are, but we may remark that we still read, and read, and read again the poetry of Keats, and that we no longer read the poetry of Alexander Smith. But it is through the growth of the truly great upon his mature perception that the aging reader finds novel excellences in them. It was only the other day that we picked up Hawthorne's *Scarlet Letter,* and realized in it, from a chance page or two, a sardonic quality of insurpassable subtlety and reach. This was something quite new to us in it. We had known the terrible pathos of the story, its immeasurable tragedy, but that deadly, quiet, pitiless, freezing irony of a witness holding himself aloof from its course, and losing, for that page or two, the moralist in the mere observer, was a revelation that had come to that time of life in us when you think the tastes stiffen and one refuses new pleasures because they are new."

Our visitor yawned visibly, audibly. "And what is all this you have been saying? You have made yourself out an extraordinary example of what may be done by guarding against the stiffening of the tastes after the end of second youth. But have you proved that there is no such danger? Or was your idea simply to celebrate yourself? At moments I fancied something like that."

We owned the stroke with an indulgent smile. "No, not exactly that. The truth is we have been very much interested by your notion—if it was yours, which is not altogether probable—and we have been turning its light upon our own experience, in what we should not so much call self-celebration as self-exploitation. One uses one's self as the stuff for knowledge of others, or for the solution of any given problem. There is no other way of getting at the answers to the questions."

SCLEROSIS OF THE TASTES

"And what is your conclusion as to my notion, if it is mine?" the veteran observer asked, with superiority.

"That there is nothing in it. The fact is that the tastes are never so tolerant, so liberal, so generous, so supple as they are at that time of life when they begin, according to your notion, to stiffen, to harden, to contract. We have in this very period formed a new taste—or taken a new lease of an old one—for reading history, which had been dormant all through our first and second youth. We expect to see the time when we shall read the Elizabethan dramatists with avidity. We may not improbably find a delight in statistics; there must be a hidden charm in them. We may even form a relish for the vagaries of pseudo-psychology—"

At this point we perceived the veteran observer had vanished and that we were talking to ourselves.

IV

THE PRACTICES AND PRECEPTS OF VAUDEVILLE

A FRIEND of the Easy Chair came in the other day after a frost from the magazine editor which had nipped a tender manuscript in its bloom, and was received with the easy hospitality we are able to show the rejected from a function involving neither power nor responsibility.

" Ah !" we breathed, sadly, at the sight of the wilted offering in the hands of our friend. " What is it he won't take *now?*"

" Wait till I get my second wind," the victim of unrequited literature answered, dropping into the Easy Chair, from which the occupant had risen; and he sighed, pensively, " I felt so sure I had got him this time." He closed his eyes, and leaned his head back against the uncomfortably carven top of the Easy Chair. It was perhaps his failure to find rest in it that restored him to animation. " It is a little thing," he murmured, " on the decline of the vaudeville."

" The decline of the vaudeville?" we repeated, wrinkling our forehead in grave misgiving. Then, for want of something better, we asked, " Do you think that is a very dignified subject for the magazine?"

" Why, bless my soul!" the rejected one cried, starting somewhat violently forward, " what is your magazine itself but vaudeville, with your contributors all doing their stunts of fiction, or poetry, or travel, or

sketches of life, or articles of popular science and so-
ciological interest, and I don't know what all! What
are your illustrations but the moving pictures of the
kalatechnoscope! Why," he said, with inspiration,
"what are you yourself but a species of Chaser that
comes at the end of the show, and helps clear the ground
for the next month's performance by tiring out the
lingering readers?"

"You don't think," we suggested, "you're being
rather unpleasant?"

Our friend laughed harshly, and we were glad to
see him restored to so much cheerfulness, at any rate.
"I think the notion is a pretty good fit, though if you
don't like to wear it I don't insist. Why should you
object to being likened to those poor fellows who come
last on the programme at the vaudeville? Very often
they are as good as the others, and sometimes, when I
have determined to get my five hours' enjoyment to the
last moment before six o'clock, I have had my reward
in something unexpectedly delightful in the work of the
Chasers. I have got into close human relations with
them, I and the half-dozen brave spirits who have
stuck it out with me, while the ushers went impatiently
about, clacking the seats back, and picking up the pro-
grammes and lost articles under them. I have had the
same sense of kindly comradery with you, and now
and then my patience has been rewarded by you, just
as it has been by the Chasers at the vaudeville, and
I've said so to people. I've said: 'You're wrong to put
down the magazine the way most of you do before you
get to those departments at the end. Sometimes there
are quite good things in them.' "

"Really," said the unreal editor, "you seem to have
had these remarks left over from your visit to the real
editor. We advise you to go back and repeat them.

They may cause him to revise his opinion of your contribution."

"It's no use my going back. I read finality in his eye before I left him, and I feel that no compliment, the most fulsome, would move him. Don't turn me out! I take it all back about your being a Chaser. You are the first act on the bill for me. I read the magazine like a Chinese book—from the back. I always begin with the Easy Chair."

"Ah, now you are talking," we said, and we thought it no more than human to ask, "What is it you have been saying about the vaudeville, anyway?"

The rejected one instantly unfolded his manuscript. "I will just read—"

"No, no!" we interposed. "Tell us about it—give us the general drift. We never can follow anything read to us."

The other looked incredulous, but he was not master of the situation, and he resigned himself to the secondary pleasure of sketching the paper he would so much rather have read.

"Why, you know what an inveterate vaudeville-goer I have always been?"

We nodded. "We know how you are always trying to get us to neglect the masterpieces of our undying modern dramatists, on the legitimate stage, and go with you to see the ridiculous stunts you delight in."

"Well, it comes to the same thing. I am an inveterate vaudeville-goer, for the simple reason that I find better acting in the vaudeville, and better drama, on the whole, than you ever get, or you generally get, on your legitimate stage. I don't know why it is so very legitimate. I have no doubt but the vaudeville, or continuous variety performance, is the older, the

34

more authentic form of histrionic art. Before the
Greek dramatists, or the longer-winded Sanskrit play-
wrights, or the exquisitely conventionalized Chinese
and Japanese and Javanese were heard of, it is probable that there were companies of vaudeville artists
going about the country and doing the turns that they
had invented themselves, and getting and giving the
joy that comes of voluntary and original work, just as
they are now. And in the palmiest days of the Greek
tragedy or the Roman comedy, there were, of course,
variety shows all over Athens and Rome where you
could have got twice the amusement for half the money
that you would at the regular theatres. While the
openly wretched and secretly rebellious actors whom
Euripides and Terence had cast for their parts were
going through rôles they would never have chosen themselves, the wilding heirs of art at the vaudeville were
giving things of their own imagination, which they had
worked up from some vague inspiration into a sketch
of artistic effect. No manager had foisted upon them
his ideals of 'what the people wanted,' none had
shaped their performance according to his own notion
of histrionics. They had each come to him with his or
her little specialty, that would play fifteen or twenty
minutes, and had, after trying it before him, had it
rejected or accepted in its entirety. Then, author and
actor in one, they had each made his or her appeal to
the public."

"There were no hers on the stage in those days," we
interposed.

"No matter," the rejected contributor retorted.
"There are now, and that is the important matter.
I am coming to the very instant of actuality, to the
show which I saw yesterday, and which I should have
brought my paper down to mention if it had been ac-

cepted." He drew a long breath, and said, with a dreamy air of retrospect: "It is all of a charming unity, a tradition unbroken from the dawn of civilization. When I go to a variety show, and drop my ticket into the chopping-box at the door, and fastidiously choose my unreserved seat in the best place I can get, away from interposing posts and persons, and settle down to a long afternoon's delight, I like to fancy myself a far-fetched phantom of the past, who used to do the same thing at Thebes or Nineveh as many thousand years ago as you please. I like to think that I too am an unbroken tradition, and my pleasure will be such as shaped smiles immemorially gone to dust."

We made our reflection that this passage was probably out of the rejected contribution, but we did not say anything, and our visitor went on.

"And what a lot of pleasure I did get, yesterday, for my fifty cents! There were twelve stunts on the bill, not counting the kalatechnoscope, and I got in before the first was over, so that I had the immediate advantage of seeing a gifted fellow-creature lightly swinging himself between two chairs which had their outer legs balanced on the tops of caraffes full of water, and making no more of the feat than if it were a walk in the Park or down Fifth Avenue. How I respected that man! What study had gone to the perfection of that act, and the others that he equally made nothing of! He was simply billed as 'Equilibrist,' when his name ought to have been blazoned in letters a foot high if they were in any wise to match his merit. He was followed by 'Twin Sisters,' who, as 'Refined Singers and Dancers,' appeared in sweeping confections of white silk, with deeply drooping, widely spreading white hats, and long-fringed white parasols heaped with

artificial roses, and sang a little tropical romance, whose
burden was

> 'Under the bámboo-trée,'

brought in at unexpected intervals. They also danced
this romance with languid undulations, and before you
could tell how or why, they had disappeared and re-
appeared in short green skirts, and then shorter white
skirts, with steps and stops appropriate to their cos-
tumes, but always, I am bound to say, of the refinement promised. I can't tell you in what their refinement consisted, but I am sure it was there, just as I
am sure of the humor of the two brothers who next
appeared as 'Singing and Dancing Comedians' of the
coon type. I know that they sang and they danced,
and worked sable pleasantries upon one another with
the help of the pianist, who often helps out the dialogue
of the stage in vaudeville. They were not so good as
the next people, a jealous husband and a pretty wife,
who seized every occasion in the slight drama of 'The
Singing Lesson,' and turned it to account in giving
their favorite airs. I like to have a husband disguise
himself as a German maestro, and musically make out
why his wife is so zealous in studying with him, and
I do not mind in the least having the sketch close without reason: it leaves something to my imagination.
Two of 'America's Leading Banjoists' charmed me
next, for, after all, there is nothing like the banjo.
If one does not one's self rejoice in its plunking, there
are others who do, and that is enough for my altruistic
spirit. Besides, it is America's leading instrument,
and those who excel upon it appeal to the patriotism
which is never really dormant in us. Its close association with color in our civilization seemed to render
it the fitting prelude of the next act, which consisted

of 'Monologue and Songs' by a divine creature in lampblack, a shirt-waist worn outside his trousers, and an exaggerated development of stomach. What did he say, what did he sing? I don't know; I only know that it rested the soul and brain, that it soothed the conscience, and appeased the hungerings of ambition. Just to sit there and listen to that unalloyed nonsense was better than to 'sport with Amaryllis in the shade, or with the tangles of Neæra's hair,' or to be the object of a votive dinner, or to be forgiven one's sins; there is no such complete purgation of care as one gets from the real Afro-American when he is unreal, and lures one completely away from life, while professing to give his impressions of it. You, with your brute preferences for literality, will not understand this, and I suppose you would say I ought to have got a purer and higher joy out of the little passage of drama, which followed, and I don't know but I did. It was nothing but the notion of a hapless, half-grown girl, who has run away from the poorhouse for a half-holiday, and brings up in the dooryard of an old farmer of the codger type, who knew her father and mother. She at once sings, one doesn't know why, 'Oh, dear, what can the matter be,' and she takes out of her poor little carpet-bag a rag-doll, and puts it to sleep with 'By low, baby,' and the old codger puts the other dolls to sleep, nodding his head, and kicking his foot out in time, and he ends by offering that poor thing a home with him. If he had not done it, I do not know how I could have borne it, for my heart was in my throat with pity, and the tears were in my eyes. Good heavens! What simple instruments we men are! The falsest note in all Hamlet is in those words of his to Guildenstern: 'You would play upon me; you would seem to know my stops; you would pluck out the heart

of my mystery; you would sound me from my lowest
note to the top of my compass. . . . 'S blood, do you
think I am easier to be played on than a pipe?' Guildenstern ought to have said: ' Much, my lord! Here is
an actor who has been summering in the country, and
has caught a glimpse of pathetic fact commoner than
the dust in the road, and has built it up in a bit of
drama as artless as a child would fancy, and yet it
swells your heart and makes you cry. Your mystery?
You have *no* mystery to an honest man. It is only
fakes and frauds who do not understand the soul. The
simplest willow whistle is an instrument more complex
than man.' That is what I should have said in Guildenstern's place if I had had Hamlet with me there at
the vaudeville show.

" In the pretty language of the playbill," the contributor went on, " this piece was called ' A Pastoral
Playlet,' and I should have been willing to see ' Mandy
Hawkins ' over again, instead of the ' Seals and Sea
Lions,' next placarded at the sides of the curtain immediately lifted on them. Perhaps I have seen too
much of seals, but I find the range of their accomplish-
ments limited, and their impatience for fish and lump
sugar too frankly greedy before and after each act.
Their banjo-playing is of a most casual and irrelevant
sort; they ring bells, to be sure; in extreme cases they
fire small cannon; and their feat of balancing large
and little balls on their noses is beyond praise. But it
may be that the difficulties overcome are too obvious in
their instances; I find myself holding my breath, and
helping them along too strenuously for my comfort. I
am always glad when the curtain goes down on them;
their mere flumping about the stage makes me unhappy; but they are not so bad, after all, as trained
dogs. They were followed by three ' Artistic Euro-

pean Acrobats,' who compensated and consoled me for the seals, by the exquisite ease with which they wrought the impossibilities of their art, in the familiar sack-coats and top-coats of every day. I really prefer tights and spangles, but I will not refuse impossibilities simply because they are performed, as our diplomats are instructed to appear at European courts, in the ordinary dress of a gentleman; it may even add a poignancy to the pleasure I own so reluctantly.

"There came another pair of 'Singers and Dancers,' and then a 'Trick Cyclist,' but really I cannot stand trick cycling, now that plain cycling, glory be! has so nearly gone out. As soon as the cyclist began to make his wheel rear up on its hind leg and carry him round the stage in that posture, I went away. But I had had enough without counting him, though I left the kalatechnoscope, with its shivering and shimmering unseen. I had had my fill of pleasure, rich and pure, such as I could have got at no legitimate theatre in town, and I came away opulently content."

We reflected awhile before we remarked: "Then I don't see what you have to complain of or to write of. Where does the decline of the vaudeville come in?"

"Oh," the rejected contributor said, with a laugh, "I forgot that. It's still so good, when compared with the mechanical drama of the legitimate theatre, that I don't know whether I can make out a case against it now. But I think I can, both in quality and quantity. I think the change began insidiously to steal upon the variety show with the increasing predominance of short plays. Since they were short, I should not have minded them so much, but they were always so bad! Still, I could go out, when they came on, and return for the tramp magician, or the comic musician, who played upon joints of stovepipe and the legs of reception-chairs

and the like, and scratched matches on his two days'
beard, and smoked a plaintive air on a cigarette. But
when the 'playlets' began following one another in
unbroken succession, I did not know what to do. Almost before I was aware of their purpose three of the
leading vaudeville houses threw off the mask, and gave
plays that took up the whole afternoon; and though
they professed to intersperse the acts with what they
called 'big vaudeville,' I could not be deceived, and
I simply stopped going. When I want to see a four-
act play, I will go to the legitimate theatre, and see
something that I can smell, too. The influence of the
vaudeville has, on the whole, been so elevating and
refining that its audiences cannot stand either the im-
purity or the imbecility of the fashionable drama. But
now the vaudeville itself is beginning to decline in
quality as well as quantity."

" Not toward immodesty ?"

" No, not so much that. But the fine intellectual
superiority of the continuous performance is beginning to suffer contamination from the plays where
there are waits between the acts. I spoke just now
of the tramp magician, but I see him no longer at the
variety houses. The comic musician is of the rarest
occurrence; during the whole season I have as yet heard
no cornet solo on a revolver or a rolling-pin. The most
dangerous acts of the trapeze have been withdrawn.
The acrobats still abound, but it is three long years
since I looked upon a coon act with real Afro-Amer-
icans in it, or saw a citizen of Cincinnati in a fur
overcoat keeping a silk hat, an open umbrella, and a
small wad of paper in the air with one hand. It is
true that the conquest of the vaudeville houses by
the full-fledged drama has revived the old-fashioned
stock companies in many cases, and has so far worked

for good, but it is a doubtful advantage when compared with the loss of the direct inspiration of the artists who created and performed their stunts."

"Delightful word!" we dreamily noted. "How did it originate?"

"Oh, I don't know. It's probably a perversion of stint, a task or part, which is also to be found in the dictionary as stent. What does it matter? There is the word, and there is the thing, and both are charming. I approve of the stunt because it is always the stuntist's own. He imagined it, he made it, and he loves it. He seems never to be tired of it, even when it is bad, and when nobody in the house lends him a hand with it. Of course, when it comes to that, it has to go, and he with it. It has to go when it is good, after it has had its day, though I don't see why it should go; for my part there are stunts I could see endlessly over again, and not weary of them. Can you say as much of any play?"

"Gilbert and Sullivan's operas," we suggested.

"That is true. But without the music? And even with the music, the public won't have them any longer. I would like to see the stunt fully developed. I should like to have that lovely wilding growth delicately nurtured into drama as limitless and lawless as life itself, owing no allegiance to plot, submitting to no rule or canon, but going gayly on to nothingness as human existence does, full of gleaming lights, and dark with inconsequent glooms, musical, merry, melancholy, mad, but never-ending as the race itself."

"You would like a good deal more than you are ever likely to get," we said; and here we thought it was time to bring our visitor to book again. "But about the decline of vaudeville?"

"Well, it isn't grovelling yet in the mire with popular fiction, but it is standing still, and whatever is standing still is going backward, or at least other things are passing it. To hold its own, the vaudeville must grab something more than its own. It must venture into regions yet unexplored. It must seize not only the fleeting moments, but the enduring moments of experience; it should be wise not only to the whims and moods, but the passions, the feelings, the natures of men; for it appeals to a public not sophisticated by mistaken ideals of art, but instantly responsive to representations of life. Nothing is lost upon the vaudeville audience, not the lightest touch, not the airiest shadow of meaning. Compared with the ordinary audience at the legitimate theatres—"

"Then what you wish," we concluded, "is to elevate the vaudeville."

The visitor got himself out of the Easy Chair, with something between a groan and a growl. "You mean to kill it."

V

INTIMATIONS OF ITALIAN OPERA

WHETHER pleasure of the first experience is more truly pleasure than that which comes rich in associations from pleasures of the past is a doubt that no hedonistic philosopher seems to have solved yet. We should, in fact, be sorry if any had, for in that case we should be without such small occasion as we now have to suggest it in the forefront of a paper which will not finally pass beyond the suggestion. When the reader has arrived at our last word we can safely promise him he will still have the misgiving we set out with, and will be confirmed in it by the reflection that no pleasure, either of the earliest or the latest experience, can be unmixed with pain. One will be fresher than the other; that is all; but it is not certain that the surprise will have less of disappointment in it than the unsurprise. In the one case, the case of youth, say, there will be the racial disappointment to count with, and in the other, the case of age, there will be the personal disappointment, which is probably a lighter thing. The racial disappointment is expressed in what used to be called, somewhat untranslatably, *Weltschmerz*. This was peculiarly the appanage of youth, being the anticipative melancholy, the pensive foreboding, distilled from the blighted hopes of former generations of youth. Mixed with the effervescent blood

44

of the young heart, it acted like a subtle poison, and
eventuated in more or less rhythmical deliriums, in
cynical excesses of sentiment, in extravagances of behavior, in effects which commonly passed when the
subject himself became ancestor, and transmitted his
inherited burden of *Weltschmerz* to his posterity. The
old are sometimes sad, on account of the sins and follies
they have personally committed and know they will
commit again, but for pure gloom—gloom positive, absolute, all but palpable—you must go to youth. That
is not merely the time of disappointment, it is in itself
disappointment; it is not what it expected to be; and
it finds nothing which confronts it quite, if at all,
responsive to the inward vision. The greatest, the love-
liest things in the world lose their iridescence or dwindle before it. The old come to things measurably prepared to see them as they are, take them for what they
are worth; but the young are the prey of impassioned
prepossessions which can never be the true measures.

The disadvantage of an opening like this is that it
holds the same quality, if not quantity, of disappointment as those other sublime things, and we earnestly
entreat the reader to guard himself against expecting
anything considerable from it. Probably the inexperi-
enced reader has imagined from our weighty prologue
something of signal importance to follow; but the
reader who has been our reader through thick and thin
for many years will have known from the first that
we were not going to deal with anything more vital,
say, than a few emotions and memories, prompted, one
night of the other winter, by hearing one of the old-
fashioned Italian operas which a more than commonly
inspired management had been purveying to an over-
Wagnered public. In fact, we had a sense that this

sort of reader was there with us the night we saw
" L' Elisir d' Amore," and that it was in his personality
we felt and remembered many things which we could
have fancied personal only to ourselves.

He began to take the affair out of our keeping from
the first moment, when, after passing through the
crowd arriving from the snowy street, we found our
way through the distracted vestibule of the opera-
house into the concentred auditorium and hushed ourselves in the presence of the glowing spectacle of the
stage. " Ah, this is the real thing," he whispered, and
he would not let us, at any moment when we could
have done so without molesting our neighbors, censure
the introduction of Alpine architecture in the entour-
age of an Italian village piazza. " It is a village at
the foot of the Alps probably," he said, " and if not,
no matter. It is as really the thing as all the rest:
as the chorus of peasants and soldiers, of men and
women who impartially accompany the orchestra in
the differing sentiments of the occasion; as the rivals
who vie with one another in recitative and aria; as the
heroine who holds them both in a passion of suspense
while she weaves the enchantment of her trills and
runs about them; as the whole circumstance of the
divinely impossible thing which defies nature and triumphs over prostrate probability. What does a little
Swiss Gothic matter? The thing is always opera, and
it is always Italy. I was thinking, as we crowded in
there from the outside, with our lives in our hands,
through all those trolleys and autos and carriages and
cabs and sidewalk ticket - brokers, of the first time
I saw this piece. It was in Venice, forty-odd years
ago, and I arrived at the theatre in a gondola, slipping
to the water-gate with a waft of the gondolier's oar that
was both impulse and arrest, and I was helped up the

sea-weedy, slippery steps by a beggar whom age and sorrow had bowed to just the right angle for supporting my hand on the shoulder he lent it. The blackness of the tide was pierced with the red plunge of a few lamps, and it gurgled and chuckled as my gondola lurched off and gave way to another; and when I got to my box—a box was two florins, but I could afford it—I looked down on just this scene, over a pit full of Austrian officers and soldiers, and round on a few Venetians darkling in the other boxes and half-heartedly enjoying the music. It was the most hopeless hour of the Austrian occupation, and the air was heavy with its oppression and tobacco, for the officers smoked between the acts. It was only the more intensely Italian for that; but it was not more Italian than this; and when I see those impossible people on the stage, and hear them sing, I breathe an atmosphere that is like the ether beyond the pull of our planet, and is as far from all its laws and limitations."

Our friend continued to talk pretty well through the whole interval between the first and second acts; and we were careful not to interrupt him, for from the literary quality of his diction we fancied him talking for publication, and we wished to take note of every turn of his phrase.

"It's astonishing," he said, "how little art needs in order to give the effect of life. A touch here and there is enough; but art is so conditioned that it has to work against time and space, and is obliged to fill up and round out its own body with much stuff that gives no sense of life. The realists," he went on, "were only half right."

"Isn't it better to be half right than wrong altogether?" we interposed.

"I'm not sure. What I wanted to express is that every now and then I find in very defective art of all kinds that mere *look* of the real thing which suffices. A few words of poetry glance from the prose body of verse and make us forget the prose. A moment of dramatic motive carries hours of heavy comic or tragic performance. Is any piece of sculpture or painting altogether good? Or isn't the spectator held in the same glamour which involved the artist before he began the work, and which it is his supreme achievement to impart, so that it shall hide all defects? When I read what you wrote the other month, or the other year, about the vaudeville shows—"

"Hush!" we entreated. "Don't bring those low associations into this high presence."

"Why not? It is all the same thing. There is no inequality in the region of art; and I have seen things on the vaudeville stage which were graced with touches of truth so exquisite, so ideally fine, that I might have believed I was getting them at first hand and pure from the street-corner. Of course, the poor fellows who had caught them from life had done their worst to imprison them in false terms, to labor them out of shape, and build them up in acts where anything less precious would have been lost; but they survived all that and gladdened the soul. I realized that I should have been making a mistake if I had required any 'stunt' which embodied them to be altogether composed of touches of truth, of moments of life. We can stand only a very little radium; the captured sunshine burns with the fires that heat the summers of the farthest planets; and we cannot handle the miraculous substance as if it were mere mineral. A touch of truth is perhaps not only all we need, but all we can endure in any one example of art."

" You are lucky if you get so much," we said, " even at a vaudeville show."

" Or at an opera," he returned, and then the curtain rose on the second act. When it fell again, he resumed, as if he had been interrupted in the middle of a sentence. " What should you say was the supreme moment of this thing, or was the radioactive property, the very soul? Of course, it is there where Nemorino drinks the elixir and finds himself freed from Adina; when he bursts into the joyous song of liberation and gives that delightful caper

> ' Which signifies indifference, indifference,
> Which signifies indifference,'

and which not uncommonly results from a philter composed entirely of claret. When Adina advances in the midst of his indifference and breaks into the lyrical lament

> ' Neppur mi guarda!'

she expresses the mystery of the sex which can be best provoked to love by the sense of loss, and the vital spark of the opera is kindled. The rest is mere incorporative material. It has to be. In other conditions the soul may be disembodied, and we may have knowledge of it without the interposition of anything material; but if there are spiritual bodies as there are material bodies, still the soul may wrap itself from other souls and emit itself only in gleams. But putting all that aside, I should like to bet that the germ, the vital spark of the opera, felt itself life, felt itself flame, first of all in that exquisite moment of release which Nemorino's caper conveys. Till then it must have been rather blind groping, with nothing better in hand than that old, worn-out notion of a love-philter. What will you bet?"

"We never bet," we virtuously replied. "We are principled against it in all cases where we feel sure of losing; though in this case we could never settle it, for both composer and librettist are dead."

"Yes, isn't it sad that spirits so gay should be gone from a world that needs gayety so much? That is probably the worst of death; it is so indiscriminate," the reader thoughtfully observed.

"But aren't you," we asked, "getting rather far away from the question whether the pleasure of experience isn't greater than the pleasure of inexperience— whether later operas don't give more joy than the first?"

"Was that the question?" he returned. "I thought it was whether Italian opera was not as much at home in exile as in its native land."

"Well, make it that," we responded, tolerantly.

"Oh no," he met us half-way. "But it naturalizes itself everywhere. They have it in St. Petersburg and in Irkutsk, for all I know, and certainly in Calcutta and Australia, the same as in Milan and Venice and Naples, or as here in New York, where everything is so much at home, or so little. It's the most universal form of art."

"Is it? Why more so than sculpture or painting or architecture?"

Our demand gave the reader pause. Then he said: "I think it is more immediately universal than the other forms of art. These all want time to denationalize themselves. It is their nationality which first authorizes them to be; but it takes decades, centuries sometimes, for them to begin their universal life. It seems different with operas. 'Cavalleria Rusticana'

50

was as much at home with us in its first year as
'L'Elisir d'Amore' is now in its sixtieth or seven-
tieth."

"But it isn't," we protested, "denationalized. What
can be more intensely Italian than an Italian opera is
anywhere?"

"You're right," the reader owned, as the reader always must, if honest, in dealing with the writer. "It
is the operatic audience, not the opera, which is denationalized when the opera becomes universal. We
are all Italians here to-night. I only wish we were in
our native land, listening to this musical peal of ghost-
ly laughter from the past."

The reader was silent a moment while the vast house
buzzed and murmured and babbled from floor to roof.
Perhaps the general note of the conversation, if it
could have been tested, would have been found voluntary rather than spontaneous; but the sound was gay,
and there could be no question of the splendor of the
sight. We may decry our own almost as much as we
please, but there is a point where we must cease to
depreciate ourselves; even for the sake of evincing our
superiority to our possessions, we must not undervalue
some of them. One of these is the Metropolitan Opera
House, where the pride of wealth, the vanity of fashion, the beauty of youth, and the taste and love of
music fill its mighty cup to the brim in the propor-
tions that they bear to one another in the community.
Wherever else we fail of our ideal, there we surely
realize it on terms peculiarly our own. Subjec-
tively the scene is intensely responsive to the New
York spirit, and objectively it is most expressive of
the American character in that certain surface effect of thin brilliancy which remains with the spec-

tator the most memorable expression of its physiognomy.

No doubt something like this was in the reader's mind when he resumed, with a sigh: "It's rather pathetic how much more magnificently Italian opera has always been circumstanced in exile than at home. It had to emigrate in order to better its fortunes; it could soon be better seen if not heard outside of Italy than in its native country. It was only where it could be purely conventional as well as ideal that it could achieve its greatest triumphs. It had to make a hard fight for its primacy among the amusements that flatter the pride as well as charm the sense. You remember how the correspondents of Mr. Spectator wrote to him in scorn of the affected taste of ' the town ' when the town in London first began to forsake the theatre and to go to the opera?"

"Yes, they were very severe on the town for pretending to a pleasure imparted in a language it could not understand a word of. They had all the reason on their side, and they needed it; but the opera is independent of reason, and the town felt that for its own part it could dispense with reason, too. The town can always do that. It would not go seriously or constantly to English opera, though ever so much invited to do so, for all the reasons, especially the patriotic reasons. Isn't it strange, by-the-way, how English opera is a fashion, while Italian opera remains a passion? We had it at its best, didn't we, in the Gilbert and Sullivan operas, which were the most charming things in the world; but they charmed only for a while, and it may be doubted whether they ever greatly charmed the town. The manager of the Metropolitan replaces German with Italian opera, and finds his account in it, but could he find his account in it if he put on ' The Mikado ' instead of 'L'Elisir d'Amore'? If he did so, the town would not be here. Why?"

The reader did not try to answer at once. He seemed to be thinking, but perhaps he was not; other readers may judge from his reply, which, when it came, was this: "There seems to be something eternally as well as universally pleasing in Italian opera; but what the thing is, or how much of a thing it is, I wouldn't undertake to say. Possibly the fault of English opera is its actuality. It seizes upon a contemporaneous mood or fad, and satirizes it; but the Italian opera at its lightest deals with a principle of human nature, and it is never satirical; it needn't be, for it is as independent of the morals as of the reasons. It isn't obliged, by the terms of its existence, to teach, any more than it is obliged to convince. It's the most absolute thing in the world; and from its unnatural height it can stoop at will in moments of enrapturing naturalness without ever losing poise. Wasn't that delightful where Caruso hesitated about his encore, and then, with a shrug and a waft of his left hand to the house, went off in order to come back and give his aria with more effect? That was a touch of naturalness not in the scheme of the opera."

"Yes, but it was more racial, more personal, than natural. It was delicious, but we are not sure we approved of it."

"Ah, in Italian opera you're not asked to approve; you're only desired to enjoy!"

"Well, then that bit of racial personality was of the effect of actuality, and it jarred."

"Perhaps you're right," the reader sighed, but he added: "It was charming; yes, it made itself part of the piece. Nemorino would have done just as Caruso did."

At the last fall of the curtain the reader and the writer rose in unison, a drop of that full tide of life which ebbed by many channels out of the vast auditorium, and in two or three minutes left it dry. They stayed in their duplex personality to glance at the silken evanescences from the boxes, and then, being in the mood for the best society, they joined the shining presences in the vestibule where these waited for their carriages and automobiles. Of this company the interlocutors felt themselves so inseparably part that they could with difficulty externate themselves so far as to observe that it was of the quality of " the town " which had gone to Italian opera from the first.

In Mr. Spectator's time the town would have been lighted by the smoky torches of linkboys to its chairs; now it was called to its electric autos in the blaze of a hundred incandescent bulbs; but the difference was not enough to break the tradition. There was something in the aspect of that patrician throng, as it waited the turn of each, which struck the reader and writer jointly as a novel effect from any American crowd, but which the writer scarcely dares intimate to the general reader, for the general reader is much more than generally a woman, and she may not like it. Perhaps we can keep it from offending by supposing that the fact can be true only of the most elect socially, but in any case the fact seemed to be that the men were handsomer than the women. They were not only handsomer, but they were sweller (if we may use a comparative hitherto unachieved) in look, and even in dress.

How this could have happened in a civilization so peculiarly devoted as ours to the evolution of female beauty and style is a question which must be referred to scientific inquiry. It does not affect the vast average of woman's loveliness and taste among us in ranks below the very highest; this remains unquestioned and unquestionable; and perhaps, in the given instance, it was an appearance and not a fact, or .perhaps the joint spectator was deceived as to the supreme social value of those rapidly dwindling and dissolving groups.

The reader and the writer were some time in finding their true level, when they issued into the common life of the street, and they walked home as much like driving home as they could. On the way the reader, who was so remotely lost in thought that the writer could scarcely find him, made himself heard in a musing suspiration: " There was something missing. Can you think what it was ?"

" Yes, certainly; there was no ballet."

" Ah, to be sure: no ballet! And there used always to be a ballet! You remember," the reader said, " how beatific it always was to have the minor coryphees subside in nebulous ranks on either side of the stage, and have the great planetary splendor of the *prima ballerina* come swiftly floating down the centre to the very footlights, beaming right and left? Ah, there's nothing in life now like that radiant moment! But even that was eclipsed when she rose on tiptoe and stubbed it down the scene on the points of her slippers, with the soles of her feet showing vertical in the act. Why couldn't we have had that to-night? Yes, we have been cruelly wronged."

" But you don't give the true measure of our injury. You forget that supreme instant when the master-spirit of the ballet comes skipping suddenly forward, and leaping into the air with calves that exchange a shimmer of kisses, and catches the *prima ballerina* at the waist, and tosses her aloft, and when she comes down supports her as she bends this way and that way, and all at once stiffens for her bow to the house. Think of our having been defrauded of that!"

"Yes, we have been wickedly defrauded." The reader was silent for a while, and then he said: "I wonder if anybody except the choreographic composer ever knew what the story of any ballet was? Were you ever able to follow it?"

"Certainly not. It is bad enough following the opera. All that one wishes to do in one case is to look, just as in the other case all one wishes to do is to listen. We would as lief try to think out the full meaning of a Browning poem in the pleasure it gave us, as to mix our joy in the opera or the ballet with any severe question of their purport."

VI

THE SUPERIORITY OF OUR INFERIORS

The satirical reader introduced himself with a gleam in his eye which kindled apprehension in the unreal editor's breast, and perhaps roused in him a certain guilty self-consciousness.

"I didn't know," the reader said, "that you were such a well-appointed *arbiter elegantiarum*."

"Meaning our little discourse last month on the proper form of addressing letters?" the editor boldly grappled with the insinuation. "Oh yes; etiquette is part of our function. We merely hadn't got round to the matter before. You liked our remarks?"

"Very much," our visitor said, with the fine irony characteristic of him. "All the more because I hadn't expected that sort of thing of you. What I have expected of you hitherto was something more of the major morality."

"But the large-sized morals did not enter into that scheme. We deal at times with the minor morality, too, if the occasion demands, as we have suggested. You should not have been surprised to find politeness, as well as righteousness, advocated or applauded here. Naturally, of course, we prefer the larger-sized morals as questions for discussion. Had you one of the larger-sized questions of morality to present?"

"I was thinking it was a larger-sized question of manners."

5   57

" For example."

" The experience of one of those transatlantic celebrities who seem to be rather multiplying upon us of late, and who come here with a proclamation of their worship of American women ready to present, as if in print, to the swarming interviewers on the pier, and who then proceed to find fault with our civilization on every other point, almost before they drive up to their hotels."

" But isn't that rather an old story?"

" I suppose it *is* rather old, but it always interests us; we are never free from that longing for a flattered appearance in the eyes of others which we so seldom achieve. This last, or next to last, celebrity—in the early winter it is impossible to fix their swift succession—seems to have suffered amaze at the rude behavior of some dairymaids in the milk-room of the lady who was showing the celebrity over her premises. I didn't understand the situation very clearly. The lady must have been a lady farmer, in order to have a milk-room with dairymaids in it; but in any case the fact is that when the lady entered with the celebrity the maids remained seated, where they were grouped together, instead of rising and standing in the presence of their superiors, as they would have done in the hemisphere that the celebrity came from."

" Well, what came of it?"

" Oh, nothing. It was explained to the celebrity that the maids did not rise because they felt themselves as good as their mistress and her guest, and saw no reason for showing them a servile deference: that this was the American ideal."

" In the minds of those Swedish, Irish, English, Polish, German, or Bohemian dairymaids," we murmured, dreamily, and when our reader roused us from our muse with a sharp "What?" we explained, "Of course they were not American dairymaids, for it stands to reason that if they were dairymaids they could not be Americans, or if Americans they could not be dairymaids."

"True," our friend assented, "but all the same you admit that they were behaving from an American ideal?"

"Yes."

"Well, that ideal is what the celebrity objects to. The celebrity doesn't like it—on very high grounds."

"The grounds of social inequality, the inferiority of those who work to those who pay, and the right of the superiors to the respect of the inferiors?"

"No, the politeness due from one class to another."

"Such as lives between classes in Europe, we suppose. Well, that is very interesting. Is it of record that the lady and her guest, on going into the milk-room where the dairymaids remained rudely seated, bowed or nodded to them or said, 'Good-day, young ladies'?"

"No, that is not of record."

"Their human quality, their human equality, being altogether out of the question, was probably in no wise recognized. Why, then, should they have recognized the human quality of their visitors?" Our satirical reader was silent, and we went on. "There is something very droll in all that. We suppose you have often been vexed, or even outraged, by the ingratitude of the waiter whom you had given a handsome tip, over and above the extortionate charge of the house, and who gathered up your quarter or half-dollar and slipped it into his pocket without a word, or even an inarticulate murmur, of thanks?"

"Often. Outraged is no word for it."

"Yes," we assented, feeling our way delicately. "Has it ever happened that in the exceptional case where the waiter has said, 'Thank you very much,' or the like, you have responded with a cordial, 'You're welcome,' or, 'Not at all'?"

"Certainly not."

"Why not?"

"Because—because—those are terms of politeness between—"

Our friend hesitated, and we interrogatively supplied the word, "Equals? There are always difficulties between unequals. But try this, some day, and see what a real gratitude you will get from the waiter. It isn't infallible, but the chances are he will feel that you have treated him like a man, and will do or say something to show his feeling: he will give a twitch to your under-coat when he has helped you on with your top-coat, which will almost pull you over. We have even tried saying 'You are welcome' to a beggar. It's astonishing how they like it. By-the-way, have you the habit of looking at your waiter when he comes to take your order; or do you let him stand facing you, without giving him a glance above the lower button of his poor, greasy waistcoat?"

"No, the theory is that he is part of the mechanism of the establishment."

"That is the theory. But it has its inconveniences. We ourselves used to act upon it, but often, when we found him long in bringing our order, we were at a loss which waiter to ask whether it would be ready some time during the evening; and occasionally we have blown up the wrong waiter, who did not fail to bring us to shame for our error."

"They do look so confoundedly alike," our visitor said, thoughtfully.

"We others look confoundedly alike to them, no doubt. If they studied us as little as we study them, if they ignored us as contemptuously as we do them, upon the theory that we, too, are part of the mechanism, the next man would be as likely as we to get our dinner."

"They are paid to study us," our visitor urged.

"Ah, *paid!* The intercourse of unequals is a commercial transaction, but when the inferiors propose to make it purely so the superiors object: they want something to boot, something thrown in, some show of respect, some appearance of gratitude. Perhaps those dairymaids did not consider that they were paid to stand up when their employer and the visiting celebrity came into the milk-room, and so, unless they were civally recognized—we don't say they weren't in this case—they thought they would do some of the ignoring, too. It is surprising how much the superiors think they ought to get for their money from the inferiors in that commercial transaction. For instance, they think they buy the right to call their inferiors by their first names, but they don't think they sell a similar right with regard to themselves. They call them Mary and John, but they would be surprised and hurt if the butler and waitress addressed them as Mary and John. Yet there is no *reason* for their surprise. Do you remember in that entrancing and edifying comedy of ' Arms and the Man '—Mr. Bernard Shaw's very best, as we think—the wild Bulgarian maid calls the daughter of the house by her Christian name? ' But you mustn't do that,' the mother of the house instructs her. ' Why not?' the girl demands. ' *She calls me Louka.*' "

"Capital!" our friend agreed. "But, of course, Shaw doesn't mean it."

"You never can tell whether he means a thing or

not. We think he meant in this case, as Ibsen means in all cases, that you shall look where you stand."

Our satirist seemed to have lost something of his gayety. "Aren't you taking the matter a little too seriously?"

"Perhaps. But we thought you wanted us to be more serious than we were about addressing letters properly. This is the larger-sized morality, the real No. 11 sort, and you don't like it, though you said you expected it of us."

"Oh, but I do like it, though just at present I hadn't expected it. But if you're in earnest you must admit that the lower classes with us are abominably rude. Now, I have the fancy—perhaps from living on the Continent a good deal in early life, where I formed the habit—of saying good-morning to the maid or the butler when I come down. But they never seem to like it, and I can't get a good-morning back unless I dig it out of them. I don't want them to treat me as a superior; I only ask to be treated as an equal."

"We have heard something like that before, but we doubt it. What you really want is to have your condescension recognized; they *feel* that, if they don't *know* it. Besides, their manners have been formed by people who don't ask good-morning from them; they are so used to being treated as if they were not there that they cannot realize they *are* there. We have heard city people complain of the wane of civility among country people when they went to them in the summer to get the good of their country air. They say that the natives no longer salute them in meeting, but we never heard that this happened when they first saluted the natives. Try passing the time of day with the next farmer you meet on a load of wood, and you will find that the old-fashioned civility is still to be had for the asking. But it won't be offered without the asking; the American who thinks from your dress and address that you don't regard him as an equal will not treat you as one at the risk of a snub; and he is right. As for domestics—or servants, as we insolently call them—their manners are formed on their masters', and are often very bad. But they are not always bad. We, too, have had that fancy of yours for saying good-morning when we come down; it doesn't always work, but it oftener works than not. A friend of ours has tried some such civility at others' houses: at his host's house when the door was opened to him, arriving for dinner, and he was gloomily offered a tiny envelope with the name of the lady he was to take out. At first it surprised, but when it was imagined to be well meant it was apparently liked; in extreme cases it led to note of the weather; the second or third time at the same house it established something that would have passed, with the hopeful spectator, for a human relation. Of course, you can't carry this sort of thing too far. You can be kind, but you must not give the notion that you do not know your place."

"Ah! You draw the line," our friend exulted. "I thought so. But where?"

"At the point where you might have the impression that you respected butlers, when you merely loved your fellow-men. You see the difference?"

"But isn't loving your fellow-men enough? Why should you respect butlers?"

"To be sure. But come to think of it, why shouldn't you? What is it in domestic employ that degrades, that makes us stigmatize it as 'service'? As soon as you get out-of-doors the case changes. You must often have seen ladies fearfully snubbed by their coachmen; and as for chauffeurs, who may kill you or somebody else at any moment, the mental attitude of the average automobilaire toward them must be one of abject deference. But there have been some really heroic, some almost seraphic, efforts to readjust the terms of a relation that seems to have something essentially odious in it. In the old times, the times of the simple life now passed forever, when the daughter of one family 'lived out' in another, she ate with the family and shared alike with them. She was their help, but she became their hindrance when she insisted upon the primitive custom after 'waiting at table' had passed the stage when the dishes were all set down, and the commensals 'did their own stretching.' Heroes and seraphs did their utmost to sweeten and soften the situation, but the unkind tendency could not be stayed. The daughter of the neighbor who 'lived out' became 'the hired girl,' and then she became the waitress, especially when she was of neighbors beyond seas; and then the game was up. Those who thought humanely of the predicament and wished to live humanely in it tried one thing and tried another. That great soul of H. D. L., one of the noblest and wisest of our economic reformers, now gone to the account which any might envy him, had a usage which he practised with all guests who came to his table. Before they sat down he or his wife said, looking at the maid who was to serve the dinner, 'This is our friend, Miss Murphy'; and then the guests were obliged in some sort to join the host and hostess in recognizing the human quality of the attendant. It was going rather far, but we never heard that any harm came of it. Some thought it rather odd, but most people thought it rather nice."

"And you advocate the general adoption of such a custom?" our friend asked, getting back to the sarcasm of his opening note. "Suppose a larger dinner, a fashionable dinner, with half a dozen men waiters? That sort of thing might do at the table of a reformer, which only the more advanced were invited to; but it wouldn't work with the average retarded society woman or clubman."

"What good thing works with *them?*" we retorted, spiritedly. "But no, the custom would not be readily adopted even among enlightened thinkers. We do not insist upon it; the men and the maids might object; they might not like knowing the kind of people who are sometimes asked to quite good houses. To be sure, they are not obliged to recognize them out of the house."

"But what," our friend asked, "has all this got to do with the question of 'the decent respect' due from domestics, as you prefer to call them, to their employers?"

"As in that case of the dairymaids which we began with? But why was any show of respect due from them? Was it nominated in the bond that for their four or five dollars a week they were to stand up when their 'mistress' and her 'company' entered the room? Why, in fine, should any human being respect another, seeing what human beings generally are? We may love one another, but *respect!* No, those maids might, and probably did, love their mistress; but they felt that they could show their love as well sitting down as standing up. They would not stand up to show their love for one another."

"Then you think there is some love lost between the master and man or mistress and maid nowadays," our beaten antagonist feebly sneered.

"The masters and mistresses may not, but the men and maids may, have whole treasures of affection ready to lavish at the first sign of a desire for it; they do not say so, for they are not very articulate. In the mean time the masters and mistresses want more than they have paid for. They want honor as well as obedience, respect as well as love, the sort of thing that money used to buy when it was worth more than it is now. Well, they won't get it. They will get it less and less as time goes on. Whatever the good new times may bring, they won't bring back the hypocritical servility of the good old times. They—"

We looked round for our visiting reader, but he had faded back into the millions of readers whom we are always addressing in print.

VII

UNIMPORTANCE OF WOMEN IN REPUBLICS

A VISITOR of the Easy Chair who seemed to have no
conception of his frequency, and who was able to supply from his imagination the welcome which his host
did not always hurry to offer him, found a place for
himself on the window-sill among the mistaken MSS.
sent in the delusion that the editor of the Chair was the
editor of the magazine.

"I have got a subject for you," he said.

"Have you ever heard," we retorted, " of carrying
coals to Newcastle? What made you think we wanted
a subject?"

"Merely that perfunctory air of so many of your
disquisitions. I should think you would feel the want
yourself. Your readers all feel it for you."

"Well, we can tell you," we said, " that there could
be no greater mistake. We are turning away subjects
from these premises every day. They come here, hat
in hand, from morning till night, asking to be treated;
and after dark they form a Topic Line at our door,
begging for the merest pittance of a notice, for the
slightest allusion, for the most cursory mention. Do
you know that there are at least two hundred thousand
subjects in this town out of a job now? If you have
got a subject, you had better take it to the country
press; the New York magazines and reviews are over-

stocked with them; the newspapers, morning and evening, are simply inundated with subjects; subjects are
turned down every Sunday in the pulpits; they cannot
get standing-room in the theatres. Why, we have just
this moment dismissed a subject of the first interest. Have you heard how at a late suffrage meeting
one lady friend of votes for women declared herself
an admirer of monarchies because they always gave
women more recognition, more honor, than republics?"

"No, I haven't," our visitor said.

"Well, it happened," we affirmed. "But every nook
and cranny of our brain was so full of subjects that
we simply could not give this a moment's consideration, and we see that all the other editors in New York
were obliged to turn the cold shoulder to it, though
they must have felt, as we did, that it was of prime
importance."

From a position of lounging ease our visitor sat up,
and began to nurse one of his knees between his clasped
hands. "But if," he asked, "you had been able to consider the subject, what should you have said?"

"There are a great many ways of considering a
subject like that," we replied. "We might have taken
the serious attitude, and inquired how far the female
mind, through the increasing number of Anglo-Amer-
ican marriages in our international high life, has become honeycombed with monarchism. We might have
held that the inevitable effect of such marriages was to
undermine the republican ideal at the very source of
the commonwealth's existence, and by corrupting the
heart of American motherhood must have weakened the
fibre of our future citizenship to the point of supinely
accepting any usurpation that promised ranks and titles
and the splendor of court life."

"Wouldn't you have been rather mixing your metaphors?" our visitor asked, with an air of having followed us over a difficult country.

"In a cause like that, no patriotic publicist would have minded mixing his metaphors. He would have felt that the great thing was to keep his motives pure; and in treating such a subject our motives would have remained the purest, whatever became of our metaphors. At the same time this would not have prevented our doing justice to the position taken by that friend of votes for women. We should have frankly acknowledged that there was a great deal to be said for it, and that republics had hitherto been remiss in not officially acknowledging the social primacy of woman, but, in fact, distinctly inviting her to a back seat in public affairs. We should then have appealed to our thoughtful readers to give the matter their most earnest attention, and with the conservatism of all serious inquirers we should have urged them to beware of bestowing the suffrage on a class of the community disposed so boldly to own its love of the splendors of the state. Would it be sage, would it be safe, to indulge with democratic equality a sex which already had its eyes on the flattering inequality of monarchy? Perhaps at this point we should digress a little and mention Montesquieu, whose delightful *Spirit of Laws* we have lately been reading. We should remind the reader, who would like to think he had read him too, how Montesquieu distinguishes between the principles on which the three sorts of government are founded: civic virtue being the base of a republic, honor the ruling motive in the subjects of a monarchy, and fear the dominant passion in the slaves of a despotism. Then we should ask whether men were prepared to intrust the reins of government to women when they had received this timely intimation that women were more eager to arrive splendidly than to bring the car of state in safety to the goal. How long would it be, we should poignantly demand, before in passing from the love of civic virtue to the ambition of honor, we should sink in the dread of power?"

Our visitor was apparently not so deeply impressed by the treatment of the subject here outlined as we had been intending and expecting he should be. He asked, after a moment, " Don't you think that would be rather a heavy-handed way of dealing with the matter?"

" Oh," we returned, " we have light methods of treating the weightiest questions. There is the semi-ironical vein, for instance, which you must have noticed a good deal in us, and perhaps it would be better suited to the occasion."

" Yes?" our visitor suggested.

" Yes," we repeated. " In that vein we should question at the start whether any such praise of monarchy had been spoken, and then we should suppose it had, and begin playfully to consider what the honors and distinctions were that women had enjoyed under monarchy. We should make a merit at the start of throwing up the sponge for republics. We should own they had never done the statesmanlike qualities of women justice. We should glance, but always a little mockingly, at the position of woman in the Greek republics, and contrast, greatly to the republican disadvantage, her place in the democracy of Athens with that she held in the monarchy of Sparta. We should touch upon the fact that the Athenian women were not only not in politics, but were not even in society, except a class which could be only fugitively mentioned, and we should freely admit that the Spartan women were the heroic inspiration of the men in all the virtues of patriotism at home as well as in the field. We should recognize the sort of middle station women held in the Roman republic, where they were not shut up in the almost Oriental seclusion of Athenian wives, nor invited to a share in competitive athletics like the Spartan daughters. We should note that if a Spartan mother had the habit of bidding her son return with his shield or on it, a Roman mother expressed a finer sense of her importance in the state when she intimated that it was enough for her to be the parent of the Gracchi. But we should not insist upon our point, which, after all, would not prove that the decorative quality of women in public life was recognized in Rome as it always has been in monarchies, and we should recur to the fact that this was the point which had been made against all republics. Coming down to the Italian republics, we should have to own that Venice, with her ducal figurehead, had practically a court at which women shone as they do in monarchies; while in Florence, till the Medici established themselves in sovereign rule, women played scarcely a greater part than in Athens. It was only with the Medici that we began to hear of such distinguished ladies as Bianca Cappello; and in the long, commonplace annals of the Swiss commonwealth we should be able to recall no female name that lent lustre to any epoch. We should contrast this poverty with the riches of the French monarchy, adorned with the memories of Agnes Sorel, of Diane de Poitiers, of Madame de Montespan, of Madame de Pompadour, following one another in brilliant succession, and sharing not only the glory but the authority of the line of princes whose affections they ruled. Of course, we should have to use an ironical gravity in concealing their real quality and the character of the courts where they flourished; and in comparing the womanless obscurity of the English Commonwealth with the feminine effulgence of the Restoration, we should seek a greater effect in our true aim by concealing the name and nature of the ladies who illustrated the court of Charles II."

"And what would your true aim be?" our visitor pressed, with an unseemly eagerness which we chose to snub by ignoring it.

"As for the position of women in despotisms," we continued, "we should confess that it seemed to be as ignobly subordinate as that of women in republics. They were scarcely more conspicuous than the Citizenesses who succeeded in the twilight of the One and Indivisible the marquises and comtesses and duchesses of the Ancien Régime, unless they happened, as they sometimes did, to be the head of the state. Without going back to the semi-mythical Semiramis, we should glance at the characters of Cleopatra and certain Byzantine usurpresses, and with a look askance at the two empresses of Russia, should arrive at her late imperial majesty of China. The poor, bad Isabella of Spain would concern us no more than the great, good Victoria of England, for they were the heads of monarchies and not of despotisms; but we should subtly insinuate that the reigns of female sovereigns were nowhere adorned by ladies of the distinction so common as hardly to be distinction in the annals of kings and emperors. What famous beauty embellished the court of Elizabeth or either Mary? Even Anne's Mrs. Masham was not a shining personality, and her Sarah of Marlborough was only a brilliant shrew.

"At this point we should digress a little, but we should pursue our inquiry in the same satirical tenor. We hope we are not of those moralists who assume a merit in denouncing the international marriages which have brought our women, some to think tolerantly and

72

some to think favorably of a monarchy as affording greater scope for their social genius. But we should ask, with the mock-seriousness befitting such a psychological study, how it was that, while American girls married baronets and viscounts and earls and dukes, almost none, if any, of their brothers married the sisters or daughters of such noblemen. It could not be that they were not equally rich and therefore equally acceptable, and could it be that they made it a matter of conscience not to marry ladies of title? Were our men, then, more patriotic than our women? Were men naturally more republican than women?

" This question would bring us to the pass where we should more or less drop the mocking mask. We should picture a state of things in which we had actually arrived at a monarchy of our own, with a real sovereign and a nobility and a court, and the rest of the tradition. With a sudden severity we should ask where, since they could not all be of the highest rank, our women would consent to strike the procession of precedence? How, with their inborn and inbred notions of the deference due their sex, with that pride of womanhood which our republican chivalry has cherished in them, they would like, when they went to court, to stand, for hours perhaps, while a strong young man, or a fat old man, or a robust man in the prime of life, remained seated in the midst of them? Would it flatter their hopes of distinction to find the worst scenes of trolley-car or subway transit repeated at the highest social function in the land, with not even a hanging-strap to support their weariness, their weakness, or, if we must say it, their declining years? Would the glory of being part of a spectacle testifying in our time to the meanness and rudeness of the past be a compensation for the aching legs and breaking backs under the trailing robes and the nodding plumes of a court dress?"

"That would be a telling stroke," our visitor said, "but wouldn't it be a stroke retold? It doesn't seem to me very new."

"No matter," we said. "The question is not what a thing is, but how it is done. You asked how we should treat a given subject, and we have answered."

"And is that all you could make of it?"

"By no means. As subjects are never exhausted, so no subject is ever exhausted. We could go on with this indefinitely. We could point out that the trouble was, with us, not too much democracy, but too little; that women's civic equality with men was perhaps the next step, and not the social inequality among persons of both sexes. Without feeling that it affected our position, we would acknowledge that there was now greater justice for women in a monarchy like Great Britain than in a republic like the United States; with shame we would acknowledge it; but we would never admit that it was so because of the monarchism of the first or the republicanism of the last. We should finally be very earnest with this phase of our subject, and we should urge our fair readers to realize that citizenship was a duty as well as a right. We should ask them before accepting the suffrage to consider its responsibilities and to study them in the self-sacrificing attitude of their husbands and fathers, or the brothers of one another, toward the state. We should make them observe that the actual citizen was not immediately concerned with the pomps and glories of public life; that parties and constituencies were not made up of one's fellow-aristocrats, but were mostly composed of plebeians very jealous of any show of distinction, and that, in spite of the displeasures of political association with them, there was no present disposition in American men to escape to monarchy from them. We cannot, we should remind them, all be of good family; that takes time, or has taken it; and without good family the chances of social eminence, or even prominence, are small at courts. Distinction is more evenly distributed in a democracy like ours; everybody has a chance at it. To be sure, it is not the shining honor bestowed by kings, but when we remember how often the royal hand needs washing we must feel that the honor from it may have the shimmer of putrescence. This is, of course, the extreme view of the case; and the condition of the royal hand is seldom scrutinized by those who receive or those who witness the honor bestowed. But the honor won from one's fellow-citizens is something worth having, though it is not expressed in a ribbon or a title. Such honor, it seems probable, will soon be the reward of civic virtue in women as well as men, and we hope women will not misprize it. The great end to be achieved for them by the suffrage is self-government, but with this goes the government of others, and that is very pleasant. The head of our state may be a woman, chosen at no far-distant election; and though it now seems droll to think of a woman being president, it will come in due time to seem no more so than for a woman to be a queen or an empress. At any rate, we must habituate our minds to the idea; we must realize it with the hope it implies that no woman will then care socially to outshine her sister; at the most she will be emulous of her in civic virtue, the peculiar grace and glory of republics. We understand that this is already the case in New Zealand and Colorado and Wyoming. It is too soon, perhaps, to look for the effect of suffrage on the female character in Denmark; it may be mixed, because there the case is complicated by the existence of a king, which may contaminate that civic virtue by the honor which is the moving principle in a monarchy. And now," we turned lightly to our visitor, " what is the topic you wish us to treat ?"

" Oh," he said, rising, " you have put it quite out of my head; I've been so absorbed in what you were saying. But may I ask just where in your treatment of the theme your irony ends ?"

" Where yours begins," we neatly responded.

VIII

HAVING JUST GOT HOME

THE air of having just got home from Europe was very evident in the friend who came to interview himself with us the other day. It was not, of course, so distinguishing as it would have been in an age of less transatlantic travel, but still, as we say, it was evident, and it lent him a superiority which he could not wholly conceal. His superiority, so involuntary, would, if he had wished to dissemble, have affirmed itself in the English cut of his clothes and in the habit of his top-hat, which was so newly from a London shop as not yet to have lost the whiteness of its sweat-band. But his difference from ourselves appeared most in a certain consciousness of novel impressions, which presently escaped from him in the critical tone of his remarks.

"Well," we said, with our accustomed subtlety, "how do you find your fellow-savages on returning to them after a three months' absence?"

"Don't ask me yet," he answered, laying his hat down on a pile of rejected MSS., delicately, so as not to dim the lustre of its nap. "I am trying to get used to them, and I have no doubt I shall succeed in time. But I would rather not be hurried in my opinions."

"You find some relief from the summer's accumulation of sky-scrapers amid the aching void of our manners?" we suggested.

77

" Oh, the fresh sky-scrapers are not so bad. You won't find the English objecting to them half so much as some of our own fellows. But you are all right about the aching void of manners. That is truly the bottomless pit with us."

" You think we get worse ?"

" I don't say that, exactly. How could we ?"

" It might be difficult."

" I will tell you what," he said, after a moment's muse. " There does not seem to be so much an increase of bad manners, or no manners, as a diffusion. The foreigners who come to us in hordes, but tolerably civil hordes, soon catch the native unmannerliness, and are as rude as the best of us, especially the younger generations. The older people, Italians, Czechs, Poles, Greeks, Assyrians, or whatever nationalities now compose those hordes, remain somewhat in the tradition of their home civility; but their children, their grandchildren, pick up our impoliteness with the first words of our language, or our slang, which they make their adoptive mother-tongue long before they realize that it is slang. When they do realize it, they still like it better than language, and as no manners are easier than manners, they prefer the impoliteness they find waiting them here. I have no doubt that their morals improve; we have morals and to spare. They learn to carry pistols instead of knives; they shoot instead of stabbing."

" Have you been attacked with any particular type of revolver since your return ?" we inquired, caustically.

" I have been careful not to give offence."

" Then why are you so severe upon your fellow-savages, especially the minors of foreign extraction ?"

" I was giving the instances which I supposed I was
asked for; and I am only saying that I have found
our manners merely worse quantitatively, or in the
proportion of our increasing population. But this
prompt succession of the new Americans to the heri-
tage of the old Americans is truly grievous. They must
so soon outnumber us, three to one, ten to one, twenty,
fifty, and they must multiply our incivilities in geo-
metrical ratio. At Boston, where I landed—"

" Oh, you landed at Boston!" we exclaimed, as if
this accounted for everything; but we were really only
trying to gain time. " If you had landed at New
York, do you think your sensibilities would have suffered in the same degree?" We added, inconsequently
enough, " We always supposed that Boston was exemplary in the matters you are complaining of."

" And when you interrupted me, with a want of
breeding which is no doubt national rather than in-
dividual, I was going on to say that I found much al-
leviation from a source whose abundant sweetness I had
forgotten. I mean the sort of caressing irony which
has come to be the most characteristic expression of
our native kindliness. There can be no doubt of our
kindliness. Whatever we Americans of the old race-
suicidal stock are not, we are kind; and I think that
our expression of our most national mood has acquired
a fineness, a delicacy, with our people of all degrees,
unknown to any other irony in the world. Do you
remember *The House with the Green Shutters*—I can
never think of the book without a pang of personal
grief for the too-early death of the author—how the
bitter, ironical temper of the Scotch villagers is realized? Well, our ironical temper is just the antithesis
of that. It is all sweetness, but it is of the same origin
as that of those terrible villagers: it comes from that

perfect, that familiar understanding, that penetrating reciprocal intelligence, of people who have lived intimately in one another's lives, as people in small communities do. We are a small community thrown up large, as they say of photographs; we are not so much a nation as a family; we each of us know just what any other, or all others, of us intend to the finest shade of meaning, by the lightest hint."

" Ah!" we breathed, quite as if we were a character in a novel which had inspired the author with a new phrase. " Now you are becoming interesting. Should you mind giving a few instances?"

" Well, that is not so easy. But I may say that the friendly ironies began for us as soon as we were out of the more single-minded keeping of the ship's stewards, who had brought our hand-baggage ashore, and, after extracting the last shilling of tip from us, had delivered us over to the keeping of the customs officers. It began with the joking tone of the inspectors, who surmised that we were not trying to smuggle a great value into the country, and with their apologetic regrets for bothering us to open so many trunks. They implied that it was all a piece of burlesque, which we were bound mutually to carry out for the gratification of a Government which enjoyed that kind of thing. They indulged this whim so far as to lift out the trays, to let the Government see that there was nothing dutiable underneath, where they touched or lifted the contents with a mocking hand, and at times carried the joke so far as to have some of the things removed. But they helped put them back with a smile for the odd taste of the Government. I do not suppose that an exasperating duty was ever so inexasperatingly fulfilled."

" Aren't you rather straining to make out a case?

We have heard of travellers who had a very different experience."

"At New York, yes, where we are infected with the foreign singleness more than at Boston. Perhaps a still livelier illustration of our ironical temperament was given me once before when I brought some things into Boston. There were some Swiss pewters, which the officers joined me for a moment in trying to make out were more than two hundred years old; but failing, jocosely levied thirty per cent. *ad valorem* on them; and then in the same gay spirit taxed me twenty per cent. on a medallion of myself done by an American sculptor, who had forgotten to verify an invoice of it before the American consul at the port of shipment."

"It seems to us," we suggested, "that this was a piece of dead earnest."

"The fact was earnest," our friend maintained, "but the spirit in which it was realized was that of a brotherly persuasion that I would see the affair in its true light, as a joke that was on me. It was a joke that cost me thirty dollars."

"Still, we fail to see the irony of the transaction."

"Possibly," our friend said, after a moment's muse, "I am letting my sense of another incident color the general event too widely. But before I come to that I wish to allege some proofs of the national irony which I received on two occasions when landing in New York. On the first of these occasions the commissioner who came aboard the steamer, to take the sworn declaration of the passengers that they were not smugglers, recognized my name as that of a well-known financier who had been abroad for a much-needed rest, and personally welcomed me home in such terms that I felt sure of complete exemption from the duties levied on others. When we landed I found that this good friend had looked out for me to the extent of getting me the first inspector, and he had guarded my integrity to the extent of committing me to a statement in severalty of the things my family had bought abroad, so that I had to pay twenty-eight dollars on my daughter's excess of the hundred dollars allowed free, although my wife was bringing in only seventy-five dollars' value, and I less than fifty."

" You mean that you had meant to lump the imports and escape the tax altogether ?" we asked.

" Something like that."

" And the officer's idea of caressing irony was to let you think you could escape equally well by being perfectly candid ?"

" Something like that."

" And what was the other occasion ?"

" Oh, it was when I had a letter to the customs officer, and he said it would be all right, and then furnished me an inspector who opened every piece of my baggage just as if I had been one of the wicked."

We could not help laughing, and our friend grinned appreciatively. " And what was that supreme instance of caressing irony which you experienced in Boston ?" we pursued.

" Ah, *there* is something I don't think you can question. But I didn't experience it; I merely observed it. We were coming down the stairs to take our hack at the foot of the pier, and an elderly lady who was coming down with us found the footing a little insecure. The man in charge bade her be careful, and then she turned upon him in severe reproof, and scolded him well. She told him that he ought to have those stairs looked after, for otherwise somebody would be killed one of these days. ' Well, ma'am,' he said, ' I shouldn't like that. I was in a railroad accident once.

But I tell you what you do. The next time you come over here, you just telephone me, and I'll have these steps fixed. Or, I'll tell you: you just write me a letter and let me know exactly how you want 'em fixed, and I'll see to it myself.' "

"That was charming," we had to own, "and it was of an irony truly caressing, as you say. Do you think it was exactly respectful?"

"It was affectionate, and I think the lady liked it as much as any of us, or as the humorist himself."

"Yes, it was just so her own son might have joked her," we assented. "But tell us, Crœsus," we continued, in the form of Socratic dialogue, "did you find at Boston that multiple unmannerliness which you say is apparent from the vast increase of adoptive citizens? We have been in the habit of going to Boston when we wished to refresh our impression that we had a native country; when we wished to find ourselves in the midst of the good old American faces, which were sometimes rather arraigning in their expression, but not too severe for the welfare of a person imaginably demoralized by a New York sojourn."

Our friend allowed himself time for reflection. "I don't think you could do that now with any great hope of success. I should say that the predominant face in Boston now was some type of Irish face. You know that the civic affairs of Boston are now in the hands of the Irish. And with reason, if the Irish are in the majority."

"In New York it has long been the same without the reason," we dreamily suggested.

"In Boston," our friend went on, without regarding us, "the Catholics outvote the Protestants, and not because they vote oftener, but because there are more of them."

" And the heavens do not fall ?"

" It is not a question of that; it is a question of whether the Irish are as amiable and civil as the Americans, now they are on top."

" We always supposed they were one of the most amiable and civil of the human races. Surely you found them so ?"

" I did at Queenstown, but at Boston I had not the courage to test the fact. I would not have liked to try a joke with one of them as I would at Queenstown, or as I would at Boston with an American. Their faces did not arraign me, but they forbade me. It was very curious, and I may have misread them."

" Oh, probably not," we lightly mocked. " They were taking it out of you for ages of English oppression; they were making you stand for the Black Cromwell."

" Oh, very likely," our friend said, in acceptance of our irony, because he liked irony so much. " But, all the same, I thought it a pity, as I think it a pity when I meet a surly Italian here, who at home would be so sweet and gentle. It is somehow our own fault. We have spoiled them by our rudeness; they think it is American to be as rude as the Americans. They mistake our incivility for our liberty."

" There is something in what you say," we agreed, " if you will allow us to be serious. They are here in our large, free air, without the parasites that kept them in bounds in their own original habitat. We must invent some sort of culture which shall be constructive and not destructive, and will supply the eventual good without the provisional evil."

" Then we must go a great way back, and begin with our grandfathers, with the ancestors who freed us from Great Britain, but did not free themselves from the illusion that equality resides in incivility and honesty in bluntness. That was something they transmitted to us intact, so that we are now not only the best-hearted but the worst-mannered of mankind. If our habitual carriage were not rubber-tired by irony, we should be an intolerable offence, if not to the rest of the world, at least to ourselves. By-the-way, since I came back I have been reading a curious old book by James Fenimore Cooper, which I understand made a great stir in its day. Do you know it?—*Home as Found?*"

"We know it as one may know a book which one has not read. It pretty nearly made an end of James Fenimore Cooper, we believe. His fellow-countrymen fell on him, tooth and nail. We didn't take so kindly to criticism in those days as we do now, when it merely tickles the fat on our ribs, and we respond with the ironic laughter you profess to like so much. What is the drift of the book besides the general censure?"

"Oh, it is the plain, dull tale of an American family returning home after a long sojourn in Europe so high-bred that you want to kill them, and so superior to their home-keeping countrymen that, vulgarity for vulgarity, you much prefer the vulgarity of the Americans who have not been away. The author's unconsciousness of the vulgarity of his exemplary people is not the only amusing thing in the book. They arrive for a short stay in New York before they go to their country-seat somewhere up the State, and the sketches of New York society as it was in the third or fourth decade of the nineteenth century are certainly delightful: society was then so exactly like what it is now in spirit. Of course, it was very provincial, but society is always and everywhere provincial. One thing about it then was different from what it is now: I mean the attitude of the stay-at-homes toward the been-abroads.

They revered them and deferred to them, and they called them Hajii, or travellers, in a cant which must have been very common, since George William Curtis used the same Oriental term for his *Howadji in Syria* and his *Nile Notes of a Howadji.*"

"We must read it," we said, with the readiness of one who never intends to read the book referred to. "What you say of it is certainly very suggestive. But how do you account for the decay of the reverence and deference in which the Hajii were once held?"

"Well, they may have overworked their superiority."

"Or?" we prompted.

"The stay - at - homes may have got onto the been-abroads in a point where we all fail, unless we have guarded ourselves very scrupulously."

"And that is?"

"There is something very vulgarizing for Americans in the European atmosphere, so that we are apt to come back worse-mannered than we went away, and vulgarer than the untravelled, in so far as it is impoliter to criticise than to be criticised."

"And is that why your tone has been one of universal praise for your countrymen in the present interview?"

Our friend reached for his hat, smoothed a ruffled edge of the crown, and blew a speck of dust from it. "One reasons to a conclusion," he said, "not from it."

IX

NEW YORK TO THE HOME-COMER'S EYE

OUR friend came in with challenge in his eye, and though a month had passed, we knew, as well as if it were only a day, that he had come to require of us the meaning in that saying of ours that New York derived her inspiration from the future, or would derive it, if she ever got it.

"Well," he said, "have you cleared your mind yet sufficiently to 'pour the day' on mine? Or hadn't you any meaning in what you said? I've sometimes suspected it."

The truth is that we had not had very much meaning of the sort that you stand and deliver, though we were aware of a large, vague wisdom in our words. But we perceived that our friend had no intention of helping us out, and on the whole we thought it best to temporize.

"In the first place," we said, "we should like to know what impression New York made on you when you arrived here, if there was any room left on your soul-surface after the image of Boston had been imprinted there."

No man is unwilling to expatiate concerning himself, even when he is trying to corner a fellow-man. This principle of human nature perhaps accounts for the frequent failure of thieves to catch thieves, in spite of the proverb; the pursuit suggests somehow the pleasures of autobiography, and while they are reminded of this and that the suspects escape the detectives. Our friend gladly paused to reply:

"I wish I could say! It was as unbeautiful as it could be, but it was wonderful! Has anybody else ever said that there is no place like it? On some accounts I am glad there isn't; one place of the kind is enough; but what I mean is that I went about all the next day after arriving from Boston, with Europe still in my brain, and tried for something suggestive of some other metropolis, and failed. There was no question of Boston, of course; that was clean out of it after my first glimpse of Fifth Avenue in taxicabbing hotelward from the Grand Central Station. But I tried with Berlin, and found it a drearier Boston; with Paris, and found it a blonder and blither Boston; with London, and found it sombrely irrelevant and incomparable. New York is like London only in not being like any other place, and it is next to London in magnitude. So far, so good; but the resemblance ends there, though New York is oftener rolled in smoke, or mist, than we willingly allow to Londoners. Both, however, have an admirable quality which is not beauty. One might call the quality picturesque immensity in London, and in New York one might call it—"

He compressed his lips, and shut his eyes to a fine line for the greater convenience of mentally visioning.

"What?" we impatiently prompted.

"I was going to say, sublimity. What do you think of sublimity?"

"We always defend New York against you. We accept sublimity. How?"

"I was thinking of the drive up or down Fifth Avenue, the newer Fifth Avenue, which has risen in marble

FIFTH AVENUE AT THIRTY-FOURTH STREET

and Indiana limestone from the brownstone and brick of a former age, the Augustan Fifth Avenue which has replaced that old Lincolnian Fifth Avenue. You get the effect best from the top of one of the imperial motor-omnibuses which have replaced the consular two-horse stages; and I should say that there was more sublimity to the block between Sixteenth Street and Sixtieth than in the other measures of the city's extent."

"This is very gratifying to us as a fond New-Yorker; but why leave out of the reach of sublimity the region of the sky - scrapers, and the spacious, if specious, palatiality of the streets on the upper West Side ?"

"I don't, altogether," our friend replied. "Especially I don't leave out the upper West Side. That has moments of being even beautiful. But there is a point beyond which sublimity cannot go; and that is about the fifteenth story. When you get a group of those sky-scrapers, all soaring beyond this point, you have, in an inverted phase, the unimpressiveness which Taine noted as the real effect of a prospect from the summit of a very lofty mountain. The other day I found myself arrested before a shop-window by a large photograph labelled 'The Heart of New York.' It was a map of that region of sky-scrapers which you seem to think not justly beyond the scope of attributive sublimity. It was a horror; it set my teeth on edge; it made me think of scrap-iron—heaps, heights, pinnacles of scrap-iron. Don't ask me why scrap-iron! Go and look at that photograph and you will understand. Below those monstrous cliffs the lower roofs were like broken foot-hills; the streets were chasms, gulches, gashes. It looked as if there had been a conflagration, and the houses had been burned into the cellars; and the eye sought the nerve-racking tangle of

7

pipe and wire which remains among the ruins after a great fire. Perhaps this was what made me think of scrap-iron—heaps, heights, pinnacles of it. No, there was no sublimity there. Some astronomers have latterly assigned bounds to immensity, but the sky-scrapers go beyond these bounds; they are primordial, abnormal."

"You strain for a phrase," we said, "as if you felt the essential unreality of your censure. Aren't you aware that mediæval Florence, mediæval Siena, must have looked, with their innumerable towers, like our sky - scrapered New York? They must have looked quite like it."

"And very ugly. It was only when those towers, which were devoted to party warfare as ours are devoted to business warfare, were levelled, that Florence became fair and Siena superb. I should not object to a New York of demolished sky - scrapers. They would make fine ruins; I would like to see them as ruins. In fact, now I think of it, ' The Heart of New York ' reminded me of the Roman Forum. I wonder I didn't think of that before. But if you want sublimity, the distinguishing quality of New York, as I feel it more and more, while I talk of it, you must take that stretch of Fifth Avenue from a motor-bus top."

"But that stretch of Fifth Avenue abounds in sky-scrapers!" we lamented the man's inconsistency.

"Sky-scrapers in subordination, yes. There is one to every other block. There is that supreme sky-scraper, the Flatiron. But just as the Flatiron, since the newspapers have ceased to celebrate its pranks with men's umbrellas, and the feathers and flounces and ' tempestuous petticoats ' of the women, has sunk back into a measurable inconspicuity, so all the other tall

buildings have somehow harmonized themselves with
the prospect and no longer form the barbarous architectural chaos of lower New York. I don't object
to their being mainly business houses and hotels; I
think that it is much more respectable than being palaces or war-like eminences, Guelf or Ghibelline; and
as I ride up-town in my motor-bus, I thrill with their
grandeur and glow with their condescension. Yes, they
condescend; and although their tall white flanks climb
in the distance, they seem to sink on nearer approach,
and amiably decline to disfigure the line of progress,
or to dwarf the adjacent edifices. Down-town, in the
heart of New York, poor old Trinity looks driven into
the ground by the surrounding heights and bulks; but
along my sublime upper Fifth Avenue there is spire
after spire that does not unduly dwindle, but looks as
if tenderly, reverently, protected by the neighboring
giants. They are very good and kind giants, apparently. But the acme of the sublimity, the quality in
which I find my fancy insisting more and more, is in
those two stately hostelries, the Gog and Magog of that
giant company, which guard the approach to the Park
like mighty pillars, the posts of vast city gates folded
back from them."

"Come!" we said. "This is beginning to be something like."

"In November," our friend said, taking breath for
a fresh spurt of praise, "there were a good many sympathetic afternoons which lent themselves to motor-
bus progress up that magnificent avenue, and if you
mounted to your place on top, about three o'clock, you
looked up or down the long vista of blue air till it
turned mirk at either vanishing-point under a sky of
measureless cloudlessness. That dimness, almost smoki-
ness at the closes of the prospect, was something un-

speakably rich. It made me think, quite out of relation or relevance, of these nobly mystical lines of Keats:

> ' His soul shall know the sadness of her night,
> And be among her cloudy trophies hung.' "

We closed our eyes in the attempt to grope after him. " Explain, O Howadji!"

" I would rather not, as you say when you can't," he replied. " But I will come down a little nearer earth, if you prefer. Short of those visionary distances there are features of the prospect either way in which I differently rejoice. One thing is the shining black roofs of the cabs, moving and pausing like processions of huge turtles up and down the street; obeying the gesture of the mid-stream policemen where they stand at the successive crossings to stay them, and floating with the coming and going tides as he drops his inhibitory hand and speeds them in the continuous current. That is, of course, something you get in greater quantity, though not such intense quality, in a London ' block,' but there is something more fluent, more mercurially impatient, in a New York street jam, which our nerves more vividly partake. Don't ask me to explain! I would rather not!" he said, and we submitted.

He went on to what seemed an unjustifiable remove from the point. " Nothing has struck me so much, after a half-year's absence, in this novel revelation of sublimity in New York, as the evident increase on the street crowds. The city seems to have grown a whole new population, and the means of traffic and transportation have been duplicated in response to the demand of the multiplying freights and feet." Our friend laughed in self-derision, as he went on. " I remember when we first began to have the electric trolleys—"

"Trams, we believe you call them," we insinuated.

"Not when I'm on this side," he retorted, and he resumed: "I used to be afraid to cross the avenues where they ran. At certain junctions I particularly took my life in my hand, and my 'courage in both hands.' Where Sixth Avenue flows into Fifty-ninth Street, and at Sixth Avenue and Thirty-fourth Street, and at Dead Man's Curve (he has long been resuscitated) on Fourteenth Street, I held my breath till I got over alive, and I blessed Heaven for my safe passage at Forty-second and Twenty-third streets, and at divers places on Third Avenue. Now I regard these interlacing iron currents with no more anxiety than I would so many purling brooks, with stepping-stones in them to keep my feet from the wet: they are like gentle eddies—soft, clear, slow tides—where one may pause in the midst at will, compared with the deadly expanses of Fifth Avenue, with their rush of all manner of vehicles over the smooth asphalt surface. There I stand long at the brink; I look for a policeman to guide and guard my steps; I crane my neck forward from my coign of vantage and count the cabs, the taxicabs, the carriages, the private automobiles, the motorbuses, the express-wagons, and calculate my chances. Then I shrink back. If it is a corner where there is no policeman to bank the tides up on either hand and lead me over, I wait for some bold, big team to make the transit of the avenue from the cross-street, and then in its lee I find my way to the other side. As for the trolleys, I now mock myself of them, as Thackeray's Frenchmen were said to say in their peculiar English. (I wonder if they really did?) It is the taxicabs that now turn my heart to water. It is astonishing how they have multiplied—they have multiplied even beyond the ratio of our self-reduplicating population. There are so many already that this morning I read in my paper of a trolley-car striking a horse-cab! The reporter had written quite unconsciously, just as he used to write horseless carriage. Yes, the motor-cab is now the type, the norm, and the horse-cab is the—the—the—"

He hesitated for the antithesis, and we proposed "Abnorm?"

"*Say* abnorm! It is hideous, but I don't know that it is wrong. Where was I?"

"You had got quite away from the sublimity of New York, which upon the whole you seemed to attribute to the tall buildings along Fifth Avenue. We should like you to explain again why, if 'The Heart of New York,' with its sky-scrapers, made you think of scrap-iron, the Flatiron soothed your lacerated sensibilities?"

"The Flatiron is an incident, an accent merely, in the mighty music of the Avenue, a happy discord that makes for harmony. It is no longer nefarious, or even mischievous, now the reporters have got done attributing a malign meteorological influence to it. I wish I could say as much for the white marble rocket presently soaring up from the east side of Madison Square, and sinking the beautiful reproduction of the Giralda tower in the Garden half-way into the ground. As I look at this pale yellowish brown imitation of the Seville original, it has a pathos which I might not make you feel. But I would rather not look away from Fifth Avenue at all. It is astonishing how that street has assumed and resumed all the larger and denser life of the other streets. Certain of the avenues, like Third and Sixth, remain immutably and characteristically noisy and ignoble; and Fifth Avenue

FIFTH AVENUE FROM THE TOP OF A MOTOR-BUS

has not reduced them to insignificance as it has Broadway. That is now a provincial High Street beside its
lordlier compeer; but I remember when Broadway
stormed and swarmed with busy life. Why, I remember the party-colored 'buses which used to thun-
der up and down; and I can fancy some Rip Van
Winkle of the interior returning to the remembered
terrors and splendors of that mighty thoroughfare,
and expecting to be killed at every crossing—I can
fancy such a visitor looking round in wonder at
the difference and asking the last decaying sur-
vivor of the famous Broadway Squad what they had
done with Broadway from the Battery to Madison
Square. Beyond that, to be sure, there is a mighty flare
of electrics blazoning the virtues of the popular beers,
whiskeys, and actresses, which might well mislead my
elderly revisitor with the belief that Broadway was
only taken in by day, and was set out again after dark
in its pristine—I think pristine is the word; it used to
be—glory. But even by night that special length of
Broadway lacks the sublimity of Fifth Avenue, as I
see it or imagine it from my motor-bus top. *I* knew
Fifth Avenue in the Lincolnian period of brick and
brownstone, when it had a quiet, exclusive beauty, the
beauty of the unbroken sky-line and the regularity of
façade which it has not yet got back, and may never
get. You will get some notion of it still in Madison
Avenue, say from Twenty - eighth to Forty - second
streets, and perhaps you will think it was dull as well
as proud. It is proud now, but it is certainly not dull.
There is something of columnar majesty in the lofty
flanks of these tall shops and hotels as you approach
them, which makes you think of some capital decked
for a national holiday. But in Fifth Avenue it is
always holiday—"

"Enough of streets!" we cried, impatiently. "Now, what of men? What of that heterogeneity for which New York is famous, or infamous? You noticed the contrasting Celtic and Pelasgic tribes in Boston. What of them here, with all the tribes of Israel, lost and found, and the 'sledded Polack,' the Czech, the Hun, the German, the Gaul, the Gothic and Iberian Spaniard, and the swart stranger from our sister continent to the southward, and the islands of the seven seas, who so sorely outnumber us?"

Our friend smiled thoughtfully. "Why, that is very curious! Do you know that in Fifth Avenue the American type seems to have got back its old supremacy? It is as if no other would so well suit with that sublimity! I have not heard that race-suicide has been pronounced by the courts amenable to our wise State law against *felo de se,* but in the modern Fifth Avenue it is as if our stirp had suddenly reclaimed its old-time sovereignty. I don't say that there are not other faces, other tongues than ours to be seen, heard, there; far from it! But I do say it is a sense of the American face, the American tongue, which prevails. Once more, after long exile in the streets of our own metropolis, you find yourself in an American city. Your native features, your native accents, have returned in such force from abroad, or have thronged here in such multitude from the prospering Pittsburgs, Cincinnatis, Chicagos, St. Louises, and San Franciscos of the West, that you feel as much at home in Fifth Avenue as you would in Piccadilly, or in the Champs Elysées, or on the Pincian Hill. Yes, it is very curious."

"Perhaps," we suggested, after a moment's reflection, "it isn't true."

X

CHEAPNESS OF THE COSTLIEST CITY ON EARTH

" ONE of my surprises on Getting Back," the more
or less imaginary interlocutor who had got back from
Europe said in his latest visit to the Easy Chair, " is
the cheapness of the means of living in New York."

At this the Easy Chair certainly sat up. " Stay not
a moment, Howadji," we exclaimed, " in removing our
deep-seated prepossession that New York is the most
expensive place on the planet."

But instead of instantly complying our friend fell
into a smiling muse, from which he broke at last to
say: " I have long been touched by the pathos of a
fact which I believe is not yet generally known. Do
you know yourself, with the searching knowledge which
is called feeling it in your bones, that a good many
Southerners and Southerly Westerners make this town
their summer resort?" We intimated that want of
penetrating statistics which we perceived would gratify
him, and he went on. " They put up at our hotels
which in the ' anguish of the solstice' they find in-
vitingly vacant. As soon as they have registered the
clerk recognizes them as Colonel, or Major, or Judge,
but gives them the rooms which no amount of family or
social prestige could command in the season, and there
they stay, waking each day from unmosquitoed nights
to iced-melon mornings, until a greater anguish is tele-

graphed forward by the Associated Press. Then they
turn their keys in their doors, and flit to the neighboring Atlantic or the adjacent Catskills, till the solstice
recovers a little, and then they return to their hotel
and resume their life in the city, which they have almost to themselves, with its parks and drives and roof-
gardens and vaudevilles, unelbowed by the three or
four millions of natives whom we leave behind us
when we go to Europe, or Newport, or Bar Harbor, or
the Adirondacks. Sometimes they take furnished flats
along the Park, and settle into a greater permanency
than their hotel sojourn implies. They get the flats
at about half the rent paid by the lessees who sublet
them, but I call it pathetic that they should count it
joy to come where we should think it misery to stay.
Still, everything is comparative, and I suppose they
are as reasonably happy in New York as I am in my
London lodgings in the London season, where I sometimes stifle in a heat not so pure and clear as that I
have fled from."

" Very well," we said, dryly, " you have established
the fact that the Southerners come here for the summer and live in great luxury; but what has that to do
with the cheapness of living in New York, which you
began by boasting ?"

" Ah, I was coming back to that," the Howadji said,
with a glow of inspiration. " I have been imagining,
in the relation which you do not see, that New York
can be made the inexpensive exile of its own children
as it has been made the. summer home of those sympathetic Southerners. If I can establish the fact of its
potential cheapness, as I think I can, I shall deprive
them of some reasons for going abroad, though I'm not
sure they will thank me, when the reasons for Europe
are growing fewer and fewer. Culture can now be

acquired almost as advantageously here as there. Except for the 'monuments,' in which we include all ancient and modern masterpieces in the several arts, we have no excuse for going to Europe, and even in these masterpieces Europe is coming to us so increasingly in every manner of reproduction that we allege the monuments almost in vain. The very ruins of the past are now so accurately copied in various sorts of portable plasticity that we may know them here with nearly the same emotion as on their own ground. The education of their daughters which once availed with mothers willing to sacrifice themselves and their husbands to the common good, no longer avails. The daughters know the far better time they will have at home, and refuse to go, as far as daughters may, and in our civilization this, you know, is very far. But it was always held a prime reason and convincing argument that Dresden, Berlin, Paris, Rome, and even London, were so much cheaper than New York that it was a waste of money to stay at home."

"Well, wasn't it?" we impatiently demanded.

"I will not say, for I needn't, as yet. There were always at the same time philosophers who contended that if we lived in those capitals as we lived at home, they would be dearer than New York. But what is really relevant is the question whether New York isn't cheaper now."

"We thought it had got past a question with you. We thought you began by saying that New York *is* cheaper."

"I can't believe I was so crude," the Howadji returned, with a fine annoyance. "That is the conclusion you have characteristically jumped to without looking before you leap. I was going to approach the fact much more delicately, and I don't know but what by your haste you have shattered my ideal of the conditions. But I'll own that the great stumbling-block to my belief that the means of living in New York are cheaper than in the European capitals is that the house rents here are so incomparably higher than they are there. But I must distinguish and say that I mean flat-rents, for, oddly enough, flats are much dearer than houses. You can get a very pretty little house, in a fair quarter, with plenty of light and a good deal of sun, for two-thirds and sometimes one-half what you must pay for a flat with the same number of rooms, mostly dark or dim, and almost never sunny. Of course, a house is more expensive and more difficult to ' run,' but even with the cost of the greater service and of the furnace heat the rent does not reach that of a far less wholesome and commodious flat. There is one thing to be said in favor of a flat, however, and that is the women are in favor of it. The feminine instinct is averse to stairs; the sex likes to be safely housed against burglars, and when it must be left alone, it desires the security of neighbors, however strange the neighbors may be; it likes the authority of a jan-itor, the society of an elevator-boy. It hates a lower door, an area, an ash-barrel, and a back yard. But if it were willing to confront all these inconveniences, it is intimately, it is osseously, convinced that a house is not cheaper than a flat. As a matter of fact, neither a house nor a flat is cheap enough in New York to bear me out in my theory that New York is no more expensive than those Old World cities. To aid ef-ficiently in my support I must invoke the prices of provisions, which I find, by inquiry at several markets on the better avenues, have reverted to the genial level of the earlier nineteen-hundreds, before the cattle com-bined with the trusts to send them up. I won't prosily rehearse the quotations of beef, mutton, pork, poultry, and fish; they can be had at any dealer's on demand; and they will be found less, on the whole, than in London, less than in Paris, less even than in Rome. They are greater no doubt than the prices in our large Western cities, but they are twenty per cent. less than the prices in Boston, and in the New England towns which hang upon Boston's favor for their marketing. I do not know how or why it is that while we wicked New-Yorkers pay twenty-five cents for our beefsteak, these righteous Bostonians should have to pay thirty, for the same cut and quality. Here I give twenty - eight a pound for my Java coffee; in the summer I live near an otherwise delightful New Hampshire town where I must give thirty-eight. It is strange that the siftings of three kingdoms, as the Rev. Mr. Higginson called his fellow-Puritans, should have come in their great-grandchildren to a harder fate in this than the bran and shorts and middlings of such harvestings as the fields of Ireland and Italy, of Holland and Hungary, of Poland and Transylvania and Muscovy afford. Perhaps it is because those siftings have run to such a low percentage of the whole New England population that they must suffer, along with the refuse of the mills—the Mills of the Gods—abounding in our city and its dependencies.

"I don't know how much our housekeepers note the fall of the prices in their monthly bills, but in browsing about for my meals, as I rather like to do, I distinctly see it in the restaurant rates. I don't mean the restaurants to which the rich or reckless resort, but those modester places which consult the means of the careful middle class to which I belong. As you know, I live ostensibly at the Hotel Universe. I have a room there, and that is my address—"

" We know," we derisively murmured. " So few of
our visitors can afford it."

" I can't afford it myself," our friend said. " But
I save a little by breakfasting there, and lunching and
dining elsewhere. Or, I did till the eggs got so bad that
I had to go out for my breakfast, too. Now I get perfect eggs, of the day before, for half the price that the
extortionate hens laying for the Universe exact for
their last week's product. At a very good Broadway
hotel, which simple strangers from Europe think first
class, I get a ' combination ' breakfast of fresh eggs,
fresh butter, and fresh rolls, with a pot of blameless
Souchong or Ceylon tea, for thirty cents; if I plunge
to the extent of a baked apple, I pay thirty-five. Do
you remember what you last paid in Paris or Rome
for coffee, rolls, and butter?"

" A franc fifty," we remembered.

" And in London for the same with eggs you paid
one and six, didn't you?"

" Very likely," we assented.

" Well, then, you begin to see. There are several
good restaurants quite near that good hotel where I
get the same combination breakfast for the same price;
and if I go to one of those shining halls which you find
in a score of places, up and down Broadway and the
side streets, I get it for twenty-five cents. But though
those shining halls glare at you with roofs and walls of
stainless tile and glass, and tables of polished marble,
their bill of fare is so inflexibly adjusted to the general demand that I cannot get Souchong or Ceylon tea
for any money; I can only get Oolong; otherwise I
must take a cup of their excellent coffee. If I wander
from my wonted breakfast, I can get almost anything
in the old American range of dishes for five or ten
cents a portion, and the quality and quantity are both

all I can ask. As I have learned upon inquiry, the great basal virtues of these places are good eggs and good butter: I like to cut from the thick slice of butter under the perfect cube of ice, better than to have my butter pawed into balls or cut into shavings, as they serve your butter in Europe. But I prefer having a small table to myself, with my hat and overcoat vis-à-vis on the chair opposite, as I have it at that good hotel. In those shining halls I am elbowed by three others at my polished marble table; but if there were more room I should never object to the company. It is the good, kind, cleanly, comely American average, which is the best company in the world, with a more than occasional fine head, and faces delicately sculptured by thought and study. I address myself fearlessly to the old and young of my own sex, without ever a snub such as I might get from the self-respectful maids or matrons who resort to the shining halls, severally or collectively, if I ventured upon the same freedom with them. I must say that my commensals lunch or dine as wisely as I do for the most part, but sometimes I have had to make my tacit criticisms; and I am glad that I forbore one night with a friendly young man at my elbow, who had just got his order of butter-cakes—"

"Butter-cakes?" we queried.

"That is what they call a rich, round, tumid product of the griddle, which they serve very hot, and open to close again upon a large lump of butter. For two of those cakes and his coffee my unknown friend paid fifteen cents, and made a supper, after which I should not have needed to break my fast the next morning. But he fearlessly consumed it, and while he ate he confided that he was of a minor clerical employ in one of the great hotels near by, and when I praised our shining hall and its guests he laughed and said he came regularly, and he always saw people there who were registered at his hotel: they found it good and they found it cheap. I suppose you know that New York abounds in tables d'hôte of a cheapness unapproached in the European capitals?"

We said we had heard so; at the same time we tried to look as if we always dined somewhere in society, but Heaven knows whether we succeeded.

"The combination breakfast is a form of table d'hôte; and at a very attractive restaurant in a good place I have seen such a breakfast—fruit, cereal, eggs, rolls, and coffee — offered for fifteen cents. I have never tried it, not because I had not the courage, but because I thought thirty cents cheap enough; those who do not I should still hold worthy of esteem if they ate the fifteen-cent breakfast. I have also seen placarded a 'business men's lunch' for fifteen cents, which also I have not tried; I am not a business man. I make bold to say, however, that I often go for my lunch or my dinner to a certain Italian place on a good avenue, which I will not locate more definitely lest you should think me a partner of the enterprise, for fifty and sixty cents, ' vino compreso.' The material is excellent, and the treatment is artistic; the company of a simple and self-respectful domesticity which I think it an honor to be part of: fathers and mothers of families, aunts, cousins, uncles, grandparents. I do not deny a Merry Widow hat here and there, but the face under it, though often fair and young, is not a Merry Widow face. Those people all look as kind and harmless as the circle which I used to frequent farther downtown at a fifty-cent French table d'hôte, but with a bouillabaisse added which I should not, but for my actual experiences, have expected to buy for any money. But there are plenty of Italian and French tables d'hôte for the same price all over town. If you venture outside of the Latin race, you pay dearer and you fare worse, unless you go to those shining halls which I have been praising. If you go to a German place, you get grosser dishes and uncouth manners for more money; I do not know why that amiable race should be so dear and rude in its feeding-places, but that is my experience."

"You wander, you wander!" we exclaimed. "Why should we care for your impressions of German cooking and waiting, unless they go to prove or disprove that living in New York is cheaper than in the European capitals?"

"Perhaps I was going to say that even those Germans are not so dear as they are in the fatherland, though rude. They do not tend much if at all to tables d'hôte, but the Italians and the French who do, serve you a better meal for a lower price than you would get in Paris, or Rome, or Naples. There the prevalent ideal is five francs, with neither wine nor coffee included. I'll allow that the cheap table d'hôte is mainly the affair of single men and women, and does not merit the consideration I've given it. If it helps a young couple to do with one maid, or with none, instead of two, it makes for cheapness of living. Service is costly and it is greedy, and except in large households its diet is the same as the family's, so that anything which reduces it is a great saving. But the table d'hôte which is cheap for one or two is not cheap for more, and it is not available if there are children. Housing and raw-provisioning and serving are the main questions, and in Europe the first and last are apparently much less expensive. Marketing is undoubtedly cheaper with us, and if you count in what you get with the newness, the wholesomeness, and handiness of an

8

American flat, the rent is not so much greater than that
of a European flat, with its elementary bareness. You
could not, here, unless you descended from the apartment to the tenement, hire any quarter where you
would not be supplied with hot and cold water, with
steam heating, with a bath-room, and all the rest of it."

" But," we said, " you are showing that we are more
comfortably housed than the Europeans, when you
should be treating the fact of relative cheapness."

" I was coming to that even in the matter of
housing—"

" It is too late to come to it in this paper. You
have now talked three thousand words, and that is
the limit. You must be silent for at least another
month."

" But if I have something important to say at this
juncture? If I may not care to recur to the subject
a month hence? If I may have returned to Europe by
that time?"

" Then you can the better verify your statistics.
But the rule in this place is inflexible. Three thousand
words, neither more nor less. The wisdom of Solomon
would be blue-pencilled if it ran to more."

XI

WAYS AND MEANS OF LIVING IN NEW YORK

THE Howadji, or the Hajii, as people called his sort in the days of *Home as Found,* was prompt to the hour when his month's absence was up, and he began without a moment's delay: " But of course the lion in the way of my thesis that New York is comparatively cheap is the rent, the rent of flats or houses in the parts of the town where people of gentle tastes and feelings are willing to live. Provisions are cheap; furnishings of all kinds are cheap; service, especially when you mainly or wholly dispense with it, is cheap, for one maid here will do the work of two abroad, and if the mistress of the house does her own work she can make the modern appliances her handmaids at no cost whatever. It is ridiculous, in fact, leaving all those beautiful and ingenious helps in housework to the hirelings who work only twice as hard with them for more wages than the hirelings of countries where they don't exist."

" Don't be so breathless," we interposed. " You will only be allowed to talk three thousand words, whether you talk fast or slow, and you might as well take your ease."

" That is true," the Howadji reflected. " But I am full of my subject, and I have the feeling that I am getting more out, even if I can't get more in, by talking fast. The rent question itself," he hurried on,

" has been satisfactorily solved of late in the new invention of co-operative housing which you may have heard of."

We owned that we had, with the light indifference of one whom matters of more money or less did not concern, and our friend went on.

" The plan was invented, you know, by a group of artists who imagined putting up a large composite dwelling in a street where the cost of land was not absolutely throat-cutting, and finishing it with tasteful plainness in painted pine and the like, but equipping it with every modern convenience in the interest of easier housekeeping. The characteristic and imperative fact of each apartment was a vast and lofty studio whose height was elsewhere divided into two floors, and so gave abundant living-rooms in little space. The proprietorial group may have been ten, say, but the number of apartments was twice as many, and the basic hope was to let the ten other apartments for rents which would carry the expense of the whole, and house the owners at little or no cost. The curious fact is that this apparently too simple-hearted plan worked. The Philistines, as the outsiders may be called, liked being near the self-chosen people; they liked the large life-giving studio which imparted light and air to the two floors of its rearward division, and they eagerly paid the sustaining rents. The fortunate experience of one æsthetic group moved others to like enterprises; and now there are eight or ten of these co-operative studio apartment-houses in different parts of the town."

" With the same fortunate experience for the owners ?" we queried, with suppressed sarcasm.

" Not exactly," our friend assented to our intention. " The successive groups have constantly sought more central, more desirable, more fashionable situations.

They have built not better than they knew, for that could not be, but costlier, and they have finished in hard woods, with marble halls and marbleized hall-boys, and the first expense has been much greater; but actual disaster has not yet followed; perhaps it is too soon; we must not be impatient; but what has already happened is what happens with other beautiful things that the æsthetic invent. It has happened notoriously with all the most lovable and livable summer places which the artists and authors find out and settle themselves cheaply and tastefully in. The Philistines, a people wholly without invention, a cuckoo tribe incapable of self - nesting, stumble upon those joyous homes by chance, or by mistaken invitation. They submit meekly enough at first to be sub-neighbors ruled in all things by the genius of the place; but once in, they begin to lay their golden eggs in some humble cottage, and then they hatch out broods of palatial villas equipped with men and maid servants, horses, carriages, motors, yachts; and if the original settlers remain it is in a helpless inferiority, a broken spirit, and an overridden ideal. This tragical history is the same at Magnolia, and at York Harbor, and at Dublin, and at Bar Harbor; even at Newport itself; the co-operative housing of New York is making a like history. It is true that the Philistines do not come in and dispossess the autochthonic groups; these will not sell to them; but they have imagined doing on a sophisticated and expensive scale what the æsthetics have done simply and cheaply. They are buying the pleasanter sites, and are building co-operatively; though they have already eliminated the studio and the central principle, and they build for the sole occupancy of the owners. But the cost of their housing then is such that it puts them out of the range of our inquiry as their riches has

already put them beyond the range of our sympathy.
It still remains for any impecunious group to buy the
cheaper lots, and build simpler houses on the old studio
principle, with rents enough to pay the cost of operation, and leave the owners merely the interest and taxes,
with the eventual payment of these also by the tenants.
Some of the studio apartments are equipped with
restaurants, and the dwellers need only do such light
housekeeping as ladies may attempt without disgrace,
or too much fatigue."

"Or distraction from their duties to society," we
suggested.

"It depends upon what you mean by society; it's
a very general and inexact term. If you mean formal
dinners, dances, parties, receptions, and all that, the
lightest housekeeping would distract from the duties to
it; but if you mean congenial friends willing to come
in for tea in the afternoon, or to a simple lunch, or
not impossibly a dinner, light housekeeping is not in-
compatible with a conscientious recognition of society's
claims. I think of two ladies, sisters, one younger and
one older than the other, who keep house not lightly,
but in its full weight of all the meals, for their father
and brother, and yet are most gracefully and most ac-
ceptably in the sort of society which Jane Austen says
is, if not good, the best: the society of gifted, cultivated,
travelled, experienced, high-principled people, capable
of respecting themselves and respecting their qualities
wherever they find them in others. These ladies do
not pretend to 'entertain,' but their table is such that
they are never afraid to ask a friend to it. In a moment, if there is not enough or not good enough, one of
them conjures something attractive out of the kitchen,
and you sit down to a banquet. The sisters are both
of that gentle class of semi-invalids whose presence in

our civilization enables us to support the rudeness of the general health. They employ æsthetically the beautiful alleviations with which science has rescued domestic drudgery from so much of the primal curse; it is a pleasure to see them work; it is made so graceful, so charming, that you can hardly forbear taking hold yourself."

"But you do forbear," we interposed; "and do you imagine that their example is going to prevail with the great average of impecunious American housewives, or sisters, or daughters?"

"No, they will continue to 'keep a girl' whom they will enslave to the performance of duties which they would be so much better for doing themselves, both in body and mind, for that doing would develop in them the hospitable soul of those two dear ladies. They will be in terror of the casual guest, knowing well that they cannot set before him things fit to eat. They have no genius for housekeeping, which is one with home-making: they do not love it, and those ladies do love it in every detail, so that their simple flat shines throughout with a lustre which pervades the kitchen and the parlor and the chamber alike. It is the one-girl household, or the two-girl, which makes living costly because it makes living wasteful; it is not the luxurious establishments of the rich which are to blame for our banishment to the mythical cheapness of Europe."

We were not convinced by the eloquence which had overheated our friend, and we objected: "But those ladies you speak of give their whole lives to house-keeping, and ought cheapness to be achieved at such an expense?"

"In the first place, they don't; and, if they do, what do the one-girl or the two-girl housekeepers give their lives to? or, for the matter of that, the ten or twenty girl housekeepers? The ladies of whom I speak have always read the latest book worth reading; they have seen the picture which people worth while are talking of; they know through that best society which likes a cup of their tea all the æsthetic gossip of the day; they are part of the intellectual movement, that part which neither the arts nor the letters can afford to ignore; they help to make up the polite public whose opinions are the court of final appeal."

"They strike us," we said, stubbornly, "as rather romantic."

"Ah, there you are! Well, they *are* romantic— romantic like a gentle poem, like an idyllic tale; but I deny that they are romanticistic. Their whole lives deal with realities, the every-other-day as well as the every-day realities. But the lives of those others who make all life costly by refusing their share of its work dwell in a web of threadbare fictions which never had any color of truth in this country. They are trying to imitate poor imitations, to copy those vulgar copies of the European ideal which form the society-page's contribution to the history of our contemporary civilization."

We were so far moved as to say, "We think we see what you mean," and our friend went on.

"Speaking of civilization, do you know what a genial change the tea-room is working in our morals and manners? There are many interesting phases of its progress among us, and not the least interesting of these is its being so largely the enterprise of ladies who must not only save money, but must earn money, in order to live, not cheaply, but at all. Their fearlessness in going to work has often the charm of a patrician past, for many of them are Southern women who have come

to New York to repair their broken fortunes. The
tea-room has offered itself as a graceful means to this
end, and they have accepted its conditions, which are
mainly the more delicate kinds of cookery, with those
personal and racial touches in which Southern women
are so expert. But there are tea-rooms managed by
Western women, if I may judge from the accents involuntarily overheard in their talk at the telephone.
The tea of the tea-room means lunch, too, and in some
places breakfast and dinner, or rather supper, on much
the plan of the several Women's Exchanges; but these
are mostly of New England inspiration and operation,
and their cooking has a Northern quality. They, as
well as the tea-rooms, leave something to be desired in
cheapness, though they might be dearer; in some you
get tea for fifteen cents, in others a no better brew for
twenty-five. But they are all charmingly peaceful, and
when at the noon hour they overflow with conversation,
still there is a prevailing sense of quiet, finely qualified
by the feminine invention and influence. Mere men
are allowed to frequent these places, not only under the
protection of women, but also quite unchaperoned, and
when one sees them gently sipping their Souchong or
Oolong, and respectfully munching their toasted muf-
fins or their chicken-pie, one remembers with tender
gratitude how recently they would have stood crooking
their elbows at deleterious bars, and visiting the bowls
of cheese and shredded fish and crackers to which their
drink freed them, while it enslaved them to the witchery
of those lurid ladies contributed by art to the evil at-
tractions of such places: you see nowhere else ladies
depicted with so little on, except in the Paris salon.
The New York tea-rooms are not yet nearly so frequent
as in London, but I think they are on the average
cosier, and on the whole I cannot say that they are

dearer. They really cheapen the midday meal to many who would otherwise make it at hotels and restaurants, and, so far as they contribute to the spread of the afternoon-tea habit, they actually lessen the cost of living: many guests can now be fobbed off with tea who must once have been asked to lunch."

"But," we suggested, "isn't that cheapness at the cost of shabbiness, which no one can really afford?"

"No, I don't think so. Whatever lightens hospitality of its cumbrousness makes for civilization, which is really more compatible with a refined frugality than with an unbridled luxury. If every à-la-carte restaurant, in the hotels and out of them, could be replaced by tea-rooms, and for the elaborate lunches and dinners of private life the informality and simplicity of the afternoon tea were substituted, we should all be healthier, wealthier, and wiser; and I should not be obliged to protract this contention for the superior cheapness of New York."

"But, wait!" we said. "There is something just occurs to us. If you proved New York the cheapest great city in the world, wouldn't it tend to increase our population even beyond the present figure, which you once found so deplorable?"

"No, I imagine not. Or, rather, it would add to our population only those who desire to save instead of those who desire to waste. We should increase through the new-comers in virtuous economy, and not as now in spendthrift vainglory. In the end the effect would be the same for civilization as if we shrank to the size of Boston."

"You will have to explain a little, Howadji," we said, "if you expect us to understand your very interesting position."

"Why, you know," he answered, with easy su-

114

periority, "that now our great influx is of opulent strangers who have made a good deal of money, and of destitute strangers willing to help them live on it. The last we needn't take account of; they are common to all cities in all ages; but the first are as new as any phenomenon can be in a world of such tiresome tautologies as ours. They come up from our industrial provinces, eager to squander their wealth in the commercial metropolis; they throw down their purses as the heroes of old threw down their gantlets for a gage of battle, and they challenge the local champions of extortion to take them up. It is said that they do not want a seasonable or a beautiful thing; they want a costly thing. If, for instance, they are offered a house or an apartment at a rental of ten or fifteen thousand, they will not have it; they require a rental of fifteen or twenty thousand, so that it may be known, 'back home,' that they are spending that much for rent in New York, and the provincial imagination taxed to proportion the cost of their living otherwise to such a sum. You may say that it is rather splendid, but you cannot deny that it is also stupid."

"Stupid, no; but barbaric, yes," we formulated the case. "It is splendid, as barbaric pearls and gold are splendid."

"But you must allow that nothing could be more mischievous. When next we go with our modest incomes against these landlords, they suppose that we too want rentals of fifteen thousand, whereas we would easily be satisfied with one of fifteen hundred or a thousand. The poor fellows' fancy is crazed by those prodigals, and we must all suffer for their madness. The extravagance of the new-comers does not affect the price of provisions so much, or of clothes; the whole population demands food and raiment within the general means, however much it must exceed its means in the cost of shelter. The spendthrifts cannot set the pace for such expenditures, no matter how much they lavish on their backs and—"

"Forbear!" we cried. "Turning from the danger we have saved you from, you will say, we suppose, that New York would be the cheapest of the great cities if it were not for the cost of shelter."

"Something like that," he assented.

"But as we understand, that difficulty is to be solved by co-operative, or composite, housing?"

"Something like that," he said again, but there was a note of misgiving in his voice.

"What is the 'out'?" we asked.

"There is no 'out,'" he said, with a deep, evasive sigh.

XII

THE QUALITY OF BOSTON AND THE QUANTITY
OF NEW YORK

LATER in the summer, or earlier in the fall, than
when we saw him newly returned from Europe, that
friend whom the veteran reader will recall as having
so brashly offered his impressions of the national com-
plexion and temperament looked in again on the Easy
Chair.

" Well," we said, " do you wish to qualify, to hedge,
to retract? People usually do after they have been at
home as long as you."

" But I do not," he said. He took his former
seat, but now laid on the heap of rejected MSS., not
the silken cylinder he had so daintily poised there before, but a gray fedora that fell carelessly over in lazy
curves and hollows. " I wish to modify by adding the
effect of further observation and adjusting it to my first
conclusions. Since I saw you I have been back to Boston; in fact, I have just come from there."

We murmured some banality about not knowing a
place where one could better come from than Boston.
But he brushed it by without notice.

" To begin with, I wish to add that I was quite wrong
in finding the typical Boston face now prevalently
Celtic."

" You call that adding?" we satirized.

He ignored the poor sneer.

"My earlier observation was correct enough, but it was a result of that custom which peoples the hills, the shores, and the sister continent in summer with the New-Englanders of the past, and leaves their capital to those New-Englanders of the future dominantly represented by the Irish. At the time of my second visit the exiles had returned, and there were the faces again that, instead of simply forbidding me, arraigned me and held me guilty till I had proved myself innocent."

"Do you think," we suggested, "that you would find this sort of indictment in them if you had a better conscience?"

"Perhaps not. And I must own I did not find them so accusing when I could study them in their contemplation of some more important subject than myself. One such occasion for philosophizing them distinctly offered itself to my chance witness when an event of the last seriousness had called some hundreds of them together. One sees strong faces elsewhere; I have seen them assembled especially in England; but I have never seen such faces as those Boston faces, so intense, so full of a manly dignity, a subdued yet potent personality, a consciousness as far as could be from self-consciousness. I found something finely visionary in it all, as if I were looking on a piece of multiple portraiture such as you see in those Dutch paintings of companies at Amsterdam, for instance. It expressed purity of race, continuity of tradition, fidelity to ideals such as no other group of faces would now express. You might have had the like at Rome, at Athens, at Florence, at Amsterdam, in their prime, possibly in the England of the resurgent parliament, though there it would have been mixed with a fanaticism absent in

Boston. You felt that these men no doubt had their limitations, but their limitations were lateral, not vertical."

"Then why," we asked, not very relevantly, "don't you go and live in Boston?"

"It wouldn't make me such a Bostonian if I did; I should want a half-dozen generations behind me for that. Besides, I feel my shortcomings less in New York."

"You are difficult. Why not fling yourself into the tide of joy here, instead of shivering on the brink in the blast of that east wind which you do not even find regenerative? Why not forget our inferiority, since you cannot forgive it? Or do you think that by being continually reminded of it we can become as those Bostonians are? Can we reduce ourselves, by repenting, from four millions to less than one, and by narrowing our phylacteries achieve the unlimited Bostonian verticality, and go as deep and as high?"

"No," our friend said. "Good as they are, we can only be better by being different. We have our own message to the future, which we must deliver as soon as we understand it."

"Is it in Esperanto?"

"It is at least polyglot. But you are taking me too seriously. I wished merely to qualify my midsummer impressions of a prevailing Celtic Boston by my autumnal impressions of a persisting Puritanic Boston. But it is wonderful how that strongly persistent past still characterizes the present in every development. Even those Irish faces which I wouldn't have ventured a joke with were no doubt sobered by it; and when the Italians shall come forward to replace them it will be with no laughing Pulcinello masks, but visages as severe as those that first challenged the wilderness of

119

Massachusetts Bay, and made the Three Hills tremble to their foundations."

"It seems to us that you are yielding to rhetoric a little, aren't you?" we suggested.

"Perhaps I am. But you see what I mean. And I should like to explain further that I believe the Celtic present and the Pelasgic future will rule Boston in their turn as the Puritanic past learned so admirably to rule it: by the mild might of irony, by the beneficent power which in the man who sees the joke of himself enables him to enter brotherly into the great human joke, and be friends with every good and kind thing."

"Could you be a little more explicit?"

"I would rather not for the moment. But I should like to make you observe that the Boston to be has more to hope and less to fear from the newer Americans than this metropolis where these are so much more heterogeneous. Here salvation must be of the Jews among the swarming natives of the East Side; but in Boston there is no reason why the artistic instincts of the Celtic and Pelasgic successors of the Puritans should not unite in that effect of beauty which is an effect of truth, and keep Boston the first of our cities in good looks as well as good works. With us here in New York a civic job has the chance of turning out a city joy, but it is a fighting chance. In Boston there is little doubt of such a job turning out a joy. The municipality of Boston has had almost the felicity of Goldsmith—it has touched nothing which it has not adorned. Wherever its hand has been laid upon Nature, Nature has purred in responsive beauty. They used to talk about the made land in Boston, but half Boston is the work of man, and it shows what the universe might have been if the Bostonians had been taken into the

CHARLES EMBANKMENT, BELOW HARVARD BRIDGE

confidence of the Creator at the beginning. The Back Bay was only the suggestion of what has since been done; and I never go to Boston without some new cause for wonder. There is no other such charming union of pleasaunce and residence as the Fenways; the system of parks is a garden of delight; and now the State has taken up the work, no doubt at the city's suggestion, and, turning from the land to the water, has laid a restraining touch on the tides of the sea, which, ever since the moon entered on their management, have flowed and ebbed through the channel of the Charles. The State has dammed the river; the brine of the ocean no longer enters it, but it feeds itself full of sweet water from the springs in the deep bosom of the country. The Beacon Street houses back upon a steadfast expanse as fresh as the constant floods of the Great Lakes."

"And we dare say that it looks as large as Lake Superior to Boston eyes. What do they call their dam? The Charlesea?"

"You may be sure they will call it something tasteful and fit," our friend responded, in rejection of our feeble mockery. "Charlesea would not be bad. But what I wish to make you observe is that all which has yet been done for beauty in Boston has been done from the unexhausted instinct of it in the cold heart of Puritanism, where it 'burns frore and does the effect of fire.' As yet the Celtic and Pelasgic agencies have had no part in advancing the city. The first have been content with voting themselves into office, and the last with owning their masters out-of-doors; for the Irish are the lords, and the Italians are the landlords. But when these two gifted races, with their divinely implanted sense of art, shall join forces with the deeply conscienced taste of the Puritans, what mayn't we expect Boston to be?"

9 121

" And what mayn't we expect New York to be on
the same terms, or, say, when the Celtic and Pelasgic
and Hebraic and Slavic elements join with the old
Batavians, in whom the love of the artistic is by right
also native? Come! Why shouldn't we have a larger
Boston here?"

" Because we are *too* large," our friend retorted, un-
dauntedly. " When graft subtly crept among the nobler motives which created the park system of Boston
the city could turn for help to the State and get it;
but could our city get help from our State? Our city
is too big to profit by that help; our State too small
to render it. The commonwealth of Massachusetts is
creating a new Garden of Eden on the banks of the
Charlesea; but what is the State of New York doing
to emparadise the shores of the Hudson?"

" All the better for us, perhaps," we stubbornly, but
not very sincerely, contended, " if we have to do our
good works ourselves."

" Yes, if we do them. But shall they remain un-
done if we don't do them? The city of New York is
so great that it swings the State of New York. The
virtues that are in each do not complement one another,
as the virtues of Boston and Massachusetts do. Where
shall you find, in our house or in our grounds, the city
and the State joining to an effect of beauty? When
you come to New York, what you see of grandeur is the
work of commercialism; what you see of grandeur in
Boston is the work of civic patriotism. We hire the
arts to build and decorate the homes of business; the
Bostonians inspire them to devote beauty and dignity
to the public pleasure and use. No," our friend concluded with irritating triumph, " we are too vast, too
many, for the finest work of the civic spirit. Athens
could be beautiful—Florence, Venice, Genoa were—but

122

Rome, which hired or enslaved genius to create beautiful palaces, temples, columns, statues, could only be immense. She could only huddle the lines of Greek loveliness into a hideous agglomeration, and lose their effect as utterly as if one should multiply Greek noses and Greek chins, Greek lips and Greek eyes, Greek brows and Greek heads of violet hair, in one monstrous visage. No," he exulted, in this mortifying image of our future ugliness, " when a city passes a certain limit of space and population, she adorns herself in vain. London, the most lovable of the mighty mothers of men, has not the charm of Paris, which, if one cannot quite speak of her virgin allure, has yet a youth and grace which lend themselves to the fondness of the arts. Boston is fast becoming of the size of Paris, but if I have not misread her future she will be careful not to pass it, and become as New York is."

We were so alarmed by this reasoning that we asked in considerable dismay: " But what shall we do? We could not help growing; perhaps we wished to overgrow; but is there no such thing as ungrowing? When the fair, when the sex which we instinctively attribute to cities, finds itself too large in its actuality for a Directoire ideal, there are means, there are methods, of reduction. Is there no remedy, then, for municipal excess of size? Is there no harmless potion or powder by which a city may lose a thousand inhabitants a day, as the superabounding fair loses a pound of beauty? Is there nothing for New York analogous to rolling on the floor, to the straight-front corset, to the sugarless, starchless diet? Come, you must not deny us all hope! How did Boston manage to remain so small? What elixirs, what exercises, did she take or use? Surely she did not do it all by reading and thinking!" Our friend continued somewhat inexorably silent, and we pursued: "Do you think that by laying waste our Long Island suburbs, by burning the whole affiliated Jersey shore, by strangling the Bronx, as it were, in its cradle, and by confining ourselves rigidly to our native isle of Manhattan, we could do something to regain our lost opportunity? We should then have the outline of a fish; true, a nondescript fish; but the fish was one of the Greek ideals of the female form." He was silent still, and we gathered courage to press on. "As it is, we are not altogether hideous. We doubt whether there are not more beautiful buildings in New York now than there are in Boston; and as for statues, where are the like there of our Macmonnies Hale, of our Saint-Gaudens Farragut and Sherman, of our Ward Indian Hunter?"

"The Shaw monument blots them all out," our friend relentlessly answered. "But these are merely details. Our civic good things are accidental. Boston's are intentional. That is the great, the vital difference."

It did not occur to us that he was wrong, he had so crushed us under foot. But, with the trodden worm's endeavor to turn, we made a last appeal. "And with the sky-scraper itself we still expect to do something, something stupendously beautiful. Say that we have lost our sky-line! What shall we not have of grandeur, of titanic loveliness, when we have got a sky-scraper-line?"

It seemed to us that here was a point which he could not meet; and, in fact, he could only say, whether in irony or not, "I would rather not think."

We were silent, and, upon the reflection to which our silence invited us, we found that we would rather not ourselves think of the image we had invoked. We preferred to take up the question at another point.

124

"Well," we said, "in your impressions of Bostonian greatness we suppose that you received the effect of her continued supremacy in authors as well as authorship, in artists as well as art? You did not meet Emerson or Longfellow or Lowell or Prescott or Holmes or Hawthorne or Whittier about her streets, but surely you met their peers, alive and in the flesh?"

"No," our friend admitted, "not at every corner. But what I did meet was the effect of those high souls having abode there while on the earth. The great Boston authors are dead, and the great Boston artists are worse—they have come to New York; they have not even waited to die. But whether they have died, or whether they have come to New York, they have left their inspiration in Boston. In one sense the place that has known them shall know them no more forever; but in another sense it has never ceased to know them. I can't say how it is, exactly, but though you don't see them in Boston, you feel them. But here in New York—our dear, immense, slattern mother—who feels anything of the character of her great children? Who remembers in these streets Bryant or Poe or Hallock or Curtis or Stoddard or Stedman, or the other poets who once dwelt in them? Who remembers even such great editors as Greeley or James Gordon Bennett or Godkin or Dana? What malignant magic, what black art, is it that reduces us all to one level of forgottenness when we are gone, and even before we are gone? Have those high souls left their inspiration here, for common men to breathe the breath of finer and nobler life from? I won't abuse the millionaires who are now our only great figures; even the millionaires are gone when they go. They die, and they leave no sign, quite as if they were so many painters and poets. You can recall some of their names, but not easily. No, if New York has any hold upon the present from the past, it isn't in the mystical persistence of such spirits among us."

"Well," we retorted, hardily, "we have no need of them. It is the high souls of the future which influence us."

Our friend looked at us as if he thought there might be something in what we said. "Will you explain?" he asked.

"Some other time," we consented.

XIII

THE WHIRL OF LIFE IN OUR FIRST CIRCLES

ONE of those recurrent selves who frequent the habitat of the Easy Chair, with every effect of exterior identities, looked in and said, before he sat down, and much before he was asked to sit down, "Are you one of those critics of smart or swell society (or whatever it's called now) who despise it because they can't get into it, or one of those censors who won't go into it because they despise it?"

"Your question," we replied, "seems to be rather offensive, but we don't know that it's voluntarily so, and it's certainly interesting. On your part, will you say what has prompted you, just at the moment, to accost us with this inquiry?" Before he could answer, we hastened to add: "By-the-way, what a fine, old-fashioned, gentlemanly word *accost* is! People used to accost one another a great deal in polite literature. 'Seeing her embarrassment from his abrupt and vigorous stare, he thus accosted her.' Or, 'Embarrassed by his fixed and penetrating regard, she timidly accosted him.' It seems to us that we remember a great many passages like these. Why has the word gone out? It was admirably fitted for such junctures, and it was so polished by use that it slipped from the pen without any effort of the brain, and—"

"I have no time for idle discussions of a mere literary nature," our other self returned. "I am very full of the subject which I have sprung upon you, and which I see you are trying to shirk."

"Not at all," we smilingly retorted. "We will answer you according to your folly without the least reluctance. We are not in smart or swell society because we cannot get in; but at the same time we would not get in if we could, because we despise it too much. We wonder," we continued, speculatively, "why we always suspect the society satirist of suffering from a social snub? It doesn't in the least follow. Was Pope, when he invited his S'in' John to

> 'leave all meaner things
> To low ambition and the pride of kings'

goaded to magnanimity by a slight from royalty? Was Mr. Benson when he came over here from London excluded from the shining first circles of New York and Newport, which are apparently reflected with such brilliant fidelity in *The Relentless City,* and was he wreaking an unworthy resentment in portraying our richly moneyed, blue-blooded society to the life? How are manners ever to be corrected with a smile if the smile is always suspected of being an agonized grin, the contortion of the features by the throes of a mortified spirit? Was George William Curtis in his amusing but unsparing *Potiphar Papers*—"

"Ah, now you are shouting!" our other self exclaimed.

"Your slang is rather antiquated," we returned, with grave severity. "But just what do you mean by it in this instance?"

"I mean that manners are never corrected with a smile, whether of compassion or of derision. The man-

128

ners that are bad, that are silly, that are vulgar, that are vicious, go on unchastened from generation to generation. Even the good manners don't seem to decay: simplicity, sincerity, kindness, don't really go out, any more than the other things, and fortunately the other things are confined only to a small group in every civilization, to the black sheep of the great, whity-brown or golden-fleeced human family."

"What has all this vague optimism to do with the *Potiphar Papers* and smart society and George William Curtis?" we brought the intruder sharply to book.

"A great deal, especially the part relating to the continuity of bad manners. I've just been reading an extremely clever little book by a new writer, called *New York Society on Parade,* which so far as its basal facts are concerned might have been written by the writer of ' Our Best Society' and the other *Potiphar Papers.* The temperament varies from book to book; Mr. Ralph Pulitzer has a neater and lighter touch than George William Curtis; his book is more compact, more directly and distinctly a study, and it is less alloyed with the hopes of society reform which could be more reasonably indulged fifty-six years ago. Do you remember when ' Our Best Society' came out in the eldest *Putnam's Magazine,* that phœnix of monthlies which has since twice risen from its ashes? Don't pretend that our common memory doesn't run back to the year 1853! We have so many things in common that I can't let you disgrace the firm by any such vain assumption of extreme youth!"

"Why should we assume it? The Easy Chair had then been three years firmly on its legs, or its rockers, and the succession of great spirits, now disembodied, whom its ease invited, were all more or less in mature flesh. We remember that paper on ' Our Best Society' vividly, and we recall the shock that its facts concerning the Upper Ten Thousand of New York imparted to the innocent, or at least the virtuous, Lower Twenty Millions inhabiting the rest of the United States. Do you mean to say that the Four Hundred of this day are no better than the Ten Thousand of that? Has nothing been gained for quality by that prodigious reduction in quantity?"

"On the contrary, the folly, the vanity, the meanness, the heartlessness, the vulgarity, have only been condensed and concentrated, if we are to believe Mr. Pulitzer; and I don't see why we should doubt him. Did you say you hadn't seen his very shapely little study? It takes, with all the unpitying sincerity of a kodak, the likeness of our best society in its three most characteristic aspects; full-face at dinner, three-quarters-face at the opera, and profile at a ball, where proud beauty hides its face on the shoulder of haughty commercial or financial youth, and moneyed age dips its nose in whatever symbolizes the Gascon wine in the paternal library. Mr. Pulitzer makes no attempt at dramatizing his persons. There is no ambitious Mrs. Potiphar with a longing for fashionable New York worlds to conquer, yet with a secret heartache for the love of her country girlhood; no good, kind, sordid Potiphar bewildered and bedevilled by the surroundings she creates for him; no soft Rev. Cream Cheese, tenderly respectful of Mammon while ritually serving God; no factitious Ottoman of a Kurz Pasha, laughingly yet sadly observant of us playing at the forms of European society. Those devices of the satirist belonged to the sentimentalist mood of the Thackerayan epoch. But it is astonishing how exactly history repeats itself in the facts of the ball in 1910 from the ball of 1852. The motives, the *personnel,* almost the *matériel,* the incidents, are the same. I should think it would amuse Mr. Pulitzer, imitating nature from his actual observation, to find how essentially his study is the same with that of Curtis imitating nature fifty-seven years ago. There is more of nature in bulk, not in variety, to be imitated now, but as Mr. Pulitzer studies it in the glass of fashion, her mean, foolish, selfish face is the same. He would find in the sketches of the Mid-Victorian satirist all sorts of tender relentings and generous hopes concerning the 'gay' New York of that time which the Early Edwardian satirist cannot indulge concerning the gay New York of this time. It seems as if we had really gone from bad to worse, not qualitatively—we couldn't—but quantitatively. There is more money, there are more men, more women, but otherwise our proud world is the proud world of 1853."

"You keep saying the same thing with 'damnable iterance,'" we remarked. "Don't you suppose that outside of New York there is now a vast society, as there was then, which enjoys itself sweetly, kindly, harmlessly? Is there no gentle Chicago or kind St. Louis, no pastoral Pittsburg, no sequestered Cincinnati, no bucolic Boston, no friendly Philadelphia, where 'the heart that is humble may look for' disinterested pleasure in the high-society functions of the day or night? Does New York set the pace for all these places, and are dinners given there as here, not for the delight of the guests, but as the dire duty of the hostesses? Do the inhabitants of those simple sojourns go to the opera to be seen and not to hear? Do they follow on to balls before the piece is done only to bear the fardels of ignominy heaped upon them by the german's leaders, or to see their elders and fatters getting all the beautiful and costly favors while their own

131

young and gracile loveliness is passed slighted by because they give no balls where those cruel captains can
hope to shine in the van? It seems to us that in our
own far prime—now well-nigh lost in the mists of antiquity—life was ordered kindlier; that dinners and
opera-parties and dances were given

'To bless and never to ban.'"

"Very likely, on the low society level on which our
joint life moved," our other self replied, with his unsparing candor. "You know we were a country village, city-of-the-second-class personality. Even in the
distant epoch painted in the *Potiphar Papers* the motives of New York society were the same as now. It
was not the place where birth and rank and fame relaxed or sported, as in Europe, or where ardent innocence played and feasted as in the incorrupt towns
of our interior. If Curtis once represented it rightly,
it was the same ridiculous, hard-worked, greedy, costly,
stupid thing which Mr. Pulitzer again represents it."

"And yet," we mused aloud, "this is the sort of
thing which the ' unthinking multitude' who criticise,
or at least review, books are always lamenting that our
fiction doesn't deal with. Why, in its emptiness and
heaviness, its smartness and dulness, it would be the
death of our poor fiction!"

"Well, I don't know," our counterpart responded.
"If our fiction took it on the human ground, and ascertained its inner pathos, its real lamentableness, it
might do a very good thing with those clubmen and
society girls and *grandes dames*. But that remains to
be seen. In the mean time it is very much to have
such a study of society as Mr. Pulitzer has given us.
For the most part it is ' satire with no pity in it,' but

there's here and there a touch of compassion, which moves the more because of its rarity. When the author notes that here and there a pretty dear finds herself left with no one to take her out to supper at the ball, his few words wring the heart. 'These poor victims of their sex cannot, like the men, form tables of their own. All that each can do is to disappear as swiftly and as secretly as possible, hurrying home in humiliation for the present and despair for the future.' "

"Do such cruel things really happen in our best society ?" we palpitated, in an anguish of sympathy.

"Such things and worse," our other self responded, "as when in the german the fair débutante sees the leader advancing toward her with a splendid and costly favor, only to have him veer abruptly off to bestow it on some fat elderling who is going to give the next ball. But Mr. Pulitzer, though he has these spare intimations of pity, has none of the sentiment which there is rather a swash of in the *Potiphar Papers*. It's the difference between the Mid-Victorian and the Early Edwardian point of view. Both satirists are disillusioned, but in the page of Curtis there is

'The tender grace of a day that is dead'

and the soft suffusion of hope for better things, while in the page of Mr. Pulitzer there is no such qualification of the disillusion. Both are enamoured of the beauty of those daughters of Mammon, and of the distinction of our iron-clad youth, the athletic, well-groomed, well-tailored worldlings who hurry up-town from their banks and brokers' offices and lawyers' offices to the dinners and opera - boxes and dances of fashion. 'The girls and women are of a higher average of beauty than any European ball-room could produce. The men, too, are generally well built, tall, and handsome, easily distinguishable from the waiters,' Mr. Pulitzer assures us."

" Well, oughtn't that to console ?" we defied our other self. " Come! It's a great thing to be easily distinguishable from the waiters, when the waiters are so often disappointed ' remittance men ' of good English family, or the scions of Continental nobility. We mustn't ask everything."

" No, and apparently the feeding is less gross than it was in Curtis's less sophisticated time. Many of the men seem still to smoke and booze throughout the night with the host in his ' library,' but the dancing youth don't get drunk as some of them did at Mrs. Potiphar's supper, and people don't throw things from their plates under the table."

" Well, why do you say, then, that there is no change for the better in our best society, that there is no hope for it ?"

" Did I say that ? If I did, I will stick to it. We must let our best society be as it now imagines itself. I don't suppose that in all that gang of beautiful, splendid, wasteful, expensively surfeited people there are more than two or three young men of intellectual prowess or spiritual distinction, though there must be some clever and brilliant toadies of the artist variety. In fact, Mr. Pulitzer says as much outright; and it is the hard lot of some of the arts to have to tout for custom among the vulgar ranks of our best society."

" Very well, then," we said, with considerable resolution, " we must change the popular ideal of the best society. We must have a four hundred made up of the most brilliant artists, authors, doctors, professors, scientists, musicians, actors, and ministers, with their wives, daughters, and sisters, who will walk to one another's dinners, or at worst go by trolley, and occupy the cheaper seats at the opera, and dance in small and early assemblages, and live in seven-room-with-bath flats. Money must not count at all in the choice of these elect and beautiful natures. The question is, how shall we get the dense, unenlightened masses to regard them as the best society; how teach the reporters to run after them, and the press to chronicle their entertainments, engagements, marriages, divorces, voyages to and from Europe, and the other facts which now so dazzle the common fancy when it finds them recorded in the society intelligence of the newspapers?"

"Yes, as General Sherman said when he had once advocated the restriction of the suffrage and had been asked how he was going to get the consent of the majority whose votes he meant to take away—'yes, that is the devil of it.'"

We were silent for a time, and then we suggested, "Don't you think that a beginning could be made by those real élite we have decided on refusing to let associate with what now calls itself our best society?"

"But hasn't our *soi-disant* best society already made that beginning for its betters by excluding them?" our other self responded.

"There is something in what you say," we reluctantly assented, "but by no means everything. The beginning you speak of has been made at the wrong end. The true beginning of society reform must be made by the moral, æsthetic, and intellectual superiors of fashionable society as we now have it. The *grandes dames* must be somehow persuaded that to be really swell, really smart, or whatever the last word for the thing is, they must search *Who's Who in New York*

for men and women of the most brilliant promise and
performance and invite them. They must not search
the banks and brokers' offices and lawyers' offices for
their dancing-men, but the studios, the editorial-rooms,
the dramatic agencies, the pulpits, for the most gifted
young artists, assignment men, interviewers, actors,
and preachers, and apply to the labor - unions for
the cleverest and handsomest artisans; they must
look up the most beautiful and intelligent girl-stu-
dents of all the arts and sciences, and department
stores for cultivated and attractive salesladies. Then,
when all such people have received cards to dinners or
dances, it will only remain for them to have previous
engagements, and the true beginning is made. Come!
You can't say the thing is impossible."

"Not impossible, no," our complementary self replied. "But difficult."

XIV

THE MAGAZINE MUSE

Two aging if not aged poets, one much better if not much older than the other, were talking of the Muse as she was in their day and of the Muse as she is in this. At the end, their common mind was that she was a far more facile Muse formerly than she is now. In other words, as the elder and better poet put it, they both decided that many, many pieces of verse are written in these times, and hidden away in the multitude of the magazines, which in those times would have won general recognition if not reputation for the authors; they would have been remembered from month to month, and their verses copied into the newspapers from the two or three periodicals then published, and, if they were not enabled to retire upon their incomes, they would have been in the enjoyment of a general attention beyond anything money can buy at the present day. This conclusion was the handsomer in the two poets, because they had nothing to gain and something to lose by it if their opinion should ever become known. It was in a sort the confession of equality, and perhaps even inferiority, which people do not make, unless they are obliged to it, in any case. But these poets were generous even beyond their unenvious tribe, and the younger, with a rashness which his years measurably excused, set about verifying his conviction in a practical way, perhaps the only practical way.

He asked his publishers to get him all the American magazines published; and has the home-keeping reader any notion of the vastness of the sea on which this poet had embarked in his daring exploration? His publishers sent him a list of some eighty-two monthly periodicals in all kinds, which, when he had begged them to confine it to the literary kind, the æsthetic kind only, amounted to some fifty. By far the greater number of these, he found, were published in New York, but two were from Philadelphia, one from Boston, one from Indianapolis, and one even from Chicago; two were from the Pacific Slope generally. That is to say, in this city there are issued every month about forty-five magazines devoted to belles-lettres, of varying degrees of excellence, not always connoted by their varying prices. Most of them are of the ten-cent variety, and are worth in most cases ten cents, and in a few cases twenty-five or thirty-five cents, quite like those which ask such sums for themselves. The cheapest are not offensive to the eye altogether, as they lie closed on the dealer's counter, though when you open them you find them sometimes printed on paper of the wood-pulp, wood-pulpy sort, and very loathly to the touch. Others of the cheapest present their literature on paper apparently as good as that of the dearest; and as it is not always money which buys literary value, especially from the beginners in literature, there seemed every reason for the poet to hope that there would be as good poetry in the one sort as in the other. In his generous animation, he hoped to find some good poetry on the wood-pulp paper just as in the Golden Age he might have found it carved by amorous shepherds on the bark of trees.

He promised himself a great and noble pleasure from his verification of the opinion he shared with that elder and better poet, and if his delight must be mixed with a certain feeling of reserved superiority, it could hardly be less a delight for that reason. In turning critic, the friendliest critic, he could not meet these dear and fair young poets on their own level, but he could at least keep from them, and from himself as much as possible, the fact that he was looking down on them. All the magazines before him were for the month of January, and though it was possible that they might have shown a certain exhaustion from their extraordinary efforts in their Christmas numbers, still there was a chance of the overflow of riches from those numbers which would trim the balance and give them at least the average poetic value. At this point, however, it ought to be confessed that the poet, or critic, was never so willing a reader as writer of occasional verse, and it cannot be denied that there was some girding up of the loins for him before the grapple with that half-hundred of magazines. Though he took them at their weakest point, might they not be too much for him?

He fetched a long breath, and opened first that magazine, *clarum et venerabile nomen*, from which he might reasonably expect the greatest surprises of merit in the verse. There were only two pieces, and neither seemed to him of the old-time quality, but neither was such as he would himself have perhaps rejected if he had been editor. Then he plunged at the heap, and in a fifteen-cent magazine of recent renown he found among five poems a good straight piece of realistic characterization which did much to cheer him. In this, a little piece of two stanzas, the author had got at the heart of a good deal of America. In another cheap magazine, professing to be devoted wholly to stories, he hoped for a breathing-space, and was tasked by nothing

139

less familiar than Swift's versification of a well-known
maxim of La Rouchefoucauld. In a ten-cent magazine
which is too easily the best of that sort, he found two
pieces of uncommon worth, which opened the way so
promisingly, indeed, for happier fortunes that he was
not as much surprised as he might later have been
in finding five poems, all good, in one of the four
greater, or at least dearer, magazines. One of these
pieces was excellent landscape, and another a capital
nature piece; if a third was somewhat strained, it was
also rather strong, and a fourth had the quiet which it
is hard to know from repose. Two poems in another
of the high-priced magazines were noticeable, one for
sound poetic thinking, and the other as very truthfully
pathetic. The two in a cheap magazine, by two Ken-
tucky poets, a song and a landscape, were one genuine-
ly a song, and the other a charming communion with
nature. In a pair of periodicals devoted to outdoor
life, on the tamer or wilder scale, there were three
poems, one celebrating the delights of a winter camp,
which he found simple, true in feeling, and informal
in phrasing; another full of the joy of a country ride,
very songy, very blithe, and original; and a third a
study of scenery which it realized to the mind's eye,
with some straining in the wording, but much felicity
in the imagining. A Mid-Western magazine had an
excellent piece by a poet of noted name, who failed to
observe that his poem ended a stanza sooner than he
did. In a periodical devoted to short stories, or abandoned to them, there were two good pieces, one of them
delicately yet distinctly reproducing certain poetic aspects of New York, and giving the sense of a fresh
talent. Where the critic would hardly have looked for
them, in a magazine of professed fashion and avowed
smartness, he came upon three pieces, one sweet and

fine, one wise and good, one fresh and well turned. A newer periodical, rather going in for literary quality, had one fine piece, with a pretty surprise in it, and another touched with imaginative observation.

The researches of the critic carried him far into the night, or at least hours beyond his bedtime, and in the dreamy mood in which he finally pursued them he was more interested in certain psychological conditions of his own than in many of the verses. Together with a mounting aversion to the work, he noted a growing strength for it. He could dispatch a dozen poems in almost as many minutes, and not slight them, either; but he no longer jumped to his work. He was aware of trying to cheat himself in it, of pretending that the brief space between titles in the table of contents, which naturally implied a poem, sometimes really indicated a short bit of prose. He would run his eye hastily over an index, and seek to miss rather than find the word "poem" repeated after a title, and when this ruse succeeded he would go back to the poem he had skipped with the utmost unwillingness. If his behavior was sinful, he was duly punished for it, in the case of a magazine which he took up well toward midnight, rejoicing to come upon no visible sign of poetry in it. But his glance fell to a grouping of titles in a small-print paragraph at the bottom of the page, and he perceived, on close inspection, that these were all poems, and that there were eighteen of them.

He calculated, roughly, that he had read from eighty-five to a hundred poems before he finished; after a while he ceased to take accurate count as he went on, but a subsequent review of the magazines showed that his guess was reasonably correct. From this review it appeared that the greater number of the magazines published two poems in each month, while several published but one, and several five or seven or four. Another remarkable fact was that the one or two in the more self-denying were as bad as the whole five or seven or nine or eighteen of those which had more freely indulged themselves in verse. Yet another singular feature of the inquiry was that one woman had a poem in five or six of the magazines, and, stranger yet, always a good poem, so that no editor would have been justified in refusing it. There was a pretty frequent recurrence of names in the title-pages, and mostly these names were a warrant of quality, but not always of the author's best quality. The authorship was rather equally divided between the sexes, and the poets were both young and old, or as old as poets ever can be.

When the explorer had returned from the search, which covered apparently a great stretch of time, but really of space, he took his notes and went with them to that elder friend of his whose generous enthusiasm had prompted his inquiry. Together they looked them over and discussed the points evolved. "Then what is your conclusion?" the elder of the two demanded. "Do you still think I was right, or have you come to a different opinion?"

"Oh, how should I safely confess that I am of a different opinion? You would easily forgive me, but what would all those hundred poets whom I thought not so promising as you believed do to my next book? Especially what would the poetesses?"

"There is something in that. But you need not be explicit. If you differ with me, you can generalize. What, on the whole, was the impression you got? Had none of the pieces what we call distinction, for want of a better word or a clearer idea?"

"I understand. No, I should say, not one; though here and there one nearly had it—so nearly that I held my breath from not being quite sure. But, on the other hand, I should say that there was a good deal of excellence, if you know what that means."

"I can imagine," the elder poet said. "It is another subterfuge. What do you really intend?"

"Why, that the level was pretty high. Never so high as the sky, but sometimes as high as the sky-scraper. There was an occasional tallness, the effect, I think, of straining to be higher than the thought or the feeling warranted. And some of the things had a great deal of naturalness."

"Come! That isn't so bad."

"But naturalness can be carried to a point where it becomes affectation. This happened in some cases where I thought I was going to have some pleasure of the simplicity, but found at last that the simplicity was a pose. Sometimes there was a great air of being untrammelled. But there is such a thing as being in-formal, and there is such a thing as being unmannerly."

"Yes?"

"I think that in the endeavor to escape from con-vention our poets have lost the wish for elegance, which was a prime charm of the Golden Age. Technically, as well as emotionally, they let themselves loose too much, and the people of the Golden Age never let themselves loose. There is too much Nature in them, which is to say, not enough; for, after all, in her little æsthetic attempts, Nature is very modest."

The elder poet brought the younger sharply to book. "Now you are wandering. Explain again."

"Why, when you and I were young—you were al-ways and always will be young—"

"None of that!"

"It seemed to me that we wished to be as careful of the form as the most formal of our poetic forebears, and that we would not let the smallest irregularity escape us in our study to make the form perfect. We cut out the tall word; we restrained the straining; we tried to keep the wording within the bounds of the dictionary; we wished for beauty in our work so much that our very roughness was the effect of hammering; the grain we left was where we had used the file to produce it."

" Was it? And you say that with these new fellows it isn't so?"

" Well, what do you say to such a word as ' danken-ing,' which occurred in a very good landscape?"

" One such word in a hundred poems?"

" One such word in a million would have been too many. It made me feel that they would all have liked to say ' dankening,' or something of the sort. And in the new poets, on other occasions, I have found faulty syntax, bad rhymes, limping feet. The editors are to blame for that, when it happens. The editor who printed ' dankening' was more to blame than the poet who wrote it, and loved the other ugly word above all his other vocables." The elder poet was silent, and the other took fresh courage. " Yes, I say it! You were wrong in your praise of the present magazine verse at the cost of that in our day. When we were commencing poets, the young or younger reputations were those of Stedman, of Bayard Taylor, of the Stoddards, of Aldrich, of Celia Thaxter, of Rose Terry, of Harriet Prescott, of Bret Harte, of Charles Warren Stoddard, of the Piatts, of Fitz James O'Brien, of Fitzhugh Ludlow, of a dozen more, whom the best of the newest moderns cannot rival. These were all delicate and devoted and indefatigable artists and lovers of form. It cannot do the later generation any good to equal them with ours."

" There is something in what you say." The elder poet was silent for a time. Then he asked, " Out of the hundred poems you read in your fifty magazines, how many did you say were what you would call good ?"

His junior counted up, and reported, " About twenty-four."

" Well, don't you call that pretty fair, in a hundred ? I do. Reflect that these were all the magazines of one month, and it is probable that there will be as many good poems in the magazines of every month in the year. That will give us two hundred and eighty-eight good poems during 1907. Before the first decade of the new century is ended, we shall have had eleven hundred and fifty-two good magazine poems. Do you suppose that as many good magazine poems were written during the last four years of the first decade of the eighteenth century ? Can you name as many yourself ?"

" Certainly not. Nobody remembers the magazine poems of that time, and nobody will remember the poems of the four years ending the present decade."

" Do you mean to say that not one of them is worth remembering ?"

The younger poet paused a moment. Then he said, with the air of a cross-examined witness, " Under advice of counsel, I decline to answer."

XV

COMPARATIVE LUXURIES OF TRAVEL

On a night well toward its noon, many years ago, a friend of the Easy Chair (so close as to be at the same time its worst enemy) was walking wearily up and down in the station at Portland, Maine, and wondering if the time for his train to start would ever come, and, if the time did come, whether his train would really take advantage of that opportunity to leave Portland. It was, of course, a night train, and of course he had engaged a lower berth in the sleeping-car; there are certain things that come by nature with the comfortable classes to which the friend of the Easy Chair belonged. He would no more have thought of travelling in one of the empty day coaches side-tracked in the station than he would have thought of going by stage, as he could remember doing in his boyhood. He stopped beside the cars and considered their potential passengers with amaze and compassion; he laughed at the notion of his being himself one of them; and, when he turned his back on them, he was arrested by the sight of an elderly pair looking from the vantage of the platform into the interior of a lighted Pullman parlor-car which, for reasons of its own, was waiting in luminous detachment apart from the day coaches. There was something engaging in the gentle humility of the elderly pair who peered into the long, brilliant saloon with an effect not so much of ignorance as of inexperience. They were apparently not so rustic as they were what another friend of the Easy Chair calls villaginous; and they seemed not of the commonest uninformed villaginosity, but of general intelligence such as comes of reading and thinking of many modern things which one has never seen. As the eavesdropper presently made out from a colloquy unrestrained by consciousness of him, they had never seen a parlor-car before, except perhaps as it flashed by their meek little home depot with the rest of some express train that never stopped there.

" It *is* splendid, John," the woman said, holding by the man's arm while she leaned forward to the window which she tiptoed to reach with her eager eyes.

" I guess it's all of that," the man consented, sadly.

" I presume we sha'n't ever go in one," she suggested.

" Not likely," he owned, in the same discouraged tone.

They were both silent for a time. Then the woman said, with a deep, hopeless aspiration, " Dear! I wish I could see inside one, once!"

The man said nothing, and if he shared her bold ambition he made no sign.

The eavesdropper faltered near their kind backs, wishing for something more from them which should give their souls away, but they remained silently standing there, and he did not somehow feel authorized to make them reflect that, if the car was lighted up, it must be open, and that the friendly porter somewhere within would not mind letting them look through it under his eye. Perhaps they did reflect, and the woman was trying to embolden the man to the hardy venture. In the end they did not attempt it, but they turned away with another sigh from the woman which found its echo in the eavesdropper's heart. Doubtless if they had penetrated that splendid interior without having paid for seats, it would, in some fine, mystical sort, have pauperized them; it would have corrupted them; they would have wished after that always to travel in such cars, when clearly they could not afford it; very possibly it might have led to their moral if not financial ruin. So he tried to still his bosom's ache, but he could never quite forget that gentle pair with their unrequited longing, and the other day they came almost the first thing into his mind when he read that a great German steamship company had some thoughts of putting on a train of Pullman cars from the port of arrival to the mercantile metropolis which was the real end of their ships' voyages. He thought, whimsically, perversely, how little difference it would make to that pair, how little to those measureless most whose journeys shall end in heaven, where Pullman passengers, or even passengers by the ordinary European first-class cars, may be only too glad to meet them. He gave a looser rein to his thoughts and considered how very little the ordinary necessities of life, such as Pullman cars and taxicabs and electric radiators and non-storage chickens and unsalted butter concern the great mass of the saints, who would find them the rarest luxuries, and could hardly be imagined coveting them; and then from this wild revery he fell to asking himself whether a Pullman train would be such a great advance or advantage over the old-fashioned European first-class carriages in which he had been so long content to travel with the native nobility. Self-brought to book on this point, he had to own that he had once had moments of thinking in a German second-class car that he would not change to an American Pullman if he could for even less than a third more money. He recalled a pleasant run from Crewe to Edinburgh in a third-class English car, when he never once thought of a Pullman car except to think it was no better. To be sure, this was after two-thirds of his third-class fellow-passengers had got out, and he was left to the sole enjoyment of two-thirds of the seats. It is the luxury of space which your more money buys you in England, where no one much lower than a duke or a prime minister now goes first class for a long haul. For short hauls it is different, and on the Continent it is altogether different. There you are often uncomfortably crowded in the first-class carriages, and doubtless would be in a Pullman if there were any, so that if you are wise, or only well informed, you will give the guard a shilling to telegraph before leaving London and get you a number on the Rapide from Calais to Paris.

It is astonishing how quickly knowledge of any such advisable precaution spreads among even such arrogantly stupid people as first-class passengers ordinarily are. By the time a certain train had started for Dover with that friend of the Easy Chair's already mentioned, every soul in his first - class compartment had telegraphed ahead, and when they arrived in Calais the earliest Englishman who got past the customs ran ahead and filled the racks of the carriage with his hand-baggage, so that the latest Frenchman was obliged to jump up and down and scream, and perhaps swear in his strange tongue, before he could find room for his valise, and then calm down and show himself the sweetest and civilest of men, and especially the obedient humble servant of the Englishman who had now made a merit of making way for his bag.

At this point the fable teaches that money will not buy everything in European travel, though some Americans imagine it will. It will not, for instance, buy comfort or decency, though it will secure privacy in a French sleeper between Paris and Marseilles either way. For an augmentation of forty-five francs, or nine dollars, on the price of a first-class ticket, it will buy you a berth in a small pen which you must share with another animal, and be tossed hither and yon, night long, as in the berth of a Bermuda steamer. Second-class passengers in France or Italy cannot buy a berth in a sleeper for any money, and they may go hang or stand, for all the International Sleeping-Car Company cares; and this suggests the question whether in our own free and equal land the passengers in the ordinary day coaches are ever invited, by the first call or the last, to share the hospitalities of our dining-cars; or are these restricted to the proud stomachs of the Pullman passengers?

No, no; the privacy of a French sleeping-car is all very well, but for decency give our friend a good, old-fashioned Pullman sleeper at a third the money, with its curtains swaying with the motion of the car and muting the long-drawn, loud-drawn breathing of the serried sleepers behind them. To be sure, in the morning, when stooping backs begin to round the curtains out, and half-shod feet to thrust into the narrow gangway between them, the effect is of a familiarity, an intimacy; but so much trust, so much brotherly kindness goes with it all that you could not call it indecency, though certainly you could not claim it privacy. It only proves, as that friend of ours was saying, that money cannot buy everything, and that, if you expect the Pullman parlor-cars to be an improvement on the German first-class cars, you will be disappointed, probably. First-class cars vary much all over Europe; even second-class cars do. In Austria they are not nearly

so good as in Germany, and in Italy—poor, dear Italy!
—they are worse still. That is because, the enemies
of socialism say, the roads are state roads, or because,
the friends of socialism say, the expropriated companies have dumped their worn-out rolling-stock on
the commonwealth, which must bear the shame of it
with the stranger. Between these clashing claims we
will not put our blade. All we say is that Italian railroad travel is as bad as heart could wish—the heart
that loves Italy and holds dear the memory of the days
when there were few railroads, if any, there, and one
still went by diligence or *vettura*. The only absolutely
good railroad travel is in England, where the corridor
car imagined from the Pullman has realized the most
exacting ideal of the traveller of any class. In the
matter of dining-cars we have stood still (having at-
tained perfection at a bound), while the English diner
has shot ahead in simplicity and quality of refection.
With us a dollar buys more dinner than you wish or
like; with them three shillings pay for an elegant sufficiency, and a tip of sixpence purchases an explicit
gratitude from the waiter which a quarter is often
helpless to win from his dark antitype with us. The
lunch served on the steamer train from London to
Liverpool leaves the swollen, mistimed dinner on the
Boston express—

"But what about that 5 P.M. breakfast which you
got, no longer ago than last September, on the express
between Salisbury and Exeter?" our friend exults to
ask; and we condescend to answer with forced candor:

"Yes, that was rather droll. No Englishman would
dream of ordering afternoon tea consisting of chops,
boiled potatoes, and a pot of souchong, and, if we chose
to do so, we took a serious chance. But starvation will
drive one to anything; we had had nothing to eat since

leaving Salisbury three hours before, and in the English air this is truly famine. Besides, the amiable agent who came to our compartment for our order pledged his word that those potatoes should be ready in twenty minutes; and so they were, and so were the chops, and so, of course, was the tea. What he had failed to specify was that the dining-car had been left, by divers defections at the junctions passed, the last car in our train, and that it was now straining at its leash in wild leaps and bounds. One reached it by passing through more corridor cars than there are Pullmans and day coaches in a west-bound Lake Shore train, and when one arrived one reeled and flounced into one's seat by such athletics as one uses in a Bermuda steamer (or did use in the old fifteen-hundred-ton kind) crossing the Gulf Stream. When once comparatively secure in one's chair, the combat with the lunch began. Mrs. Siddons would have been at home there, for there was nothing for it but to stab the potatoes, and all one's cunning of fence was needed to hold one's own with the chops. But how delicious they were! How the first mealed and the last melted in the mouth; and the tea, when once poured from the dizzy height at which the pot had to be held, and the wild whirl in which the cup had to be caught to the lips, how it cheered without inebriating, and how the spirit rose to meet it! The waiter, dancing and swaying like any ship's steward, served the stray Americans with as much respectful gravity as if they had been county-family English and he had been for generations in their service. He did not deprecate the capers of the car, but only casually owned that, when it happened to be the last in the train, it did pitch about a bit, sir.

No, England is the only country where you can get the whole worth of your money in railroad travel, and

the well-to-do sinner can enjoy the comfort which must
be his advance recompense in this world for the happiness he cannot warrantably count upon in the next.
That steamer train of Pullmans in Germany will never
contest the palm with the English corridor train; nor
will our palatial, porterless depots vie with the simplest of these English wayside stations, where the soft
endearments of the railway servants penetrate to the
very interior of the arriving stranger's compartment
and relieve him of all anxiety for his hand-baggage.
Then the cloak-room, that refuge of temporary sojourn,
where his baggage remains in the porter's charge till
it is put back into the train, who will contend that
our parcels' windows, with their high counters fencing
the depositor from the grim youths standing like re-
ceiving and paying tellers within, compare with the
English cloak-room? Its very name descends from the
balls and assemblies of the past, and graces the public
enjoyment of its convenience with something of the
courtesy and dignity of the exclusive pleasures of the
upper classes; it brings to one sense a vision of white
shoulders bent over trim maids slippering slim feet, and
to another the faint, proud odors of flowers that withered a hundred years ago.

But what vain concession is this to the outworn ideals
of a state and a condition justly superseded! How
far we have got from that gentle pair with whom we
began peering into the parlor-car in Portland, Maine!
To such as they it will matter little whether Pullman
cars are or are not put on that steamer train in North
Germany. A great danger is that the vast horde of
Americans who travel will forget the immeasurable
majority who remain at home, and will lose in
their sophistication the heaven - glimpsing American
point of view. It is very precious, that point of

view, and the foreigner who wins it is a happier man
than the native who purse-proudly puts it away. When
we part with the daily habit of trolleys and begin to
think in cabs and taxicabs; when we pass the line of
honest day coaches and buy a seat in the parlor-car;
when we turn from pie, or baked beans, and coffee at
the refreshment-counter and keep our hunger for the
table d'hôte of the dining-car; when we buy a room
in the steamboat in disdain of the berth that comes
with our ticket; when we refuse to be one of four or
even two in the cabin of the simpler steamers and will
not go abroad on any vessel of less than twenty or
thirty thousand tons, with small, separate tables and
tuxedos in the saloon; when we forsake the clothing-
store with its democratic misfit for all figures and order
our suits in London, then we begin to barter away our
birthright of republican simplicity, and there is soon
nothing for us but a coronet by marriage in the family
or a quarter - section of public land in northwestern
Canada.

There has been altogether too much talk (some of
it, we contritely own, has been ours) of the comparative comforts and discomforts of life for the better-to-
do in Europe and America. In the demand for Pullman trains between our port of arrival and the end of
our journey when we go to the Continent for a much-
needed rest, we are apt to forget the fellow - citizens
whom we saw across the impassable barrier dividing
our first class from them on the steamer, and who will
find the second-class German cars quite good enough
for them, and better than our day coaches at home.
If we cannot remember these, then let us remember
those for whom Pullmans are not good enough and
who spurn the dust of our summer ways in their automobiles, and leave the parlor-cars to our lower-class

vulgarity. Such people take their automobiles to Europe with them, and would not use that possible Pullman train if they found it waiting for them at the port of arrival in Germany. What is the use? It will soon not be an affair of automobiles, but of aeroplanes, at the ports of European arrival, and a Pullman train will look sadly strange and old to the debarking passengers. No one will want to take it, as no one would now want to take a bicycle, or even a " bicycle built for two." These things are all comparative; there is nothing positive, nothing ultimate in the luxuries, the splendors of life. Soon the last word in them takes on a vulgarity of accent; and Distinction turns from them " with sick and scornful looks averse," and listens for the

> " airy tongues that syllable men's names
> On sands and shores and desert wildernesses."

Simplicity, at the furthest possible remove from all complexity, will be the next word—the word that follows the last, the woman's word.

XVI

QUALITIES WITHOUT DEFECTS

THEY had got to that point in their walk and talk where the talk might be best carried forward by arresting the walk; and they sat down on a bench of the Ramble in Central Park, and provisionally watched a man feeding a squirrel with peanuts. The squirrel had climbed up the leg of the man's trousers and over the promontory above, and the man was holding very still, flattered by the squirrel's confidence, and anxious not to frighten it away by any untoward movement; if the squirrel had been a child bestowing its first intelligent favors upon him the man could not have been prouder. He was an old fellow, one of many who pamper the corrupt rodents of the Park, and reduce them from their native independence to something like the condition of those pauper wards of the nation on our Indian Reservations, to whom a blurred image of the chase offers itself at stated intervals in the slaughter of the Government's dole of beef-cattle.

The friend to whom this imperfect parallel occurred recalled his thoughts from it and said, with single reference to the man and the squirrel: " I suppose that's an expression of the sort of thing we've been talking about. Kindness to animals is an impulse, isn't it, of the ' nat-

THE MALL, CENTRAL PARK

ural piety' embracing the fatherhood of God and the brotherhool of man?"

"I don't think it's quite so modern as that formulation," the other friend questioned. "I was thinking it was very eighteenth-century; part of the universal humanitarian movement of the time when the master began to ask himself whether the slave was not also a man and a brother, and the philanthropist visited the frightful prisons of the day and remembered those in bonds as bound with them."

"Yes, you may say that," the first allowed. "But benevolence toward dumb creatures originated very much further back than the eighteenth century. There was St. Francis of Assisi, you know, who preached to the birds, didn't he? and Walter von der Vogelweide, who pensioned them. And several animals—cats, crocodiles, cows, and the like—enjoyed a good deal of consideration among the Egyptians. The serpent used to have a pretty good time as a popular religion. And what about the Stoics? They were rather kind to animals, weren't they? Why should Pliny's Doves have come down to us in mosaic if he cultivated them solely for the sake of broiled squabs? It's true that the modern Roman, before the extension of the S. P. C. A. to his city, used his horse cruelly upon the perfectly unquestionable ground that the poor beast was not a Christian."

"I don't remember about the Stoics exactly," the second friend mused aloud; and the first let this go, though they both understood that very likely he not only did not remember, but had never known. "They had so many virtues that they must have been kind to brutes, but I taste something more Cowperian, more Wordsworthian, than Marcus-Aurelian in our own kindness. These poets taught me, so far as I could learn, not to

> 'enter on my list of friends the man
> Who needlessly sets foot upon a worm,'

and

> 'Never to mix my pleasure or my pride
> With sorrow of the meanest thing that breathes.' "

" Yes, but I don't like giving up the Stoics; we may have to come back to their ground if things keep on going the way they have gone for the last generation. The Stoics had a high ideal of duty; it's hard to see that the Christian ideal is higher, though they taught themselves to be proudly good, and we (if we may still say we when we say Christians) are always trying to teach ourselves to be humbly good."

" What do you mean," the second of the friends demanded, " by coming back to their ground?"

" Why," the first responded, picking up a twig that opportunely dropped at his feet, and getting out his knife to whittle it, " I suppose they were the first agnostics, and we who don't so much deny the Deity as ignore Him—"

" I see," the second answered, sadly. " But aren't you throwing up the sponge for faith rather prematurely? The power of believing has a tremendous vitality. I heard a Catholic once say to a Protestant friend, ' You know the Church has outlived schisms much older than yours.' And inside of Protestantism as well as Catholicism there is a tremendous power of revival. We have seen it often. After an age of unbelief an age of belief is rather certain to follow."

" Well, well, I'm willing. I'm no more agnostic

than you are. I should be glad of an age of faith for the rest to my soul, if for no other reason. I was harking back to the Stoics not only because they were good to animals, if they were good, but because they seemed to have the same barren devotion to duty which has survived my faith as well as my creed. But why, if I neither expect happiness nor dread misery, should I still care to do my duty? And I certainly always do."

"What, always?"

"Well, nearly always."

The friends laughed together, and the first said, "What a pity the Gilbertian humor has gone out so; you can't adapt it to a daily need any longer without the risk of not being followed."

The other sighed. "Nearly everything goes out, except duty. If that went out, I don't think I should have much pleasure in life."

"No, you would be dead, without the hope of resurrection. If there is anything comes direct from the Creative Force, from

'La somma sapienza e il primo amore,'

it is the sense of duty, 'the moral law within us,' which Kant divined as unmistakably delivered from God to man. I use the old terminology."

"Don't apologize. It still serves our turn; I don't know that anything else serves it yet. And you make me think of what dear old M. D. C—— told me shortly after his wife died. He had wished, when they both owned that the end was near, to suggest some comfort in the hope of another life, to clutch at that straw to save his drowning soul; but she stopped him. She said, 'There is nothing but duty, the duty we have wished to do and tried to do.'"

The friends were silent in the pathos of the fact, and then the first said, " I suppose we all wish to do our duty, even when we don't try or don't try hard enough."

The other conjectured, " Perhaps, after all, it's a question of strength; wickedness is weakness."

" That formula won't always serve; still, it will serve in a good many cases; possibly most. It won't do to preach it, though."

" No, we must cultivate strength of character. I wonder how ?"

" Well, your Stoics—"

" *My* Stoics ?"

" *Anybody's* Stoics — did it by self - denial. When they saw a pleasure coming their way they sidestepped it; they went round the corner, and let it go by while they recruited their energies. Then when they saw a duty coming they stepped out and did it."

" It seems very simple. But aren't you rather cynical ?"

" That's what people call one when one puts ethics picturesquely. But perhaps I've rather overdone it about the Stoics. Perhaps they wouldn't have refused to enjoy a pleasure at their own expense, at their cost in some sort of suffering to themselves. They really seem to have invented the Christian ideal of duty."

" And a very good thing. It may be all that will be left of Christianity in the end, if the Christian hope of reward goes as the Christian fear of punishment has gone. It seems to have been all there was of it in the beginning."

The second of the friends said at this, " I don't know that I should go so far as that."

The first returned, " Well, I don't know that I should ask you. I don't know that I go that far myself," he said, and then they laughed together again.

The man who was feeding the squirrel seemed to have exhausted his stock of peanuts, and he went away. After some hesitation the squirrel came toward the two friends and examined their countenances with a beady, greedy eye. He was really glutted with peanuts, and had buried the last where he would forget it, after having packed it down in the ground with his paws.

"No, no," the first of the friends said to the squirrel; "we are on the way back to being Stoics and practising the more self-denying virtues. You won't get any peanuts out of us. For one thing, we haven't got any."

"There's a boy," the second friend dreamily suggested, "down by the boat-house with a basketful."

"But I am teaching this animal self-denial. He will be a nobler squirrel all the rest of his life for not having the peanuts he couldn't get. That's like what I always try to feel in my own case. It's what I call character-building. Get along!"

The squirrel, to which the last words were addressed, considered a moment. Then it got along, after having inspected the whittlings at the feet of the friends to decide whether they were edible.

"I thought," the second of the friends said, "that your humanity included kindness to animals."

"I am acting for this animal's best good. I don't say but that, if the peanut-boy had come by with his basket, I shouldn't have yielded to my natural weakness and given the little brute a paper of them to bury. He seems to have been rather a saving squirrel—when he was gorged."

The mellow sunlight of the November day came down through the tattered foliage, and threw the shadows of the friends on the path where they sat, with their soft hats pulled over their foreheads. They were silent so long that when the second of them resumed their conversation he had to ask, " Where were we ?"

" Cultivating force of character in squirrels."

" I thought we had got by that."

" Then we had come round to ourselves again."

" Something like that," the first friend reluctantly allowed.

" What a vicious circle! It seems to me that our first duty, if that's what you mean, is to get rid of ourselves."

" Whom should we have left? Other people? We mustn't pamper their egotism in chastising our own. We must use a great deal of caution in doing our duty. If I really loved that squirrel, if I were truly kind to animals, if I studied their best good, as disagreeable friends say they study ours, I should go after him and give him a hickory-nut that would wear down his teeth as nature intended; civilization is undermining the health of squirrels by feeding them peanuts, which allow their teeth to overgrow."

" That is true. Isn't it doing something of the same sort in other ways for all of us? If I hadn't lost my teeth so long ago, I'm sure I should feel them piercing from one jaw to another in their inordinate development. It's duty that keeps down the overgrowths that luxury incites. By-the-way, what set you thinking so severely about duty this beautiful Sunday morning? The neglected duty of going to church?"

" Ah, I call going to church a pleasure. No, I suppose it was an effect, a reverberation, of the tumult of my struggle to vote for the right man on Tuesday, when I knew that I was throwing my vote away if I did vote for him."

" But you voted for him?"

The first friend nodded.

" Which man was it ?"

" What's the use ? He was beaten—

    ' That is all you know or need to know.'"

" Of course he was beaten if it was your duty to vote for him," the second friend mused. " How patient the Creator must be with the result of His counsel to His creatures ! He keeps on communing, commanding, if we are to believe Kant. It is His one certain way to affirm and corroborate Himself. Without His perpetual message to the human conscience, He does not recognizably exist; and yet more than half the time His mandate sends us to certain defeat, to certain death. It's enough to make one go in for the other side. Of course, we have to suppose that the same voice which intimates duty to us intimates duty to them ?"

" And that they would like to obey it, if they could consistently with other interests and obligations ?"

" Yes, they juggle with their sense of it; they pretend that the Voice does not mean exactly what it says. They get out of it that way."

" And the great, vital difference between ourselves and them is that we promptly and explicitly obey it; we don't palter with it in the slightest; ' we don't bandy words with our sovereign,' as Doctor Johnson said. I wonder," the speaker added, with the briskness of one to whom a vivid thought suddenly occurs, " how it would work if one went and did exactly the contrary of what was intimated to the human conscience ?"

" That's not a new idea. There are people who habitually do so, or, rather, to whom an inverted moral law is delivered."

" You mean the people who beat you at the polls last Tuesday ?"

"No, I mean the people in the asylums, some of them. They are said to hear the voice that bids us do right commanding them to do wrong. 'Thou shalt kill,' they hear it say, 'thou shalt steal, thou shalt bear false witness, thou shalt commit adultery, thou shalt not honor thy father and thy mother,' and so on through the Decalogue, with the inhibition thrown off or put on, as the case may be."

"How very hideous!" the second friend exclaimed. "It's like an emanation from the Pit. I mean the Pit that used to be. It's been abolished."

"And a very good thing. The noises from it went far to drown the voice of God, and bewildered some men so that they did not rightly know what the voice was saying. Now when people hear a voice bidding them do evil, we know what to do with them."

"And you think that the fellows who outvoted you on Tuesday heard the same voice that you heard; and they disobeyed it?"

"Ah, it's hard to say. We haven't got to the bottom of such things yet. Perhaps they disobeyed the voice provisionally, expecting to make a satisfactory explanation later on. Or perhaps they had put their civic consciences in the keeping of others, who gave them an official interpretation of the command, with instructions not to take it literally."

"That's very interesting," the second friend said. "Then it's your idea that no one really prefers to do wrong?"

"Not outside of the asylums. And even there they can plead authority. No, no, no! In a world pretty full of evil there isn't any purely voluntary evil among the sane. When the 'wicked,' as we call them, do wrong, it is provisionally only; they mean to do right presently and make it up with the heavenly powers.

As long as an evil-doer lives he means to cease some time to do evil. He may put it off too long, or until he becomes ethically unsound. You know Swedenborg found that the last state of sinners was insanity."

" Dreadful!"

" But I've always thought very few reached that state. There's this curious thing about it all: we are not only ethically prompted by that inner voice, we are æsthetically prompted; it's a matter of taste as well as of conduct, too. The virtues are so clean, the vices so repulsively dirty. Justice is beautifully symmetrical; injustice is so shapeless, so unbalanced. Truth is such a pure line; falsehood is so out of drawing. The iniquities make you uncomfortable. The arts deny them."

The second friend drew a long breath. " Then I don't see why there are so many."

" Well," the first friend suggested, " there seems to be a difficulty. Some say that they have to be employed as antitheses; we can't get on without them, at least at this stage of the proceedings. Perhaps we shall advance so far that we shall be able to use historical or accomplished evil for the contrasts by which we shall know actual good."

" I don't see how you make that out."

" Why, there are already some regions of the globe where the summer does not require the antithesis of winter for its consciousness. Perhaps in the moral world there will yet be a condition in which right shall not need to contrast itself with wrong. We are still meteorologically very imperfect."

" And how do you expect to bring the condition about? By our always doing our duty?"

" Well, we sha'n't by not doing it."

XVII

A WASTED OPPORTUNITY

The Easy Chair saw at once that its friend was full of improving conversation, and it let him begin without the least attempt to stay him; anything of the kind, in fact, would have been a provocation to greater circumstance in him. He said:

"It was Christmas Eve, and I don't know whether he arrived by chance or design at a time when the heart is supposed to be softest and the mind openest. It's a time when, unless you look out, you will believe anything people tell you and do anything they ask you. I must say I was prepossessed by his appearance; he was fair and slender, and he looked about thirty-five years old; and when he said at once that he would not deceive me, but would confess that he was just out of the penitentiary of a neighboring State where he had been serving a two years' sentence, I could have taken him in my arms. Even if he had not pretended that he had the same surname as myself, I should have known him for a brother, and though I suspected that he was wrong in supposing that his surname was at all like mine, I was glad that he had sent it in, and so piqued my curiosity that I had him shown up, instead of having my pampered menial spurn him from my door, as I might if he had said his name was Brown, Jones, or Robinson."

"We dare say you have your self-justification," we put in at this point, "but you must own that it doesn't appear in what you are saying. As a good citizen, with the true interests of the poor at heart, you would certainly have had your pampered menial spurn him from your door. His being of your name, or claiming to be so, had nothing to do with his merit or want of it."

"Oh, I acknowledge that, and I'll own that there was something in his case, as he stated it, that appealed to my fancy even more than his community of surname appealed to my family affection. He said he was a Scotchman, which I am not, and that he had got a job on a cattle-steamer, to work his way back to his native port. The steamer would sail on Monday, and it was now Friday night, and the question which he hesitated, which he intimated, in terms so tacit that I should not call them an expression of it, was how he was to live till Monday.

"He left the calculation entirely to me, which he might not have done if he had known what a poor head I had for figures, and I entered into it with a reluctance which he politely ignored. I had some quite new two-dollar notes in my pocket-book, the crisp sort, which rustle in fiction when people take them out to succor the unfortunate or bribe the dishonest, and I thought I would give him one if I could make it go round for him till his steamer sailed. I was rather sorry for its being fresh, but I had no old, shabby, or dirty notes such as one gives to cases of dire need, you know."

"No, we don't know. We so seldom give paper at all; we prefer to give copper."

"Well, that is right; one ought to give copper if the need is very pressing; if not so pressing, one gives small silver, and so on up. But here was an instance

which involved a more extended application of alms.
' You know,' I told him, while I was doing my sum in
mental arithmetic, ' there are the Mills hotels, where
you can get a bed for twenty-five cents; I don't remember whether they throw in breakfast or not.' I
felt a certain squalor in my attitude, which was not
relieved by the air of gentle patience with which he
listened, my poor namesake, if not kinsman; we were
both at least sons of Adam. He looked not only gentle,
but refined; I made my reflection that this was probably the effect of being shut up for two years where the
winds were not allowed to visit him roughly, and the
reflection strengthened me to say, ' I think two dollars
will tide you over till Monday.' I can't say whether
he thought so, too, but he did not say he did not think
so. He left it quite to me, and I found another mathe-
matical difficulty. There were three nights' lodging
to be paid for, and then he would have a dollar and a
quarter for food. I often spend as much as that on a
single lunch, including a quarter to the waiter, and I
wouldn't have liked making it pay for three days'
board. But I didn't say so; I left the question entirely
to him, and he said nothing.

"In fact, he was engaged in searching himself for
credentials, first in one pocket, and then in another;
but he found nothing better than a pawn-ticket, which
he offered me. ' What's this?' I asked. ' My overcoat,'
he said, and I noted that he had borrowed a dollar and
a half on it. I did not like that; it seemed to me that
he was taking unfair advantage of me, and I said, ' Oh,
I think you can get along without your overcoat.' I'm
glad to think now that it hadn't begun to snow yet, and
that I had no prescience of the blizzard—what the papers fondly called the Baby Blizzard (such a pretty
fancy of theirs!)—which was to begin the next after-

noon, wasn't making the faintest threat from the moonlit sky then. He said, 'It's rather cold,' but I ignored his position. At the same time, I gave him a quarter."

"That was magnificent, but it was not political economy," we commented. "You should have held to your irrefutable argument that he could get along without his overcoat. You should have told him that he would not need it on shipboard."

"Well, do you know," our friend said, "I really did tell him something like that, and it didn't seem to convince him, though it made me ashamed. I suppose I was thinking how he could keep close to the reading-room fire, and I did not trouble to realize that he would not be asked to draw up his chair when he came in from looking after the cattle."

"It would have been an idle compliment, anyway," we said. "You can't draw up the reading-room chairs on shipboard; they're riveted down."

"I remembered afterward. But still I was determined not to take his overcoat out of pawn, and he must have seen it in my eye. He put back his pawn-ticket, and did not try to produce any other credentials. I had noticed that the ticket did not bear the surname we enjoyed in common; I said to myself that the name of Smith, which it did bear, must be the euphemism of many who didn't wish to identify themselves with their poverty even to a pawnbroker. But I said to him, 'Here!' and I pulled open my table drawer, and took from it a small envelope full of English coins, which I had been left stranded with on several returns from Europe; the inhuman stewards had failed to relieve me of them; and as I always vow, when I have got through our customs, that I will never go to Europe again, I had often wondered what I should do with those coins. I now took out the largest and handsomest of them: 'Do you know what that is?' 'Yes,' he said; 'it's two shillings and sixpence—what we call a half-crown.' His promptness restored my faith in him; I saw that he must be what he said; undoubtedly he had been in the penitentiary; very likely our name was the same; an emotion of kinship stirred in my heart. 'Here!' I said, and I handed him the coin; it did not seem so bad as giving him more American money. 'They can change that on the ship for you. I guess you can manage now till Monday,' and my confidence in Providence diffused such a genial warmth through my steam-heated apartment that I forgot all about his overcoat. I wish I could forget about it now."

We felt that we ought to say something to comfort a man who owned his excess of beneficence. " Oh, you mustn't mind giving him so much money. We can't always remember our duty to cut the unfortunate as close as we ought. Another time you will do better. Come! Cheer up!"

Our friend did not seem entirely consoled by our amiability. In fact, he seemed not to notice it. He heaved a great sigh in resuming: "He appeared to think I was hinting that it was time for him to go, for he got up from the lounge where I had thoughtlessly had the decency to make him sit down, and went out into the hall, thanking me as I followed him to the door. I was sorry to let him go; he had interested me somehow beyond anything particularly appealing in his personality; in fact, his personality was rather null than otherwise, as far as that asserted any claim; such a mere man and brother! Before he put his hand on my door-knob a belated curiosity stirred in me, which I tried, as delicately as I could, to appease. 'Was your trouble something about the '—I was going to say the ladies, but that seemed too mawkish, and I boldly outed with—'women?' 'Oh no,' he said, meekly; 'it was just cloth, a piece of cloth.' 'Breaking and entering?' I led on. 'Well, not exactly, but—it came to grand larceny,' and I might have fancied a touch of mounting self-respect in his confession of a considerable offence.

"I didn't know exactly what to say, so I let myself off with a little philosophy: 'Well, you see, it didn't pay, exactly.' 'Oh no,' he said, sadly enough, and he went out."

Our friend was silent at this point, and we felt that we ought to improve the occasion in his behalf. "Well, there you lost a great opportunity. You ought to have rubbed it in. You ought to have made him reflect upon the utter folly of his crime. You ought to have made him realize that for a ridiculous value of forty, or fifty, or seventy-five dollars, he had risked the loss of his liberty for two years, and not only his liberty, but his labor, for he had come out of the penitentiary after two years of hard work as destitute as he went in; he had not even the piece of cloth to show for it all. Yes, you lost a great opportunity."

Our friend rose from the dejected posture in which he had been sitting, and blazed out—we have no milder word for it—blazed out in a sort of fiery torrent which made us recoil: "Yes, I lost that great opportunity, and I lost a greater still. I lost the opportunity of telling that miserable man that, thief for thief, and robber for robber, the State which had imprisoned him for two years, and then cast him out again without a cent of pay for the wages he had been earning all that dreadful time, was a worse thief and a worse robber than he! I ought to have told him that in so far as he had been cheated of his wages by the law he was the victim, the martyr of an atrocious survival of bar-

barism. Oh, I have thought of it since with shame and sorrow! I was sending him out into the cold that was gathering for the Baby Blizzard without the hope of his overcoat, but since then I have comforted myself by considering how small my crime was compared with that of the State which had thrown him destitute upon the world after the two years' labor it had stolen from him. At the lowest rate of wages for unskilled labor, it owed him at least a thousand dollars, or, with half subtracted for board and lodging, five hundred. It was his delinquent debtor in that sum, and it had let him loose to prey upon society in my person because it had defrauded him of the money he had earned."

" But, our dear friend!" we entreated, " don't you realize that this theft, this robbery, this fraud, as you call it, was part of the sanative punishment which the State had inflicted upon him ?"

" And you don't think two years' prison, two years' slavery, was sanative enough without the denial of his just compensation ?"

We perceived that it would be useless to argue with a man in this truculent mood, and we silently forbore to urge that the vision of destitution which the criminal must have before his eyes, advancing hand in hand with liberty to meet him at the end of his term when his prison gates opened into the world which would not feed, or shelter, or clothe, or in any wise employ him, would be a powerful deterrent from future crime, and act as one of the most efficient agencies of virtue which the ingenuity of the law has ever invented. But our silence did not wholly avail us, for our poor misguided friend went on to say:

" Suppose he had a wife and children—he may have had several of both, for all I know—dependent on him, would it have been particularly sanative for them to be deprived of his earnings, too?"

"We cannot answer these sophistries," we were exasperated into replying. "All that we can say is that anything else—anything like what you call justice to the criminal, the prisoner—would disrupt society," and we felt that disrupt was a word which must carry conviction to the densest understanding. It really appeared to do so in this case, for our friend went away without more words, leaving behind him a manuscript, which we mentally rejected, while seeing our way to use the material in it for the present essay; it is the well-known custom of editors to employ in this way the ideas of rejected contributors.

A few days later we met our friend, and as we strolled beside him in the maniacal hubbub of the New York streets, so favorable to philosophic communion, we said, "Well, have you met your namesake since you came to his rescue against the robber State, or did he really sail on the cattle-steamer, as he said he was going to do?"

Our friend gave a vague, embarrassed laugh. "He didn't sail, exactly, at least not on that particular steamer. The fact is, I have just parted from him at my own door—the outside of it. It appears that the authorities of that particular line wished to take advantage of him by requiring him to pay down a sum of money as a guarantee of good faith, and that he refused to do so—not having the money, for one reason. I did not understand the situation exactly, but this was not essential to his purpose, which made itself evident through a good deal of irrelevant discourse. Since I had seen him, society had emulated the State in the practice of a truly sanative attitude toward him. At the place where he went to have his half - crown changed into American money they would only give him forty cents for it, but he was afterward assured by an acquaintance that the current rate was sixty cents. In fact, a half-crown is worth a little more."

"Well, what can you expect of money-changers?" we returned, consolingly. "And what is going to become of your unhappy beneficiary now?"

"Why, according to his report, fortune has smiled, or half-smiled, as the novelists say, upon him. He has found a berth on another line of cattle-steamers, where they don't require a deposit as a guarantee of good faith. In fact, the head steward has taken a liking to him, and he is going out as one of the table-stewards instead of one of the herdsmen; I'm not sure that herdsmen is what they call them."

We laughed sardonically. "And do you believe he is really going?"

Our friend sighed heavily. "Well, I don't believe he's coming back. I only gave him the loose change I had in my pocket, and I don't think it will support him so handsomely to the end of the week that he will wish to call upon me for more."

We were both silent, just as the characters are in a novel till the author can think what to make them say next. Then we asked, "And you still think he had been in the penitentiary?"

"I don't see why he should have said so if he wasn't."

"Well, then," we retorted bitterly, again like a character in fiction, "you have lost another great opportunity: not a moral opportunity this time, but an æsthetic opportunity. You could have got him to tell you all about his life in prison, and perhaps his whole career leading up to it, and you could have made something interesting of it. You might have written a picaresque novel or a picaresque short story, anyway."

174

Our friend allowed, with a mortified air, " It *was* rather a break."

" You threw away the chance of a lifetime. Namesakes who have been in jail don't turn up every day. In his intimate relation to you, he would have opened up, he would have poured out his whole heart to you. Think of the material you have lost."

We thought of it ourselves, and with mounting exasperation. When we reflected that he would probably have put it into his paper, and when we reflected that we could have given so much more color to our essay, we could not endure it. " Well, good-day," we said, coldly; " we are going down this way."

Our friend shook hands, lingeringly, absently. Then he came to himself with a mocking laugh. " Well, perhaps he wasn't, after all, what he said."

XVIII

A NIECE'S LITERARY ADVICE TO HER UNCLE

A VETERAN NOVELIST, who was also an intimate friend of the Easy Chair's, sat before his desk pensively supporting his cheek in his left hand while his right toyed with the pen from which, for the moment at least, fiction refused to flow. His great-niece, who seemed such a contradiction in terms, being as little and vivid personally as she was nominally large and stately, opened the door and advanced upon him.

"Do I disturb you, uncle?" she asked; she did not call him great-uncle, because that, she rightly said, was ridiculous; and now, as part of the informality, she went on without waiting for him to answer, "Because, you know, you wanted me to tell you what I thought of your last story; and I've just read it."

"Oh yes!" the Veteran Novelist assented brightly, hiding his struggle to recall which story it was. "Well?"

"Well," she said, firmly but kindly, "you want me to be frank with you, don't you?"

"By all means, my dear. It's very good of you to read my story." By this time, he had, with the help of the rather lean volume into which his publishers had expanded a long-short story, and which she now held intensely clasped to her breast, really remembered.

"Not at all!" she said. She sat down very elastically in the chair on the other side of his desk, and as she talked she accented each of her emotions by a spring from the cushioned seat. "In the first place," she said, with the effect of coming directly to business, "I suppose you know yourself that it couldn't be called virile."

"No?" he returned. "What is virile?"

"Well, I can't explain, precisely; but it's something that all the critics say of a book that is very strong, don't you know; and masterful; and relentless; and makes you feel as if somebody had taken you by the throat; and shakes you up awfully; and seems to throw you into the air, and trample you under foot."

"Good heavens, my dear!" the Veteran Novelist exclaimed. "I hope I'm a gentleman, even when I'm writing a novel."

"Your being a gentleman has nothing to do with it, uncle!" she said, severely, for she thought she perceived a disposition in the Veteran Novelist to shuffle. "You can't be virile and at the same time remember that you are a gentleman. Lots of *women* write virile books."

"Ladies?" the novelist asked.

"Don't I say that has nothing to do with it? If you wish to grip the reader's attention you must let yourself go, whether you're a gentleman or a lady. Of course," she relented, "your book's very idyllic, and delightful, and all that; but," she resumed, severely, "do you think an honest critic could say there was not a dull page in it from cover to cover?"

The novelist sighed. "I'm sure I don't know. They seem to say it—in the passages quoted in the advertisements—of all the books published. Except mine," he added, sadly.

"Well, we will pass that point," his great-niece relented again. "I didn't intend to wound your feelings, uncle."

"Oh, you haven't. I suppose I *am* a little too easy-going at times."

"Yes, that is it. One can't say dull; but too easy-going. No faithful critic could begin a notice of your book with such a passage as: 'Have you read it? No? Then hop, skip, and jump, and get it. Don't wait to find your hat or drink your coffee. March! It's going like the wind, and you must kite if you want one of the first edition of fifty thousand!' Now that," his great-niece ended, fondly, "is what I should like every critic to say of your book, uncle."

The Veteran Novelist reflected for a moment. Then he said, more spiritedly, "I don't believe *I* should, my dear."

"Then you *must;* that's all. But that's a small thing. What I really wonder at is that, with all your experience, you are not more of a stylist."

"Stylist?"

"Yes. I don't believe there's an epigram in your book from beginning to end. That's the reason the critics don't quote any brilliant sentences from it, and the publishers can't advertise it properly. It makes me mad to find the girls repeating other authors' sayings, and I never catch a word from a book of yours, though you've been writing more than a century."

"Not quite so long, my dear, I think; though very, very long. But just what do you mean by style?"

"Well, you ought to say even the simplest things in a distinguished way; and here, all through, I find you saying the most distinguished things in the simplest way. But I won't worry you about things that are not vital. I'll allow, for the sake of argument, that

178

you can't have virility if you remember that you are a gentleman even when you are writing fiction. But you *can* have *passion.* Why don't you?"

" Don't I? I thought—"

" Not a speck of it—not a single speck! It's rather a delicate point, and I don't exactly know how to put it, but, if you want me to be frank, I must." She looked at her great-uncle, and he nodded encouragement. " I don't believe there's a single place where he crushes her to his heart, or presses his lips to hers in a long kiss. He kisses her cheek once, but I don't call that anything. Why, in lots of the books, nowadays, the girls themselves cling to the men in a close embrace, or put their mouths tenderly to theirs— Well, of course, it sounds rather disgusting, but in your own earlier books, I'm sure there's more of it — of passion. Isn't there? Think!"

The Veteran Novelist tried to think. " To tell you the truth, my dear, I can't remember. I hope there was, and there always will be, love, and true love, in my novels—the kind that sometimes ends in happy marriage, but is always rather shy of showing itself off to the reader in caresses of any kind. I think passion can be intimated, and is better so than brutally stated. If you have a lot of hugging and kissing—"

" Uncle!"

" —How are your lovers different from those poor things in the Park that make you ashamed as you pass them?"

" The police ought to put a stop to it. They are perfectly disgraceful!"

" And they ought to put a stop to it in the novels. It's not only indecent, but it's highly insanitary. Nice people don't want you to kiss their children, nowadays, and yet they expect us novelists to supply them with passion of the most demonstrative sort in our fiction. Among the Japanese, who are now one of the great world-powers, kissing is quite unknown in real life. I don't know the Japanese fiction very well, but I doubt whether there's a single kiss, or double, in it. I believe that a novel full of intense passion could be written without the help of one embrace from beginning to end."

"Uncle!" the girl vividly exclaimed, "why don't you *do* it? It would be the greatest success! Just give them the wink, somehow, at the start—just hint that there was the greatest kind of passion going on all the time and never once showing itself, and the girls would be raving about it. Why *don't* you do it, uncle? You know I do so want you, for once, to write the most popular book of the month!"

"I want to do it myself, my dear. But as to my writing a book full of suppressed passion, that's a story in itself."

"Tell it!" she entreated.

"The Easy Chair wouldn't give me room for it. But I'll tell you something else. When I was a boy I had a knack at versing, which came rather in anticipation of the subjects to use it on. I exhausted Spring and Morning and Snow and Memory, and the whole range of mythological topics, and then I had my knack lying idle. I observed that there was one subject that the other poets found inexhaustible, but somehow I felt myself disqualified for treating it. How could I sing of Love when I had never been in love? For I didn't count those youthful affairs when I was only in the Third Reader and the first part of the Arithmetic. I went about trying to be in love, as a matter of business; but I couldn't manage it. Suddenly it managed itself; and then I found myself worse disqualified than ever. I didn't want to mention it; either to myself or to her, much less to the world at large. It seemed a little too personal."

"Oh, uncle! How funny you are!"

"Do you think so? I didn't think it much fun then, and I don't now. Once I didn't know what love was, and now I've forgotten!"

"No such thing, uncle! You write about it beautifully, even if you're not very virile or epigrammatic or passionate. I won't let you say so."

"Well, then, my dear, if I haven't forgotten, I'm not interested. You see, I know so much more about it than my lovers do. I can't take their point of view any longer. To tell you the truth, I don't care a rap whether they get married or not. In that story there, that you've been reading, I got awfully tired of the girl. She was such a fool, and the fellow was a perfect donkey."

"But he was the dearest donkey in the world! I wanted to h—shake hands with him, and I wanted to kiss—yes, kiss!—*her,* she was such a lovable fool."

"You're very kind to say so, my dear, but you can't keep on making delightful idiots go down with the public. That was what I was thinking when you came in and found me looking so dismal. I had stopped in the middle of a most exciting scene because I had discovered that I was poking fun at my lovers."

"And here I," the girl lamented, "didn't take the slightest notice, but began on you with the harshest criticisms!"

"I didn't mind. I dare say it was for my good."

"I'm sure I meant it so, uncle. And what are you going to do about it?"

"Well, I must get a new point of view."

"Yes?"

"I must change my ground altogether. I can't pretend any longer to be the contemporary of my lovers, or to have the least sympathy with their hopes and fears. If I were to be perfectly honest with them, I should tell them, perhaps, that disappointed love was the best thing that could happen to either of them, but, if they insisted on happiness, that a good broken engagement promised more of it than anything else I could think of."

"That is true," the girl sighed. "There are a great many unhappy marriages. Of course, people would say it was *rather* pessimistic, wouldn't they?"

"People will say anything. One mustn't mind them. But now I'll tell you what I've been thinking all the time we've been talking."

"Well? I knew you were not thinking of *my* nonsense!"

"It was very good nonsense, as nonsense goes, my dear. What I've been thinking is that I must still have the love interest in my books, and have it the main interest, but I must treat it from the vantage-ground of age; it must be something I look back upon, and a little down upon."

"I see what you mean," the girl dissentingly assented.

"I must be in the whole secret — the secret, not merely of my lovers' love, but the secret of love itself. I must know, and I must subtly intimate, that it doesn't really matter to anybody how their affair turns out; for in a few years, twenty or thirty years, it's a thousand to one that they won't care anything about it themselves. I must maintain the attitude of the sage, dealing not unkindly but truthfully with the situation."

"It would be rather sad," the girl murmured. "But one likes sad things."

"When one is young, one does; when one is old, one

likes true things. But, of course, my love-stories would be only for those who have outlived love. I ought to be fair with my readers, and forewarn them that my story was not for the young, the hopeful, the happy."

The girl jumped to her feet **and** stood magnificent. "Uncle! It's grand!"

He rose, too. "What is?" he faltered.

"The idea! Don't you see? You can have the publisher announce it as a story for the disillusioned, the wretched, and the despairing, and that would make every girl want it, for that's what every girl thinks she is, and they would talk to the men about it, and then *they* would want it, and it would be the book of the month! Don't say another word. Oh, you dear!" In spite of the insanitary nature of the action, she caught her uncle round the neck, and kissed him on his bald spot, and ran out of the room. She opened the door to call back: "Don't lose a single minute. Begin it *now!*"

But the Veteran Novelist sank again into his chair in the posture in which she had surprised him.

XIX

A SEARCH FOR CELEBRITY

WE lately received a publication which has interested us somewhat out of proportion to its size. It is called *The Way into Print,* but it does not treat, as the reader might rashly suppose, of the best method of getting your name into the newspapers, either as a lady who is giving a dinner to thirteen otherwise unknown persons, or is making a coming-out tea for her débutante daughter, or had a box full of expensively confectioned friends at the opera or the vaudeville, or is going to read a paper at a woman's club, or is in any sort figuring in the thousand and one modern phases of publicity; it does not even advise her guests or hearers how to appear among those present, or those who were invited and did not come, or those who would not have come if they had been invited. Its scope is far more restricted, yet its plane is infinitely higher, its reach incomparably further. The Print which it proposes to lead the Way into is that print where the elect, who were once few and are now many, are making the corridors of time resound to their footsteps, as poets, essayists, humorists, or other literary forms of immortality. Their procession, which from the point of the impartial spectator has been looking more and more like a cake-walk in these later years, is so increasingly the attraction of young-eyed ambition that

184

nothing interests a very large class of people more than advice for the means of joining it, and it is this advice which the publication in point supplies: supplies, we must say, with as much good sense and good feeling as is consistent with an office which does not seem so dignified as we could wish.

Inevitably the adviser must now and then stoop to the folly of the aspirant, inevitably he must use that folly from time to time with wholesome severity, but he does not feel himself equal to the work unaided. Our sudden national expansion, through the irresistible force of our imaginative work, into an intellectual world-power has thrust a responsibility upon the veterans of a simpler time which they may not shirk, and the author of *The Way into Print* calls upon them to share his task. He is not satisfied with the interesting chapters contributed by younger authors who are in the act of winning their spurs, but he appeals to those established in the public recognition to do their part in aiding us to hold our conquest through the instruction and discipline of those who must take their places when they put their armor off. He does this by means of a letter, almost an open letter, addressed personally to each veteran by means of the substitution of his typewritten name for that of some other veteran, but not differenced in the terms of the ensuing appeal to his kindness or his conscience. He puts himself upon a broad humanitarian ground, and asks that the typewritten author, who, he assumes, is " prominently before the public," shall answer certain questions to which the appellant owns that he has already received hundreds of replies.

By an odd mischance one of his half-open letters found its way to the Easy Chair, and, although that judgment-seat felt relieved from the sense of anything

like a lonely prominence before the public by the very
multitude of those similarly consulted, it did not remain as Easy as it would have liked under the erring
attribution of prominence. Yet to have refused to help
in so good a work would not have been in its nature,
and it lost as little time as possible in summoning a
real author of prominence to consider the problems so
baffling to a mere editorial effigy; for, as we ought to
explain, the *de facto* editor is to be found in the Study
next door, and never in the Easy Chair. The author
prominently before the public came at once, for that
kind of author has very little to do, and is only too
happy to respond to calls like that of the friend of
rising authorship. Most of his time is spent at sym-
posiums, imagined by the Sunday editions of the newspapers, to consider, decide the question whether fig-
paste is truly a health-food; or whether, in view of a
recent colossal gift for educational purposes, the product of the Standard Oil Company was the midnight oil
which Shakespeare had in mind when he spoke of the
scholar wasting it; or something of that kind. His
mind is whetted to the sharpest edge by its employment
with these problems, and is in prime condition for such
simple practical inquiries as those proposed by the letter we had received. But, of course, he put on an air
of great hurry, and spoke of the different poems, novels,
essays, and sketches which he had laid aside to oblige
us, and begged us to get down to business at once.

"We wish nothing better than to do so," we said, to
humor him, "for we know you are a very busy man,
and we will not keep you a moment longer than is
absolutely necessary. Would you like to have all the
questions at once, or would you rather study them one
after another?"

He said he thought he could better give an undivided

mind to each if he had them one at a time, and so we began with the first:

" ' 1. Would you advise the young story-writer to study the old masters in literature or the stories in the current magazines, in order to meet the demands of the current editors?' "

" Will you read that again?" the author prominently before the public demanded, but when we had read it a second time it seemed only to plunge him deeper into despair. He clutched his revered head with both hands, and but for an opportune baldness would probably have torn his hair. He murmured, huskily, " Do you think you have got it right?"

We avoided the response " Sure thing " by an appropriate circumlocution, and then he thundered back: " How in—nature—is a young writer to forecast the demands of current editors? If an editor is worth his salt—his Attic salt—he does not know himself what he wants, except by the eternal yearning of the editorial soul for something new and good. If he has any other demands, he is not a current editor, he is a stagnant editor. Is it possible that there is a superstition to the contrary?"

" Apparently."

" Then that would account for many things. But go on."

" Go on yourself. You have not answered the question."

" Oh, by all means," the author sardonically answered; " if the current editor has demands beyond freshness and goodness, let the young writer avoid the masters in literature and study the stories in the current magazines."

" You are not treating the matter seriously," we expostulated.

"Yes, I am — seriously, sadly, even tragically. I could not have imagined a condition of things so bad, even with the results all round us. Let us have the second question of your correspondent."

"Here it is: ' 2. Has the unknown writer an equal chance with the well-known author, provided his work is up to the standard of the latter's?' "

"Of the latter's?—of the latter's?—of the latter's?" Our friend whispered the phrase to himself before he groaned out: "What a frightful locution! Really, really, it is more than I can bear!"

"For the cause you ought to bear anything. What do you really think?"

"Why, if the former's work is as good as the latter's, why isn't the former's chance as good if the current editor's demands are for the same kind in the former's case as in the latter's? If the latter's aim is to meet the imaginary demands of the stagnant editor, then the former's work ought to be as attractive as the latter's. Ha, ha, ha!"

He laughed wildly, and in order to recall him to himself we read the third question: " ' 3. Which is the more acceptable—a well-told story with a weak plot, or a poorly told story with a strong plot?' "

"Oh, but that is a conundrum, pure and simple!" the author protested. "It is a poor parody on the old End-man pleasantry, 'Would you rather be as foolish as you look, or look as foolish as you are?' You are making it up!"

"We assure you we are not. It is no more a conundrum than the others. Come: question!"

"Well, in the first place, I should like to know what a plot is. Something that has occurred to you primarily as an effect from your experience or observation? Or something you have carpentered out of the old stuff of your reading, with a wooden hero and heroine reciprocally dying for each other, and a wooden villain trying to foil them?"

"You had better ask a current editor or a stagnant. Do you confess yourself posed by this plain problem? Do you give it up?"

"For the present. Perhaps I may gather light from the next question."

"Then here it is: '4. What do you consider the primary weakness in the average stories or verses of the old writers?"

"Oh, that is easy. The same as in the average stories and verses of the younger writers—absence of mind."

"Are you sure you are not shirking? Cannot you give a categorical answer—something that will really help some younger writer to take the place which you are now more or less fraudulently holding? The younger writers will cheerfully allow that the trouble is absence of mind, but what line of reading would you suggest which would turn this into presence of mind?"

"There is none, except to have themselves newly ancestored. Presence of mind as well as absence of mind is something derived; you cannot acquire it."

"We think you might be a little less sardonic. Now here is the next problem: '5. What are the successful author's necessary qualifications in the matters of natural ability, education, life as he sees it and lives it, technical training, etc?' "

"This will be the death of me!" the prominent author lamented. "Couldn't I skip that one?"

"It seems to cover some of the most important points. We do not think your self-respect will allow you to skip it. At any rate, make an effort to answer it."

Thus challenged, the prominent author pulled himself together. " Oh," he said, sadly, " which of us knows whether he has natural ability or not, and what is education, and what is life as one sees it, and what is technical training? Do these poor young fellows think that one is tall or short by taking thought? It is the same as that, it seems to me; or if you prefer a mystical solution, I should say, if you have a longing, from your earliest consciousness, to write poetry or fiction, and cannot keep from doing it for any long time together, you are possibly born with a gift for it. But this may be altogether a mistake; it may be the effect of your early and incessant scribblings on the minds of spectators wholly incompetent to judge of your abilities, such as your fond parents. This must rather often happen if we can judge from what nine-tenths of what is called literature is composed of. If your longing to write is the real thing, or is not, still education will not help or hinder you in doing it. No man was ever yet taught any art. He may be taught a trade, and that is what most of the versing and prosing is, I suppose. If you have the gift, you will technically train yourself: that is, you will learn how to be simple and clear and honest. Charm you will have got from your great-grandfather or great-grandmother; and life, which is only another sort of school, will not qualify you to depict life; but if you do not want to depict life, you will perhaps be able to meet the demands of what our friend calls the current editors."

Here the prominent author rose, but we stayed him with a gesture. " There is another question, the last: ' 6. Do you care to convey any hints or suggestions gleaned from your personal experiences in the climb to success that may make easier the gaining of the heights for the beginner?"

The prominent author roared with laughter. " Read that again!" But when we had done so, he became grave, even sorrowful. "Is it really true, then, as we seem to see, that there is a large body of young people taking up literature as a business? The thing that all my life I have fondly dreamed was an art, dear and almost holy! Are they going into it for the money there is in it? And am I, in my prominence—more or less fraudulent, as you say—an incentive to them to persevere in their enterprises? Is that what one has to come to after a life of conscientious devotion to—an ideal? Come, old friend, say it isn't so bad as that! It is? Then "—the prominent author paused and sank weakly into the chair from which he had risen—" perhaps I have been dreaming all these years; but in my dream it seems to me that everything outside of myself which seemed to hinder me has really helped me. There has been no obstacle in my way which if I were at the bottom of the hill, where I might very rightfully be, I would have removed. I am glad that the climb to success, as your friend calls it, has been hard and long, and I bless God for my difficulties and backsets, all of them. Sometimes they seemed cruel; they filled me with despair and shame; but there was not one that did not make me stronger and fitter for my work, if I was fit for it. You know very well that in this art of ours we need all the strength we can get from our overthrows. There is no training that can ever make the true artist's work easy to him, and if he is a true artist he will suspect everything easily done as ill done. What comes hard and slow and hopelessly, that is the thing which when we look at it we find is the thing that was worth doing. I had my downs with my ups, and when I was beginning the downs outnumbered the ups ten to one. For one manuscript accepted, and after the days of many years printed, I had a dozen rejected and rejected without delay. But every such rejection helped me. In some cases I had to swallow the bitter dose and own that the editor was right; but the bitter was wholesome. In other cases I knew that he was wrong, and then I set my teeth, and took my courage in both hands, and tried and tried with that rejected manuscript till the divinely appointed editor owned that I was right. But these are the commonplaces of literary biography. I don't brag of them; and I have always tried to keep my head in such shape that even defeat has not swelled it beyond the No. 7 I began with. Why should I be so wicked as to help another and a younger man over the bad places? If I could only gain his confidence I should like to tell him that these are the places that will strengthen his heart for the climb. But if he has a weak heart, he had better try some other road. There! I have given you all the 'hints and suggestions from my experience' that I can think of, and now let me go."

Once more he rose, and once more we stayed him. " Yes," we said, " no doubt you think you have spoken honestly and faithfully, but you have addressed your-self to the wrong audience. You have spoken to artists, born and self - made, but artists can always manage without help. Your help was invoked in behalf of artisans, of adventurers, of speculators. What was wanted of you was a formula for the fabrication of gold bricks which would meet the demands of current dealers in that sort of wares."

" But if I have never made gold bricks myself, or not knowingly?"

" Ah, that is what you say! But do you suppose anybody will believe you?"

The prominent author put on the hat which he flat-

tered himself was a No. 7, but which we could plainly
see was a No. 12, and said, with an air of patronizing
compassion, " You have sat here so long in your cushioned comfort, looking out on the publishing world,
that you have become corrupt, cynical, pessimistic."

XX

PRACTICAL IMMORTALITY ON EARTH

THE talk at a dinner given by the Easy Chair to some of its most valued friends was of the life after death, and it will not surprise any experienced observer to learn that the talk went on amid much unserious chatter, with laughing irrelevancies more appropriate to the pouring of champagne, and the changing of plates, than to the very solemn affair in hand. It may not really have been so very solemn. Nobody at table took the topic much to heart apparently. The women, some of them, affected an earnest attention, but were not uncheerful; others frankly talked of other things; some, at the farther end of the table, asked what a given speaker was saying; the men did not, in some cases, conceal that they were bored.

" No," the first speaker said, after weighing the pros and cons, " for my part, I don't desire it. When I am through, here, I don't ask to begin again elsewhere."

" And you don't expect to ?" his closest listener inquired.

" And I don't expect to."

" It is curious," the closest listener went on, " how much our beliefs are governed by our wishes in this matter. When we are young and are still hungering for things to happen, we have a strong faith in immortality. When we are older, and the whole round

194

of things, except death, has happened, we think it very
likely we shall not live again. It seems to be the same
with peoples; the new peoples believe, the old peoples
doubt. It occurs to very, very few men to be convinced, as a friend of mine has been convinced against
the grain, of the reality of the life after death. I will
not say by what means he was convinced, for that is not
pertinent; but he was fully convinced, and he said to
me: 'Personally, I would rather not live again, but it
seems that people do. The facts are too many; the
proofs I have had are irresistible; and I have had to
give way to them in spite of my wish to reject
them.'"

"Yes," the first speaker said, "that is certainly an
uncommon experience. You think that if I were perfectly honest, I should envy him his experience? Well,
then, honestly, I don't."

"No," the other rejoined, "I don't know that I accuse your sincerity. But, may I ask, what are your
personal objections to immortality?"

"It wouldn't be easy to say. If I could have had
my way, I would not have been at all. Speaking
selfishly, as we always do when we speak truly, I have
not had a great deal of happiness, though I have had a
good deal of fun. But things seem to wear out. I like
to laugh, and I have laughed, in my time, consumedly.
But I find that the laugh goes out of the specific instances of laughability, just as grieving goes out of
grief. The thing that at the first and third time
amused me enormously leaves me sad at the fourth, or
at least unmoved. You see, I can't trust immortality
to be permanently interesting. The reasonable chances
are that in the lapse of a few æons I should find
eternity hanging heavy on my hands. But it isn't
that, exactly, and it would be hard to say what my ob-

jection to immortality exactly is. It would be simpler to say what it *really* is. It is personal, temperamental, congenital. I was born, I suspect, an indifferentist, as far as this life is concerned, and as to another life, I have an acquired antipathy."

"That is curious, but not incredible, and of course not inconceivable," the closest listener assented.

"I'm not so sure of that," a light skirmisher broke his silence for the first time. "Do you mean to say," he asked of the first speaker, "that you would not mind being found dead in your bed to-morrow morning, and that you would rather like it if that were actually the end of you?"

The first speaker nodded his head over the glass he had just emptied, and having swallowed its contents hastily, replied, "Precisely."

"Then you have already, at your age, evolved that 'instinct of death,' which Metchnikoff, in his strange book, thinks the race will come to when men begin living rightly, and go living on to a hundred and fifty years or more, as they once did."

"Who is Metchnikoff, and what is the name of his strange book?" the light skirmisher cut in.

"He's the successor of Pasteur in the Pasteur Institute at Paris, and his book is called *The Nature of Man.*"

"That blighting book!" One of the women who had caught on to the drift of the talk contributed this anguished suspiration.

"Blighting? Is it blighting?" the first speaker parleyed.

"Don't you call it blighting," she returned, "to be told not only that you are the descendant of an anthropoid ape—we had got used to that—but of an anthropoid ape gone wrong?"

196

"Sort of simian degenerate," the light skirmisher formulated the case. "We are merely apes in error."

The closest listener put this playfulness by. "What seems to me a fundamental error of that book is its constant implication of a constant fear of death. I can very well imagine, or I can easily allow, that we are badly made, and that there are all sorts of 'disharmonies,' as Metchnikoff calls them, in us; but my own experience is that we are not all the time thinking about death and dreading it, either in earlier or later life, and that elderly people think less about it, if anything, than younger people. His contention for an average life four or five times longer than the present average life seems to be based upon an obscure sense of the right of a man to satisfy that instinct of life here on earth which science forbids him to believe he shall satisfy hereafter."

"Well, I suppose," the first speaker said, "that Metchnikoff may err in his premises through a temperamental 'disharmony' of Russian nature rather than of less specific human nature. The great Russian authors seem to recognize that perpetual dread of death in themselves and their readers which we don't recognize in ourselves or our Occidental friends and neighbors. Other people don't think of death so much as he supposes, and when they do they don't dread it so much. But I think he is still more interestingly wrong in supposing that the young are less afraid of death than the old because they risk their lives more readily. That is not from indifference to death, it is from inexperience of life; they haven't learned yet the dangers which beset it and the old have; that is all."

"I don't know but you're right," the first speaker said. "And I couldn't see the logic of Metchnikoff's position in regard to the 'instinct of death' which he expects us to develop after we have lived, say, a hundred and thirty or forty years, so that at a hundred and fifty we shall be glad to go, and shall not want anything but death after we die. The apparent line of his argument is that in youth we have not the instinct of life so strongly but that we willingly risk life. Then, until we live to a hundred and thirty or forty or so, we have the instinct of life so strongly that we are anxious to shun death; lastly the instinct of death grows in us and we are eager to lay down life. I don't see how or why this should be. As a matter of fact, children dread death far more than men who are not yet old enough to have developed the instinct of it. Still, it's a fascinating and suggestive book."

" But not enough so to console us for the precious hope of living again which it takes away so pitilessly," said the woman who had followed the talk.

" Is that such a very precious hope ?" the first speaker asked.

" I know you pretend not," she said, " but I don't believe you."

" Then you think that the dying, who almost universally make a good end, are buoyed up by that hope ?"

" I don't see why they shouldn't be. I know it's the custom for scientific people to say that the resignation of the dying is merely part of the general sinking and so is just physical; but they can't prove that. Else why should persons who are condemned to death be just as much resigned to it as the sick and even more exalted ?"

" Ah," the light skirmisher put in, " some of the scientific people dispose of that point very simply. They say it's self-hypnotism."

" Well, but they can't prove that, either," she retorted. Then she went on : " Besides, the dying are not almost universally willing to die. Sometimes they are very unwilling: and they seem to be unwilling because they have no hope of living again. Why wouldn't it be just as reasonable to suppose that we could evolve the instinct of death by believing in the life hereafter as by living here a hundred and fifty years? For the present, it's as easy to do the one as the other."

"But not for the future," the first speaker said. "As you suggest, it may be just as reasonable to think we can evolve the instinct of death by faith as by longevity, but it isn't as scientific."

"What M. Metchnikoff wants is the scientific certainty—which we can have only by beginning to live a century and a half apiece—that the coming man will not be afraid to die." This, of course, was from the light skirmisher.

The woman contended, "The coming man may be scientifically resigned if he prefers, but the going man, the *gone* man, was rapturously ready to die, in untold thousands of martyrdoms, because he believed that he should live again."

The first speaker smiled compassionately, and perhaps also a little patronizingly. "I'm not sure that you have met the point exactly. Metchnikoff denies, on the basis of scientific knowledge, that it is possible for a man, being dead, to live again. In those two extremely interesting chapters of his, which treat of the 'Religious Remedies' and the 'Philosophical Remedies' for the 'disharmonies of the human constitution,' he is quite as unsparing of the sages as of the saints. The Christians and the Buddhists fare no worse than Plato and the Stoics; the last are no less unscientific than the first in his view, and no less fallacious. What he asks is not that we shall be resigned or enraptured in view of death, but that we shall physically desire it when we are tired of living, just as we physically desire sleep when we are tired of waking."

"And to that end," the light skirmisher said, "he asks nothing but that we shall live a hundred and fifty years."

"No, he asks that we shall live such natural lives that we shall die natural deaths, which are voluntary deaths. He contends that most of us now die accidental and violent deaths."

The woman who had caught on demanded, "Why does he think we could live a century and a half?"

"From analogies in the lives of other animals and from the facts of our constitution. He instances the remarkable cases of longevity recorded in the Bible."

"I think he's very inconsistent," his pursuer continued. "The Bible says men lived anywhere from a hundred to nine hundred years, and he thinks it quite possible. The Bible says that men live after death, and he thinks that's impossible."

"Well, have you ever met a man who had lived after death?" the first speaker asked.

"No. Have you ever met a man two hundred years old? If it comes to undeniable proof there is far more proof of ghosts than of bicentenarians."

"Very well, then, I get out of it by saying that I don't believe in either."

"And leave Metchnikoff in the lurch!" the light skirmisher reproached him. "You don't believe in the instinct of death! And I was just going to begin living to a hundred and fifty and dying voluntarily by leaving off cheese. Now I will take some of the Gorgonzola."

Everybody laughed but the first speaker and the woman who had caught on; they both looked rather grave, and the closest listener left off laughing soonest.

"We can't be too grateful to science for its devotion to truth. But isn't it possible for it to overlook one kind of truth in looking for another? Isn't it imaginable that when a certain anthropoid ape went wrong and blundered into a man, he also blundered into a soul, and as a slight compensation for having involuntarily degenerated from his anthropoid ancestor, came into the birthright of eternal life?"

"It's imaginable," the first speaker granted. "But science leaves imagining things to religion and philosophy."

"Ah, that's just where you're mistaken!" the woman who had caught on exclaimed. "Science does nothing but imagine things!"

"Well, not quite," the light skirmisher mocked.

She persisted unheeding: "First the suggestion from the mystical somewhere—the same *where,* probably, that music and pictures and poetry come from; then the hypothesis; then the proof; then the established fact. Established till some new scientist comes along and knocks it over."

"It would be very interesting if some one would proceed hypothetically concerning the soul and its immortality, as the scientific people do in their inquiries concerning the origin of man, electricity, disease, and the rest."

"Yes," the light skirmisher agreed. "Why doesn't some fellow bet himself that he has an undying soul and then go on to accumulate the proofs?" The others seemed now to have touched bottom in the discussion, and he launched a random inquiry upon the general silence. "By-the-way, I wonder why women are so much more anxious to live again than men, as a general thing."

"Because they don't feel," one of them at table

ventured, "that they have had a fair chance here."

"Oh! I thought maybe they felt that they hadn't had their say."

"Is it quite certain," the closest listener asked, "that they *are* more anxious to live again than men?" He looked round at the ladies present, and at first none of them answered; perhaps because they feared the men would think them weak if they owned to a greater longing than themselves for immortality.

Finally the woman who had caught on said: "I don't know whether it's so or not; and I don't think it matters. But I don't mind saying that I long to live again; I am not ashamed of it. I don't think very much of myself; but I'm interested in living. Then " —she dropped her voice a little—" there are some I should like to see again. I have known people—characters—natures—that I can't believe are wasted. And those that were dear to us and that we have lost—"

She stopped, and the first speaker now looked at her with a compassion unalloyed by patronage, and did not ask, as he might, " What has all that to do with it?"

In fact, a sympathetic silence possessed the whole company. It was broken at last by the closest listener's saying: "After all, I don't know that Metchnikoff's book is so very blighting. It's certainly a very important book, and it produces a reaction which may be wholesome or unwholesome as you choose to think. And no matter what we believe, we must respect the honesty of the scientific attitude in regard to a matter that has been too much abandoned to the emotions, perhaps. In all seriousness I wish some scientific man would apply the scientific method to finding out the soul, as you "—he turned to the light skirmisher—" suggest. Why shouldn't it be investigated?"

Upon this invitation the light skirmisher tried to imagine some psychological experiments which should bear a certain analogy to those of the physicists, but he failed to keep the level of his suggestion.

" As I said," the closest listener remarked, " he produces a secondary state of revolt which is desirable, for in that state we begin to inquire not only where we stand, but where *he* *s*tands."

" And what is your conclusion as to his place in the inquiry ?"

" That it isn't different from yours or mine, really. We all share the illusion of the race from the beginning that somehow our opinion of the matter affects its reality. I should distinguish so far as to say that we think we believe, and he thinks he knows. For my own part, I have the impression that he has helped my belief."

The light skirmisher made a desperate effort to retrieve himself: " Then a few more books like his would restore the age of faith."

XXI

AROUND A RAINY-DAY FIRE

A NUMBER of the Easy Chair's friends were sitting round the fire in the library of a country-house. The room was large and full of a soft, flattering light. The fire was freshly kindled, and flashed and crackled with a young vivacity, letting its rays frolic over the serried bindings on the shelves, the glazed pictures on the walls, the cups of after-luncheon coffee in the hands of the people, and the tall jugs and pots in the tray left standing on the library table. It was summer, but a cold rain was falling forbiddingly without. No one else could come, and no one could wish to go. The conditions all favored a just self-esteem, and a sense of providential preference in the accidental assemblage of those people at that time and place.

The talk was rather naturally, though not necessarily, of books, and one of the people was noting that children seemed to like short stories because their minds had not the strength to keep the facts of a whole book. The effort tired them, and they gave it up, not because a book did not interest them, but because it exhausted their little powers. They were good for a leap, or a dash, or a short flight in literature, even very high literature, but they had not really the force for anything covering greater time and space.

Another declared this very suggestive, and declared it in such a way that the whole company perceived he had something behind his words, and besought him to say what he meant. He did so, as well as he could, after protesting that it was not very novel, or if so, perhaps not very important, and if it was important, perhaps it was not true. They said they would take the chances; and then he said that it was merely a notion which had occurred to him at the moment concerning the new reading of the new reading public, whether it might not be all juvenile literature, adapted in mature terms to people of physical adolescence but of undeveloped thinking and feeling: not really feeble-minded youth, but æsthetically and intellectually children, who might presently grow into the power of enjoying and digesting food for men. By-and-by they might gather fortitude for pleasure in real literature, in fiction which should not be a travesty of the old fairy-tales, or stories of adventures among giants and robbers and pirates, or fables with human beings speaking from the motives and passions of animals. He mentioned fiction, he said, because the new reading of the new reading public seemed to be nearly altogether fiction.

All this had so much the effect of philosophical analysis that those comfortable people were lulled into self - approving assent; and putting themselves altogether apart from the new reading public, they begged him to say what he meant. He answered that there was nothing more phenomenal in the modern American life; and he paid a pretty tribute to their ignorance in owning that he was not surprised they knew nothing of that public. He promised that he would try to define it, and he began by remarking that it seemed to be largely composed of the kind of persons who at the theatre audibly interpret the action to one another. The present company must have heard them?

His listeners again assented. Was the new reading public drawn from the theatre-going, or more definitely speaking, the matinée class?

There was something odd, there, the philosopher returned. The matinée class was as large as ever: larger; while the new reading public, perfectly interchangeable with it in its intellectual pleasure and experiences, had suddenly outnumbered it a thousandfold. The popular novel and the popular play were so entirely of one fibre and texture, and so easily convertible, that a new novel was scarcely in every one's bread-trough before it was on the boards of all the theatres. This led some to believe that we were experiencing a revival of the drama, and that if we kept on having authors who sold half a million copies we could not help having a Shakespeare by-and-by: he must follow.

One of those listening asked, But how had these people begun so instantaneously to form themselves into this new innumerable reading public? If they were of that quality of mind which requires the translation of an unmistakable meaning from the players to the play-goers, they must find themselves helpless when grappling in solitude with the sense of a book. Why did not they go increasingly to the theatre instead of turning so overwhelmingly to the printed word?

The philosopher replied that they had not now begun to do this, but only seemed to have begun, since there really was no beginning in anything. The readers had always been in the immense majority, because they could read anywhere, and they could see plays only in the cities and towns. If the theatre were universal, undoubtedly they would prefer plays, because a play makes far less draft upon the mental capacities or energies than the silliest book; and what seemed their effort to interpret it to one another might very well be the exchange of their delight in it. The books they preferred were of the nature of poor plays, full of "easy things to understand," cheap, common incidents, obvious motives, and vulgar passions, such as had been used a thousand times over in literature. They were fitted for the new reading public for this reason; the constant repetition of the same characters, events, scenes, plots, gave their infantile minds the pleasure which children find in having a story told over and over in exactly the same terms. The new reading public would rebel against any variance, just as children do.

The most of the company silently acquiesced, or at least were silent, but one of them made the speaker observe that he had not told them what this innumerable unreasoning multitude had read before the present plague of handsome, empty, foolish duodecimos had infested everybody's bread-trough.

The philosopher said the actual interior form of nonliterary literature was an effect of the thin spread of our literary culture, and outwardly was the effect of the thick spread of our material prosperity. The dollar-and-a-half novel of to-day was the dime novel of yesterday in an avatar which left its essence unchanged. It was even worse, for it was less sincerely and forcibly written, and it could not be so quickly worn out and thrown away. Its beauty of paper, print, and binding gave it a claim to regard which could not be ignored, and established for it a sort of right to lie upon the table, and then stand upon the shelf, where it seemed to relate itself to genuine literature, and to be of the same race and lineage. As for this vast new reading public, it was the vast old reading public with more means in its pocket of satisfying its crude, childish taste. Its head was the same empty head.

There was a sort of dreadful finality in this, and for a while no one spoke. Then some one tried in vain to turn the subject, while the philosopher smiled upon the desolation he had made; and then one of that sex which when satisfied of the truth likes to have its "sense of satisfaction ache" through the increase of conviction, asked him why the English reading public, which must be so much more cultivated than our new reading public, seemed to like the same sort of puerile effects in works of imagination, the stirring incidents, the well-worn plots, the primitive passions, and the robustious incentives. He owned the fact, but he contended that the fact, though interesting, was not so mysterious as it appeared at first sight. It could be explained that the English had never taken the imagination very seriously, and that in their dense, close civilization, packed tight with social, political, and material interests, they asked of the imagination chiefly excitement and amusement. They had not turned to it for edification or instruction, for that thrill of solemn joy which comes of vital truth profoundly seen and clearly shown. For this reason when all Europe besides turned her face to the light, some decades ago, in the pages of the great prose poets who made the age illustrious, England preferred the smoky links and dancing damp-fires which had pleased her immature fancy, and kept herself well in the twilight of the old ideal of imagination as the mother of unrealities. There could be no doubt, the philosopher thought, that the recrudescence which her best wits recognized as the effects of this perversity, was the origin of the preposterous fiction which we now feed to the new reading public, and which we think must somehow be right because it was hers and is ours, and has the sanction of race and tradition.

It was not, he continued, a thing to shed the tear of unavailing regret for, though it was not a transitory phase, or a state of transition, for the condition that now existed had always existed. The new reading public was larger than ever before not merely because there was a fresh demand for reading, but because more people were lettered and moneyed and leisured, and did not know what otherwise to do with themselves. It was quite simple, and the fact was less to be regretted in itself than for an indirect result which might be feared from it. He paused at this, in order to be asked what this result was, and being promptly asked he went on.

It was, he said, the degradation of authorship as a calling, in the popular regard. He owned that in the past authorship had enjoyed too much honor in the reverence and affection of the world: not always, indeed, but at certain times. As long as authors were the clients and dependents of the great, they could not have been the objects of a general interest or honor. They had then passed the stage when the simple poet or story-teller was wont to

> —sit upon the ground,
> And tell sad stories of the deaths of kings,

to wondering and admiring circles of simple listeners, and they had not yet come to that hour of authorship when it reverted to the peasantry, now turned people, and threw itself upon the people's generous acceptance and recognition for bread and fame. But when that hour came, it brought with it the honor of a reverent and persistent curiosity concerning literature and the literary life, which the philosopher said he was afraid could not survive the actual superabundance of authors and the transformation of the novelist into the artisan. There seemed, he pursued, a fixed formula for the manufacture of a work of fiction, to be studied and practised like any other. Literature was degraded from an art to a poor sort of science, in the practical application of which thousands were seen prospering; for the immense output of our press represented the industry of hundreds and thousands. A book was concocted, according to a patent recipe, advertised, and sold like any other nostrum, and perhaps the time was already here when it was no longer more creditable to be known as the author of a popular novel than as the author of a popular medicine, a Pain-killer, a Soothing Syrup, a Vegetable Compound, a Horse Liniment, or a Germicide. Was it possible, he asked, for a reader of the last book selling a hundred thousand copies to stand in the loving or thrilling awe of the author that we used to feel for Longfellow and Tennyson, for Emerson and Carlyle, for Hawthorne and George Eliot, for Irving and Scott, or for any of their great elders or youngers? He repeated that perhaps authorship had worked its worshippers too hard, but there was no doubt that their worship was a genuine devotion. For at least a hundred and fifty years it had been eagerly offered in a full acceptance of the Schiller superstition that at the sharing of the earth the poet, representing authorship, had been so much preoccupied with higher things that he had left the fleshpots and the loaves and fishes to others, and was to be compensated with a share of the divine honors paid to Jove himself. From Goethe to Carlyle, what a long roll of gods, demigods, and demisemigods it was! It might have been bad for the deities, and the philosopher rather thought it was, but burning incense on the different shrines was an excellent thing for the votaries, and kept them out of all sorts of mischiefs, low pleasures, and vain amusements. Whether that was really so or not, the doubt remained whether authorship was not now a creed outworn. Did tender maids and virtuous matrons still cherish the hope of some day meeting their literary idols in the flesh? Did generous youth aspire to see them merely at a distance, and did doting sires teach their children that it was an epoch-making event when a great poet or novelist visited the country; or when they passed afar, did they whip some favored boy, as the father of Benvenuto Cellini whipped him at sight of a salamander in the fire that he might not forget the prodigy? Now that the earth had been divided over again, and the poet in his actual guise of novelist had richly shared in its goods with the farmer, the noble, the merchant, and the abbot, was it necessary or even fair that he should be the guest of heaven? In other words, now that every successful author could keep his automobile, did any one want his autograph?

In the silence that fell upon the company at these words, the ticking of the clock under its classic pediment on the mantel was painfully audible, and had the effect of intimating that time now had its innings and eternity was altogether out of it. Several minutes seemed to pass before any one had the courage to ask whether the degradation of authorship was not partially the result of the stand taken by the naturalists in Zola, who scorned the name of art for his calling and aspired to that of science. The hardy adventurer who suggested this possibility said that it was difficult to imagine the soul stirred to the same high passion by the botanist, the astronomer, the geologist, the electrician, or even the entomologist as in former times by the poet, the humorist, the novelist, or the playwright. If the fictionist of whatever sort had succeeded in identifying himself with the scientist, he must leave the enjoyment of divine honors to the pianist, the farce-comedian, the portrait-painter, the emotional actor, and the architect, who still deigned to practise an art.

The philosopher smiled, and owned that this was very interesting, and opened up a fresh field of in-quiry. The first question there was whether the imaginative author were not rather to blame for not having gone far enough in the scientific direction in the right scientific fashion than for having taken that course at all. The famous reproach of poetry made by Huxley, that it was mostly " sensual caterwauling," might well have given the singer pause in striking the sympathetic catgut of his lyre: perhaps the strings were metallic; but no matter. The reproach had a justice in it that must have stung, and made the lyrist wish to be an atomic theorist at any cost. In fact, at that very moment science had, as it were, caught the bread out of fiction's mouth, and usurped the highest func-tions of imagination. In almost every direction of its recent advance it had made believe that such and such a thing was so, and then proceeded to prove it. To this method we owed not only the possession of our present happy abundance of microbes in every sort, but our knowledge of the universe in almost every respect. Science no longer waited for the apple to fall before inferring a law of gravitation, but went about with a stick knocking fruit off every bough in the hope that something suggestive would come of it. On make-believes of all kinds it based the edifices of all kinds of eternal veracities. It behooved poetry, or fiction, which was radically the same, to return to its earliest and simplest devices if it would find itself in the em-brace of science, and practise the make-beliefs of its infancy. Out of so many there were chances of some coming true if they were carried far enough and long

212

enough. In fact, the hypothetical method of science had apparently been used in the art of advertising the works in which the appetite of the new reading public was flattered. The publishers had hypothesized from the fact of a population of seventy millions, the existence of an immense body of raw, coarse minds, untouched by taste or intelligence, and boldly addressed the new fiction to it. As in many suppositions of science their guess proved true.

Then why, the hardy listener who had spoken before inquired, was not make-believe the right method for the author, if it was the right method for the scientist and the publisher? Why should not the novelist hypothesize cases hitherto unknown to experience, and then go on by persistent study to find them true? It seemed to this inquirer that the mistake of fiction, when it refused longer to be called an art and wished to be known as a science, was in taking up the obsolescent scientific methods, and in accumulating facts, or human documents, and deducing a case from them, instead of boldly supposing a case, as the new science did, and then looking about for occurrences to verify it.

The philosopher said, Exactly; this was the very thing he was contending for. The documents should be collected in support of the hypothesis; the hypothesis should not be based on documents already collected. First the inference, then the fact; was not that the new scientific way? It looked like it; and it seemed as if the favorite literature of the new reading public were quite in the spirit of the new science. Its bold events, its prodigious characters, its incredible motives, were not they quite of the nature of the fearless conjecture which imagined long and short electric waves and then spread a mesh of wire to intercept them and seize their message?

The hardy inquirer demanded: Then if so, why despise the literature of the new reading public? Why despise the new reading public, anyway?

The philosopher responded that he despised nothing, not even a thing so unphilosophical as modern science. He merely wished his interpellant to observe again that the unification of the literary spirit and the scientific spirit was degrading the literary man to the level of the scientific man. He thought this was bad for the small remnant of mankind, who in default of their former idolatry might take to the worship of themselves. Now, however bad a writer might be, it was always well for the reader to believe him better than himself. If we had not been brought up in this superstition, what would have become of the classics of all tongues? But for this, what was to prevent the present company from making a clearance of three-fourths of the surrounding shelves and feeding that dying flame on the hearth?

At this the host, who had been keeping himself in a modest abeyance, came forward and put some sticks on the fire. He said he would like to see any one touch his bindings; which seemed to be his notion of books. Nobody minded him; but one of those dutyolators, who abound in a certain sex, asked the philosopher what he thought we ought to do for the maintenance of author-worship among us.

He answered, he had not thought of that; his mind had been fixed upon the fact of its decay. But perhaps something could be done by looking up the author whose book had sold least during the season, and asking him candidly whether he would not like to be paid the divine honors now going begging from one big seller to another; for the decay of author-worship must be as much from the indifference of the authors as from the irreverence of the readers. If such a low-selling author did not seem to regard it as rather invidious, then pay him the divine honors; it might be a wholesome and stimulating example; but perhaps we should afterward have the demigod on our hands. Something might be safelier done by writing, as with the present company, and inquiring into "the present condition of polite learning." This would keep the sacred flame alive, and give us the comfort of refined association in an exquisite moment of joy from the sense of our superiority to other people. That, after all, was the great thing.

The company drew a little closer round the fire. The rain beat upon the panes, and the wind swept the wet leaves against them, while each exhaled a sigh of aspiration not unmixed with a soft regret.

XXII

THE ADVANTAGES OF QUOTATIONAL CRITICISM

The talk round the Easy Chair one day was of that strange passion for reading which has of late possessed the public, and the contagion or infection by which it has passed to hundreds of thousands who never read before; and then the talk was of how this prodigious force might be controlled and turned in the right way: not suffered to run to waste like water over the dam, but directed into channels pouring upon wheels that turn the mills of the gods or something like that. There were, of course, a great many words; in fact, talk is composed of words, and the people at that luncheon were there for talking as well as eating, and they did not mind how many words they used. But the sum of their words was the hope, after a due season of despair, that the present passion for reading might be made to eventuate in more civilization than it seemed to be doing, if it could be brought back to good literature, supposing it was ever there in great strength, and the question was how to do this.

One of the company said he had lately been reading a good many books of Leigh Hunt's, and after everybody had interrupted with "Delightful!" "Perfectly charming!" and the like, he went on to observe that one of the chief merits of Hunt seemed to be his aptness in quotation. That, he remarked, was almost a lost art with critics, who had got to thinking that they could tell better what an author was than the author himself could. Like every other power disused, the power of apt quotation had died, and there were very few critics now who knew how to quote: not one knew, as Hunt, or Lamb, or Hazlitt, or the least of the great quotational school of critics, knew. These had perhaps overworked their gift, and might have been justly accused, as they certainly were accused, of misleading the reader and making him think that the poets, whose best they quoted, putting the finest lines in italics so that they could not be missed, were as good throughout as in the passages given. It was this sense of having abused innocence, or ignorance, which led to the present reaction in criticism no doubt, and yet the present reaction was an error. Suppose that the poets whose best was given by quotation were not altogether as good as that? The critics never pretended they were; they were merely showing how very good these poets could be, and at the same time offering a delicate pleasure to the reader, who could not complain that his digestion was overtaxed by the choice morsels. If his pleasure in them prompted him to go to the entire poet quoted, in the hope of rioting gluttonously upon him, the reader was rightly served in one sense. In another, he was certainly not misserved or his time wasted. It would be hard for him to prove that he could have employed it more profitably.

Everybody, more or less, now sat up, and he who had the eye and ear of the table went on to remark that he had not meant to make a defence of the extinct school of quotational criticism. What he really meant to do was to suggest a way out of the present situation in which the new multitude of voracious readers were grossly feeding upon such intellectual husks as swine

would not eat, and imagining themselves nourished by
their fodder. There might be some person present who
could improve upon his suggestion, but his notion, as
he conceived it, was that something might be done in
the line of quotational criticism to restore the great
poets to the public favor, for he understood that good
authors were now proportionately less read than they
once were. He thought that a pity: and the rest of
the company joined in asking him how he proposed to
employ the quotational method for his purpose.

In answering he said that he would not go outside
of the English classics, and he would, for the present,
deal only with the greatest of these. He took it for
granted that those listening were all agreed that mankind would be advantaged in their minds or manners by a more or less familiar acquaintance with
Chaucer, Spenser, Shakespeare, Milton, Dryden, Pope,
Cowper, Burns, Byron, Wordsworth, Coleridge, Shelley, Keats, Tennyson, and Browning; he himself did
not mind adding Scott to the list, whose poetry he
found much better than his prose. To bring about an
acquaintance which might very profitably ripen into intimacy, he would have each of these poets treated in
the whole measure of his work as many or most of
them had been topically or partially treated by the
quotational critics. Some one here made him observe
that he was laying out rather a large piece of work,
and to this he answered, Not at all; the work had been
already done. Asked then, somewhat derisively, why
it need be done over again, he explained, with a modesty
and patience which restored him to the regard he had
lost by the derision (all had impartially united in it),
that though the work had already been done, there
needed some slight additions to it which would easily
fit it to his purpose. He was not thinking of going in

for one of those dreadful series of books which seemed the dismay alike of publisher and reader, and required rewriting of matter more than enough rewritten. In fact, he said, that for his purpose the writing was done fully and probably better than it could be done again, and it was only the reading and quoting that demanded editorial attention.

Another said he did not see how that could be, and the inventor of the brave scheme, which was still *in petto,* said that he would try to show him. We had, he contended, only too great riches in the criticisms of the poets open to our choice, but suppose we took Spenser and let Lowell introduce him to us. There would be needed a very brief biographical note, and then some able hand to intersperse the criticism with passages from Spenser, or with amplifications of the existing quotations, such as would give a full notion of the poet's scope and quality. The story of each of his poems could be given in a few words, where the poems themselves could not be given even in part, and with the constant help of the critic the reader could be possessed of a luminous idea of the poet, such as he probably could not get by going to him direct, though this was not to be deprecated, but encouraged, after the preparatory acquaintance. The explanatory and illustrative passages could be interpolated in the text of the criticism without interrupting the critic, and something for Spenser might thus be done on the scale of what Addison did for Milton. It was known how those successive papers in the *Spectator* had rehabilitated one of the greatest English poets, or, rather, rehabilitated the English public, and restored the poet and the public to each other. They formed almost an ideal body of criticism, and if they did not embody all that the reader need know of Milton, they embodied so much that he could no longer feel himself ignorant of Milton. In fact, they possesed him of a high degree of Miltonian culture, which was what one wanted to have with respect to any poet. They might be extended with still greater quotation, and if something more yet were needed the essay on Milton which made Macaulay's reputation might be employed as a vessel to catch the overrunnings of the precious ichor.

Who could not wish to know the poetry of Keats as we already knew his life through the matchless essay of Lowell? That might be filled out with the most striking passages of his poetry, simply let in at appropriate places, without breaking the flow of that high discourse, and forming a rich accompaniment which could leave no reader unpleasured or uninstructed. The passages given from the poet need not be relevant to the text of the critic; they might be quite irrelevant and serve the imaginable end still better. For instance, some passages might be given in the teeth of the critic, and made to gainsay what he had been saying. This would probably send the reader, if he was very much perplexed, to the poet himself, which was the imaginable end. He might be disappointed one way or he might be disappointed the other way, but in the mean while he would have passed his time, and he would have instructed if he had not amused himself.

It would be very interesting to take such a criticism as that of Lowell on Dryden and give not only the fine things from him, but the things that counted for the critic in his interesting contention that Dryden failed of being a prime poet because of the great weight of prose in him, and very good prose; or, as the critic charmingly put it, he had wings that helped him run along the ground, but did not enable him to fly. It would be most valuable for us to see how Dryden was a great literary man, but not one of the greatest poets, and yet must be ranked as a great poet. If the balance inclined now toward this opinion, and now against it, very possibly the reader would find himself impelled to turn to the poet's work, and again the imaginable end would be served.

A listener here asked why the talker went chiefly to Lowell for the illustration of his theory, and was frankly answered, For the same reason that he had first alluded to Leigh Hunt: because he had lately been reading him. It was not because he had not read any other criticism, or not that he entirely admired Lowell's; in fact, he often found fault with that. Lowell was too much a poet to be a perfect critic. He was no more the greatest sort of critic than Dryden was the greatest sort of poet. To turn his figure round, he had wings that lifted him into the air when he ought to be running along the ground.

The company laughed civilly at this piece of luck, and then they asked, civilly still, if Leigh Hunt had not done for a great many poets just what he was proposing to have done. What about the treatment of the poets and the quotations from them in the volumes on *Wit and Humor, Imagination and Fancy, A Jar of Honey from Mount Hybla,* and the rest? The talker owned that there was a great deal about these which was to his purpose, but, upon the whole, the criticism was too desultory and fragmentary, and the quotation was illustrative rather than representative, and so far it was illusory. He had a notion that Hunt's stories from the Italian poets were rather more in the line he would have followed, but he had not read these since he was a boy, and he was not prepared to answer for them.

One of the company said that she had read those Italian poets in Leigh Hunt's version of them when she was a girl, and it had had the effect of making her think she had read the poets themselves, and she had not since read directly Dante, Petrarch, Ariosto, or Tasso. She regarded that as an irreparable injury, and she doubted whether, if the great English poets could be introduced in that manner, very many people would pursue their acquaintance for themselves. They would think they were familiar with them already.

Yes, the talker assented, if that were the scheme, but it was not; or, at least, it was only part of the scheme. The scheme was to give the ever-increasing multitude of readers a chance to know something of the best literature. If they chose to pursue the acquaintance, very good; if they chose not to pursue the acquaintance, still very good; they could not have made it at all without being somewhat refined and enlightened. He felt very much about it as he felt about seeing Europe, which some people left unseen because they could not give all the time to it they would like. He always said to such people, Go if they could only be gone a month. A day in Rome, or London, or Paris, was a treasure such as a lifetime at home could not lay up; an hour of Venice or Florence was precious; a moment of Milan or Verona, of Siena or Mantua, was beyond price. So you could not know a great poet so little as not to be enriched by him. A look from a beautiful woman, or a witty word from a wise one, distinguished and embellished the life into which it fell, so that it could never afterward be so common as it was before.

Why, it was asked from a silence in which all the ladies tried to think whether the speaker had her in mind or not, and whether he ought really to be so personal, why could not Mr. Morley's *English Men of Letters* series be used to carry out the scheme proposed; and its proposer said he had nothing to say against that, except perhaps that the frames might be too much for the pictures. He would rather choose a critical essay, as he had intimated, for the frame of each picture; in this sort of thing we had an endless choice, both new and old. If he had any preference it would be for the older-fashioned critics, like Hazlitt or perhaps like De Quincey; he was not sure, speaking without the book, whether De Quincey treated authors so much as topics, but he had the sense of wonderful things in him about the eighteenth - century poets: things that made you think you knew them, and that yet made you burn to be on the same intimate terms with them as De Quincey himself.

His method of knowing the poets through the critics, the sympathetic critics, who were the only real critics, would have the advantage of acquainting the reader with the critics as well as the poets. The critics got a good deal of ingratitude from the reader generally, and perhaps in their character of mere reviewers they got no more than they merited, but in their friendly function of ushers to the good things, even the best things, in the authors they were studying, they had a claim upon him which he could not requite too generously. They acted the part of real friends, and in the high company where the reader found himself strange and alone, they hospitably made him at home. Above all other kinds of writers, they made one feel that he was uttering the good things they said. Of course, for the young reader, there was the danger of his continuing always to think their thoughts in their terms, but there were also great chances that he would begin by-and-by to think his own thoughts in terms of his own.

The more quotational the critics were, the better. For himself the speaker said that he liked that old custom of printing the very finest things in italics when it came to citing corroborative passages. It had not only the charm of the rococo, the pathos of a bygone fashion, but it was of the greatest use. No one is the worse for having a great beauty pointed out in the author one is reading or reading from. Sometimes one does not see the given beauty at first, and then he has the pleasure of puzzling it out; sometimes he never sees it, and then his life is sublimed with an insoluble conundrum. Sometimes, still, he sees what the critic means, and disagrees with him. In this case he is not likely to go to the end of his journey without finding a critic whom he agrees with about the passage in question.

After all, however, it was asked by one that had not spoken before (with that fine air of saying a novel thing which people put on who have not spoken before), would not the superficial knowledge of the poets imparted by quotational criticism result in a sort of pseudo-culture which would be rather worse than nothing, a kind of intellectual plated ware or æsthetic near-silk?

The talker said he thought not, and that he had already touched upon some such point in what he had said about going to Europe for a few months. He offered the opinion that there was no such thing as pseudo-culture; there was culture or there was not; and the reader of a quotational criticism, if he enjoyed the quotations, became, so far, cultivated. It could not be said that he knew the poets treated of, but neither could it be said that he was quite ignorant of them. As a matter of fact, he did know them in a fashion, through a mind larger and clearer than his own.

For this reason the talker favored the reading of criticism, especially the kind of criticism that quoted. He would even go so far as to say that there was no just and honest criticism without quotation. The critic was bound to make out his case, or else abdicate his function, and he could not make out his case, either for or against an author, without calling him to testify. Therefore, he was in favor of quotational criticism, for fairness' sake, as well as for his pleasure; and it was for the extension of it that he now contended. He was not sure that he wished to send the reader to the authors quoted in all cases. The reader could get through the passages cited a pretty good notion of the authors' quality, and as for their quantity, that was often made up of commonplaces or worse. In the case of the old poets, and most of the English classics, there was a great deal of filth which the reader would be better for not taking into his mind and which the most copiously quotational critics would hardly offer him. If any one said that without the filth one could not get a fair idea of those authors, he should be disposed to distinguish, and to say that without the filth one could not get a fair idea of their age, but of themselves, yes. Their beauty and their greatness were personal to them; even their dulness might be so; but their foulness was what had come off on them from living at periods when manners were foul.

XXIII

READING FOR A GRANDFATHER

A YOUNG girl (much respected by the Easy Chair) who had always had the real good of her grandfather at heart, wished to make him a Christmas present befitting his years and agreeable to his tastes. She thought, only to dismiss them for their banality, of a box of the finest cigars, of a soft flannel dressing-gown, a bath robe of Turkish towelling embroidered by herself, of a velvet jacket, and of a pair of house shoes. She decided against some of these things because he did not smoke, because he never took off his walking coat and shoes till he went to bed, and because he had an old bath robe made him by her grandmother, very short and very scant (according to her notion at the chance moments when she had surprised him in it), from which neither love nor money could part him; the others she rejected for the reason already assigned. Little or nothing remained, then, but to give him books, and she was glad that she was forced to this conclusion because, when she reflected, she realized that his reading seemed to be very much neglected, or at least without any lift of imagination or any quality of modernity in it. As far as she had observed, he read the same old things over and over again, and did not know at all what was now going on in the great world of literature. She herself was a famous reader, and an authority

226

about books with other girls, and with the young men who asked her across the afternoon tea-cups whether she had seen this or that new book, and scrabbled round, in choosing between cream and lemon, to hide the fact that they had not seen it themselves. She was therefore exactly the person to select a little library of the latest reading for an old gentleman who was so behind the times as her grandfather; but before she plunged into the mad vortex of new publications she thought she would delicately find out his preferences, or if he had none, would try to inspire him with a curiosity concerning these or those new books.

"Now, grandfather," she began, "you know I always give you a Christmas present."

"Yes, my dear," the old gentleman patiently assented, "I know you do. You are very thoughtful."

"Not at all. If there is anything I hate, it is being thoughtful. What I like is being spontaneous."

"Well, then, my dear, I don't mind saying you are very spontaneous."

"And I detest surprises. If any one wishes to make a lasting enemy of me, let him surprise me. So I am going to tell you now what I am going to give you. Do you like that?"

"I like everything you do, my child."

"Well, this time you will like it better than ever. I am going to give you books. And in order not to disappoint you by giving you books that you have read before, I want to catechise you a little. Shall you mind it?"

"Oh no, but I'm afraid you won't find me very frank."

"I shall make you be. If you are not frank, there is no fun in not surprising you, or in not giving you books that you have read."

"There is something in that," her grandfather assented. "But now, instead of finding out what I have read, or what I like, why not tell me what I ought to read and to like? I think I have seen a vast deal of advice to girls about their reading: why shouldn't the girls turn the tables and advise their elders? I often feel the need of advice from girls on all sorts of subjects, and you would find me very grateful, I believe."

The girl's eyes sparkled and then softened toward this docile ancestor. "Do you really mean it, grandfather? It would be fun if you did."

"But I should want it to be serious, my dear. I should be glad if your good counsel could include the whole conduct of life, for I am sensible sometimes of a tendency to be silly and wicked, which I am sure you could help me to combat."

"Oh, grandfather," said the girl, tenderly, "you know that isn't true!"

"Well, admit for the sake of argument that it isn't. My difficulty in regard to reading remains, and there you certainly could help me. At moments it seems to me that I have come to the end of my line."

The old gentleman's voice fell, and she could no longer suspect him of joking. So she began, "Why, what have you been reading last?"

"Well, my dear, I have been looking into the *Spectator* a little."

"The London *Spectator*? Jim says they have it at the club, and he swears by it. But I mean, what books; and that's a weekly newspaper, or a kind of review, isn't it?"

"The *Spectator* I mean was a London newspaper, and it was a kind of review, but it was a daily. Is it possible that you've never heard of it?" The young girl shook her head thoughtfully, regretfully, but upon the whole not anxiously; she was not afraid that any important thing in literature had escaped her. " But you've heard of Addison, and Steele, and Pope, and Swift ?"

" Oh yes, we had them at school, when we were reading *Henry Esmond;* they all came into that. And I remember, now: Colonel Esmond wrote a number of the *Spectator* for a surprise to Beatrix; but I thought it was all a make-up."

" And you don't know about Sir Roger de Coverley ?"

" Of course I do! It's what the English call the Virginia Reel. But why do you ask? I thought we were talking about your reading. I don't see how you could get an old file of a daily newspaper, but if it amuses you! *Is* it so amusing ?"

" It's charming, but after one has read it as often as I have one begins to know it a little too well."

" Yes; and what else have you been reading ?"

" Well, Leigh Hunt a little lately. He continues the old essayist tradition, and he is gently delightful."

" Never heard of him!" the girl frankly declared.

" He was a poet, too, and he wrote the *Story of Rimini*—about Paolo and Francesca, you know."

" Oh, there you're away off, grandfather! Mr. Philips wrote about *them;* and that horrid D'Annunzio. Why, Duse gave D'Annunzio's play last winter! What are you thinking of ?"

" Perhaps I am wandering a little," the grandfather meekly submitted, and the girl had to make him go on.

" Do you read poetry a great deal ?" she asked, and she thought if his taste was mainly for poetry, it would simplify the difficulty of choosing the books for her present.

" Well, I'm rather returning to it. I've been looking

into Crabbe of late, and I have found him full of a quaint charm."

"Crabbe? I never heard of him!" she owned as boldly as before, for if he had been worth hearing of, she knew that she would have heard of him. "Don't you like Kipling?"

"Yes, when he is not noisy. I think I prefer William Watson among your very modern moderns."

"Why, is *he* living yet? I thought he wrote ten or fifteen years ago! You don't call *him* modern! You like Stevenson, don't you? He's a great stylist; everybody says he is, and so is George Meredith. You must like *him?*"

"He's a great intellect, but a little of him goes almost as long a way as a little of Browning. I think I prefer Henry James."

"Oh yes, he's just coming up. He's the one that has distinction. But the people who write *like* him are a great deal more popular. They have all his distinction, and they don't tax your mind so much. But don't let's get off on novelists or there's no end to it. Who are really your favorite poets?"

"Well, I read Shakespeare rather often, and I read Dante by fits and starts; and I do not mind Milton from time to time. I like Wordsworth, and I like Keats a great deal better; every now and then I take up Cowper with pleasure, and I have found myself going back to Pope with real relish. And Byron; yes, Byron! But I shouldn't advise your reading *Don Juan.*"

"That's an opera, isn't it? What they call 'Don Giovanni.' I never heard of any such poem."

"That shows how careful you have been of your reading."

"Oh, we read everything nowadays—if it's up to

date; and if *Don Juan* had been, you may be sure I would have heard of it. I suppose you like Tennyson, and Longfellow, and Emerson, and those *old* poets?"

"Are they old? They used to be so new! Yes, I like them, and I like Whittier and some things of Bryant's."

At the last two names the girl looked vague, but she said: "Oh yes, I suppose so. And I suppose you like the old dramatists?"

"Some of them — Marlowe, and Beaumont and Fletcher: a few of their plays. But I can't stand most of the Elizabethans; I can't stand Ben Jonson at all."

"Oh yes—'Rasselas.' I can't stand him either, grandfather. I'm quite with you about Ben Jonson. 'Too much Johnson,' you know."

The grandfather looked rather blank. "Too *different* Johnsons, I think, my dear. But perhaps you didn't mean the Elizabethans; perhaps you mean the dramatists of the other Johnson's time. Well, I like Sheridan pretty well, though his wit strikes me as mechanical, and I really prefer Goldsmith; in his case, I prefer his *Vicar of Wakefield,* and his poems to his plays. Plays are not very easy reading, unless they are the very best. Shakespeare's are the only plays that one *wants* to read."

The young girl held up her charming chin, with the air of keeping it above water too deep for her. "And Ibsen?" she suggested. "I hope you despise Ibsen as much as I do. He's clear gone out now, thank goodness! Don't you think *Ghosts* was horrid?"

"It's dreadful, my dear; but I shouldn't say it was horrid. No, I don't despise Ibsen; and I have found Mr. Pinero's plays good reading."

231

"Oh," the girl said, getting her foot on the ground. "'The Gay Lord Quex'; Miss Vanbrugh was *great* in that. But now don't get off on the theatre, grandfather, or there will be no end to it. Which of the old, *old* poets—before Burns or Shelley even—do you like?"

"Well, when I was a boy, I read Chaucer, and liked him very much; and the other day when I was looking over Leigh Hunt's essays, I found a number of them about Chaucer with long, well-chosen extracts; and I don't know when I've found greater pleasure in poetry. If I must have a favorite among the old poets, I will take Chaucer. Of course, Spenser is rather more modern."

"Yes, but I can't bear his agnosticism, can you? And I hate metaphysics, anyway."

The grandfather looked bewildered; then he said, "Now, I'm afraid we are getting too much Spenser."

The girl went off at a tangent. "Don't you just *love* Mr. Gillette in 'Sherlock Holmes'? There's a play I should think you would like to read! They say there's a novel been made out of it. I wish I could get hold of it for you. Well, go on, grandfather!"

"No, my dear, it's for you to go on. But don't you think you've catechised me sufficiently about my reading? You must find it very old-fashioned."

"No, not at all. I like old things myself. The girls are always laughing at me because I read George Eliot, and Dickens, and Thackeray, and Charles Reade, and Wilkie Collins, and those back numbers. But I should say, if I said anything, that you were rather deficient in fiction, grandfather. You seem to have read everything but novels."

"Is that so? I was afraid I had read nothing but novels. I—"

"Tell me what novels you have read," she broke in

232

upon him imperatively. " The ones you consider the greatest."

The grandfather had to think. " It is rather a long list—so long that I'm ashamed of it. Perhaps I'd better mention only the very greatest, like *Don Quixote*, and *Gil Blas*, and *Wilhelm Meister*, and *The Vicar of Wakefield*, and *Clarissa Harlowe*, and *Emma*, and *Pride and Prejudice*, and *The Bride of Lammermoor*, and *I Promessi Sposi*, and *Belinda*, and *Frankenstein*, and *Chartreuse de Parme*, and *César Birotteau*, and *The Last Days of Pompeii*, and *David Copperfield*, and *Pendennis*, and *The Scarlet Letter*, and *Blithedale Romance*, and *The Cloister and the Hearth*, and *Middlemarch*, and *Smoke*, and *Fathers and Sons*, and *A Nest of Nobles*, and *War and Peace*, and *Anna Karénina*, and *Resurrection*, and *Doña Perfecta*, and *Marta y Maria*, and *I Malavoglia*, and *The Return of the Native*, and *L'Assomoir*, and *Madame Bovary*, and *The Awkward Age*, and *The Grandissimes*—and most of the other books of the same authors. Of course, I've read many more perhaps as great as these, that I can't think of at the moment."

The young girl listened, in a vain effort to follow her agile ancestor in and out of the labyrinths of his favorite fiction, most of which she did not recognize by the names he gave and some of which she believed to be very shocking, in a vague association of it with deeply moralized, denunciatory criticisms which she had read of the books or the authors. Upon the whole, she was rather pained by the confession which his reading formed for her grandfather, and she felt more than ever the necessity of undertaking his education, or at least his reform, in respect to it. She was glad now that she had decided to give him books for a Christmas present, for there was no time like Christmas for good resolutions, and if her grandfather was ever going to turn over a new leaf, this was the very hour to help him do it.

She smiled very sweetly upon him, so as not to alarm him too much, and said she had never been so much interested as in knowing what books he really liked. But as he had read all those he named—

" Oh, dozens of times!" he broke in.

—Then perhaps he would leave it to her to choose an entirely new list for him, so that he could have something freshly entertaining; she did not like to say more edifying for fear of hurting his feelings, and taking his silence for consent she went up and kissed him on his bald head and ran away to take the matter under immediate advisement. Her notion then was to look over several lists of the world's best hundred books which she had been keeping by her, but when she came to compare them, she found that they contained most of the books he had mentioned, besides many others. It would never do to give him any one of these libraries of the best hundred books for this reason, and for the reason that a hundred books would cost more of her grandfather's money than she felt justified in spending on him at a season when she had to make so many other presents.

Just when she was at her wit's end, a sudden inspiration seized her. She pinned on her hat, and put on her new winter jacket, and went out and bought the last number of *The Bookworm*. At the end of this periodical she had often got suggestions for her own reading, and she was sure that she should find there the means of helping her poor grandfather to a better taste in literature than he seemed to have. So she took the different letters from Chicago, San Francisco, Denver, Cincinnati, New Orleans, Cleveland, Buffalo, Boston,

Philadelphia, and up - town and down - town in New York, giving the best-selling books of the month in all those places, and compiled an eclectic list from them, which she gave to her bookseller with orders to get them as nearly of the same sizes and colors as possible. He followed her instructions with a great deal of taste and allowed her twenty-five per cent. off, which she applied toward a wedding-present she would have to give shortly. In this way she was able to provide her grandfather for the new year with reading that everybody was talking about, and that brought him up to date with a round turn.

XXIV

SOME MOMENTS WITH THE MUSE

AMONG the many letters which the Easy Chair has received after its conference on the state of poetry, one of most decided note was from a writer confessing herself of the contrary - minded. "I love some children, but not childhood in general merely because it is childhood. So I love some poems rather than poetry in general just because it is poetry. . . . I object to the tinkle. I object to the poetic license which performs a Germanic divorce between subject and verb, so that instead of a complete thought which can be mastered before another is set before the brain, there is a twist in the grammatical sequence that requires a conscious effort of will to keep the original thread. The world is too busy to do this; reading must be a relaxation, not a study. . . . When poetry conforms in its mental tone to the spirit of the times; when it reflects the life and more or less the common thought of the day, then more of the common people will read it."

There were other things in this letter which seemed to us of so much importance that we submitted it as a whole to a Woman's Club of our acquaintance. The nine ladies composing the club were not all literary, but they were all of æsthetic pursuits, and together they brought a good deal of culture to bear on the main points of the letter. They were not quite of one mind, but they were so far agreed that what they had to say might be fairly regarded as a consensus of opinion. We will not attempt to report their remarks at any length— they ran to all lengths—but in offering a résumé of what they variously said to a sole effect, we will do what we can to further the cause they joined in defending.

The Muses—for we will no longer conceal that this Woman's Club was composed of the tuneful Nine—acknowledged that there was a great deal in what their contrary-minded sister said. They did not blame her one bit for the way she felt; they would have felt just so themselves in her place; but being as it were professionally dedicated to the beautiful in all its established forms, they thought themselves bound to direct her attention to one or two aspects of the case which she had apparently overlooked. They were only sorry that she was not there to take her own part; and they confessed, in her behalf, that it *was* ridiculous for poetry to turn the language upside down, and to take it apart and put it together wrong-end to, as it did. If anybody spoke the language so, or in prose wrote it so, they would certainly be a fool; but the Muses wished the sister to observe that every art existed by its convention, or by what in the moral world Ibsen would call its life-lie. If you looked at it from the colloquial standpoint, music was the absurdest thing in the world. In the orchestral part of an opera, for instance, there were more repetitions than in the scolding of the worst kind of shrew, and if you were to go about singing what you had to say, and singing it over and over, and stretching it out by runs and trills, or even expressing yourself in *recitativo secco,* it would simply set people wild. In painting it was worse, if anything: you had to make believe that things two inches high were life-size, and that there were relief and distance where there was nothing but a flat canvas, and that colors which were really like nothing in nature were natural. As for sculpture, it was too laughable for anything, whether you took it in bass-reliefs with persons stuck onto walls, half or three-quarters out, or in groups with people in eternal action; or in single figures, standing on one leg or holding out arms that would drop off if they were not supported by stone pegs; or sitting down outdoors bareheaded where they would take their deaths of cold, or get sun-struck, or lay up rheumatism to beat the band, in the rain and snow and often without a stitch of clothes on.

All this and more the Muses freely conceded to the position of the contrary-minded correspondent of the Easy Chair, and having behaved so handsomely, they felt justified in adding that her demand seemed to them perfectly preposterous. It was the very essence and office of poetry *not* to conform to "the mental tone and spirit of the times"; and though it might very well reflect the life, it must not reflect "the common thought of the day" upon pain of vulgarizing and annulling itself. Poetry was static in its nature, and its business was the interpretation of enduring beauty and eternal veracity. If it stooped in submission to any such expectation as that expressed, and dedicated itself to the crude vaticination of the transitory emotions and opinions, it had better turn journalism at once. It had its law, and its law was distinction of ideal and elevation of tendency, no matter what material it dealt with. It might deal with the commonest, the cheapest material, but always in such a way as to dignify and beautify the material.

Concerning the first point, that modern poetry was

wrong to indulge all those inversions, those transloca-
tions, those ground and lofty syntactical tumblings
which have mainly constituted poetic license, the ladies
again relented, and allowed that there was much to say
for what our correspondent said. In fact, they agreed,
or agreed as nearly as nine ladies could, that it was
perhaps time that poetry should, as it certainly might,
write itself straightforwardly, with the verb in its true
English place, and the adjective walking soberly before
the noun; shunning those silly elisions like *ne'er* and
o'er, and, above all, avoiding the weak and loathly
omission of the definite article. Of the tinkle, by which
they supposed the contrary - minded sister meant the
rhyme, they said they could very well remember when
there was no such thing in poetry; their native Greek
had got on perfectly well without it, and even those
poets at second-hand, the Romans. They observed that
though Dante used it, Shakespeare did not, and Milton
did not, in their greatest works; and a good half of the
time the first - rate moderns managed very well with
blank verse.

The Easy Chair did not like to dissent from these
ladies, both because they were really great authorities
and because it is always best to agree with ladies when
you can. Besides, it would not have seemed quite the
thing when they were inclining to this favorable view
of their sister's contrary - mindedness, to take sides
against her. In short, the Easy Chair reserved its
misgivings for some such very intimate occasion as
this, when it could impart them without wounding the
susceptibilities of others, or risking a painful snub for
itself. But it appeared to the Chair that the Muses
did not go quite far enough in justifying the convention, or the life-lie, by which poetry, as a form, existed.
They could easily have proved that much of the mys-

tical charm which differences poetry from prose resides
in its license, its syntactical acrobatics, its affectations
of diction, its elisions, its rhymes. As a man inverting
his head and looking at the landscape between his legs
gets an entirely new effect on the familiar prospect, so
literature forsaking the wonted grammatical attitudes
really achieves something richly strange by the novel
and surprising postures permissible in verse. The
phrases, the lines, the stanzas which the ear keeps
lingering in its porches, loath to let them depart, are
usually full of these licenses. They have a witchery
which could be as little proved as denied; and when
any poet proposes to forego them, and adhere rigidly
to the law of prose in his rhythm, he practises a loyalty
which is a sort of treason to his calling and will go
far toward undoing him.

While the ladies of that club were talking, some such
thoughts as these were in our mind, suggested by sum-
mer-long reading of a dear, delightful poet, altogether
neglected in these days, who deserves to be known again
wherever reality is prized or simplicity is loved. It is
proof, indeed, how shallow was all the debate about
realism and romanticism that the poetic tales of George
Crabbe were never once alleged in witness of the charm
which truth to condition and character has, in whatever
form. But once, long before that ineffectual clamor
arose, he was valued as he should be still. Edmund
Burke was the first to understand his purpose and appreciate his work. He helped the poet not only with
praises but with pounds till he could get upon his feet.
He introduced Crabbe's verse to his great friends,
to Doctor Johnson, who perceived at once that he
would go far; to Sir Joshua Reynolds, who felt the
brother-artist in him; to the Lord Chancellor Thurlow,
whose oaths were harder than his heart toward the fear-

lessly fearful young singer. The sympathy and admiration of the highest and the best followed him through his long life to his death. The great Mr. Fox loved him and his rhyme, and wished his tales to be read to him on the bed he never left alive. Earl Grey, Lord Holland, and the brilliant Canning wrote him letters of cordial acclaim; Walter Scott, the generous, the magnanimous, hailed him brother, and would always have his books by him; none of his poems appeared without the warmest welcome, the most discriminating and applausive criticism from Jeffrey, the first critic of his long day.

Crabbe had not only this exquisitely intelligent hearing, but he was accepted on his own terms, as a poet who saw so much beauty in simple and common life that he could not help painting it. He painted it in pieces of matchless fidelity to the fact, with nothing of flattery, but everything of charm in the likeness. His work is the enduring witness of persons, circumstances, customs, experiences utterly passed from the actual world, but recognizably true with every sincere reader. These tales of village life in England a hundred years ago are of an absolute directness and frankness. They blink nothing of the sordid, the mean, the vicious, the wicked in that life, from which they rarely rise in some glimpse of the state of the neighboring gentry, and yet they abound in beauty that consoles and encourages. They are full of keen analysis, sly wit, kindly humor, and of a satire too conscientious to bear the name; of pathos, of compassion, of reverence, while in unaffected singleness of ideal they are unsurpassed.

Will our contrary-minded correspondent believe that these studies, these finished pictures, which so perfectly "reflect the common life . . . of the day," are full of the license, the tinkle, the German divorce of verb and

subject, the twisted grammatical sequence which her
soul abhors in verse? Crabbe chose for his vehicle the
heroic couplet in which English poetry had jog-trotted
ever since the time of Pope, as it often had before;
and he made it go as like Pope's couplet as he could,
with the same cæsura, the same antithetical balance, the
same feats of rhetoric, the same inversions, and the
same closes of the sense in each couplet. The most
artificial and the most natural poets were at one in their
literary convention. Yet such was the freshness of
Crabbe's impulse, such his divine authority to deal
with material unemployed in English poetry before,
that you forget all the affectations of the outward convention, or remember them only for a pleasure in the
quaintness of their use for his purposes. How im-
perishable, anyway, is the interest of things important
to the spirit, the fancy, and how largely does this interest lie in the freshness of the mind bringing itself to
the things, how little in the novelty of the things!
The demand for strangeness in the things themselves is the demand of the sophisticated mind: the
mind which has lost its simplicity in the process of
continuing unenlightened. It is this demand which be-
trays the mediocre mind of the Anglo-Saxon race, the
sophistication of the English mind, and the obfuscation
(which is sophistication at second-hand) of the American mind. The non-imaginative person is nowhere so
much at home as in a voluntary exile; and this may be
why it was sometime said that travel is the fool's paradise. For such a person to realize anything the terms
are that he shall go abroad, either into an alien scene
or into a period of the past; then he can begin to have
some pleasure. He must first of all get away from
himself, and he is not to be blamed for that; any one
else would wish to get away from him. His exaction is

not a test of merit; it is merely the clew to a psycho-logical situation which is neither so novel nor so important as to require of our hard-worked civilization the production of an order of more inspired criticism than it has worried along with hitherto.

XXV

A NORMAL HERO AND HEROINE OUT OF WORK

THEY sat together on a bench in the Park, far enough apart to distinguish themselves from the many other pairs who were but too obviously lovers. It could not be said quite that these two were actually lovers; but there was an air of passionate provisionality over and around them, a light such as in springtime seems to enfold the tree before it takes the positive color of bud or blossom; and, with an eye for literary material that had rarely failed him, he of the Easy Chair perceived that they were a hero and heroine of a kind which he instantly felt it a great pity he should not have met oftener in fiction of late. As he looked at them he was more and more penetrated by a delicate pathos in the fact that, such as he saw them, they belonged in their fine sort to the great host of the Unemployed. No one else might have seen it, but he saw, with that inner eye of his, which compassion suffused but did not obscure, that they were out of a job, and he was not surprised when he heard the young girl fetch a muted sigh and then say: "No, they don't want us any more. I don't understand why; it is very strange; but it is perfectly certain."

"Yes, there's no doubt of that," the young man returned, in a despair tinged with resentment.

She was very pretty and he was handsome, and they

were both tastefully dressed, with a due deference to
fashion, yet with a personal qualification of the cut
and color of their clothes which, if it promised more
than it could fulfil in some ways, implied a modest self-
respect, better than the arrogance of great social success or worldly splendor. She could have been the only
daughter of a widowed father in moderate circumstances; or an orphan brought up by a careful aunt,
or a duteous sister in a large family of girls, with whom
she shared the shelter of a wisely ordered, if somewhat
crowded, home; or she could have been a serious student
of any of the various arts and sciences which girls study
now in an independence compatible with true beauty of
behavior. He might have been a young lawyer or doctor or business man; or a painter or architect; or a
professor in some college or a minister in charge of his
first parish. What struck the observer in them and
pleased him was that they seemed of that finer American average which is the best, and, rightly seen,
the most interesting phase of civilized life yet
known.

"I sometimes think," the girl resumed, in the silence
of her companion, "that I made a mistake in my
origin or my early education. It's a great disadvantage, in fiction nowadays, for a girl to speak gram-
matically, as I always do, without any trace of accent
or dialect. Of course, if I had been high-born or low-
born in the olden times, somewhere or other, I shouldn't
have to be looking for a place now; or if I had been
unhappily married, or divorced, or merely separated
from my husband, the story-writers would have had
some use for me. But I have tried always to be good
and nice and ladylike, and I haven't been in a short
story for ages."

"Is it so bad as that?" the young man asked, sadly.

"Quite. If I could only have had something askew in my heredity, I know lots of authoresses who would have jumped at me. I can't do anything wildly adventurous in the Middle Ages or the Revolutionary period, because I'm so afraid; but I know that in the course of modern life I've always been fairly equal to emergencies, and I don't believe that I should fail in case of trouble, or that if it came to poverty I should be ashamed to share the deprivations that fell to my lot. I don't think I'm very selfish; I would be willing to stay in town all summer if an author wanted me, and I know I could make it interesting for his readers. I could marry an English nobleman if it was really necessary, and, if I didn't like to live in England because I was fond of my own country, I believe I could get him to stay here half the time with me; and that would appeal to a large class. I don't know whether I would care to be rescued a great deal; it would depend upon what it was from. But I could stand a great deal of pain if need be, and I hope that if it came to anything like right or wrong I should act conscientiously. In society, I shouldn't mind any amount of dancing or dining or teaing, and I should be willing to take my part in the lighter athletics. But," she ended, as she began, with a sigh, "I'm not wanted."

"Yes, I see what you mean," the young man said, with a thoughtful knot between his brows. "I'm not wanted myself, at present, in the short stories; but in the last dozen or so where I had an engagement I certainly didn't meet you; and it *is* pleasant to be paired off in a story with a heroine who has the instincts and habits of a lady. Of course, a hero is only something in an author's fancy, and I've no right to be exacting; but it does go against me to love a girl who ropes cattle, or a woman who has a past, or a husband, or something of the kind. I always do my best for the author, but I can't forget that I'm a gentleman, and it's difficult to win a heroine when the very idea of her makes you shudder. I sometimes wonder how the authors would like it themselves if they had to do what they expect of us in that way. They're generally very decent fellows, good husbands and fathers, who have married lady - like girls and wouldn't think of associating with a shady or ignorant person."

" The authoresses are quite as inconsistent," the professional heroine rejoined. " They wouldn't speak to the kind of young men whom they expect a heroine to be passionately in love with. They must know how very oddly a girl feels about people who are outside of the world she's been brought up in. It isn't enough that a man should be very noble at heart and do grand things, or save your life every now and then, or be masterful and use his giant will to make you in love with him. I don't see why they can't let one have, now and then, the kind of husbands they get for themselves. For my part, I should like always to give my heart to a normal, sensible, well-bred, conscientious, agreeable man who could offer me a pleasant home—I wouldn't mind the suburbs; and I could work with him and work for him till I dropped—the kind of man that the real world seems to be so full of. I've never had a fair chance to show what was in me; I've always been placed in such a false position. Now I have no position at all, not even a false one!"

Her companion was silent for a while. Then he said: " Yes, they all seem, authors and authoresses both, to lose sight of the fact that the constitution of our society is more picturesque, more dramatic, more poetical than any in the world. We can have the play of all the passions and emotions in ordinary, innocent love-making that other peoples can have only on the worst conditions; and yet the story-writers won't avail themselves of the beauty that lies next to their hands. They go abroad for impossible circumstances, or they want to bewitch ours with the chemistry of all sorts of eccentric characters, exaggerated incentives, morbid propensities, pathological conditions, or diseased psychology. As I said before, I know I'm only a creature of the storyteller's fancy, and a creature out of work at that; but I believe I was imagined in a good moment—I'm sure *you* were—and I should like an engagement in an honest, wholesome situation. I think I could do creditable work in it."

" I *know* you could," the heroine rejoined, fervently, almost tenderly, so that it seemed to the listener there was an involuntary *rapprochement* of their shadowy substances on the bench where they floated in a sitting posture. " I don't want to be greedy; I believe in living and letting live. I think the abnormal has just as good a right to be in the stories as the normal; but why shut the normal out altogether? What I should like to ask the short-story writers is whether they and their readers are so bored with themselves and the people they know in the real world that they have no use for anything like its average in their fiction. It's impossible for us to change—"

" I shouldn't wish *you* to change," the hero said, so fondly that the witness trembled for something more demonstrative.

" Thank you! But what I mean is, couldn't *they* change a little? Couldn't they give us another trial? They've been using the abnormal, in some shape or other, so long that I should think they would find a hero and heroine who simply fell in love at a dance or a dinner, or in a house-party or at a picnic, and worked out their characters to each other, through the natural worry and difficulty, and pleasure and happiness, till they got married—a relief from, well, the other thing. I'm sure if they offered me the chance, I could make myself attractive to their readers, and I believe I should have the charm of novelty."

"You would have more than the charm of novelty," the hero said, and the witness trembled again for the *convenances* which one so often sees offended on the benches in the Park. But then he remembered that these young people were avowedly nice, and that they were morally incapable of misbehavior. "And for a time, at least, I believe you—I believe *we,* for I must necessarily be engaged with you—would succeed. The difficulty would be to get the notion of our employment to the authors." It was on the listener's tongue to say that he thought he could manage that, when the hero arrested him with the sad misgiving, "But they would say we were commonplace, and that would kill the chance of our ever having a run."

A tremendous longing filled the witness, a potent desire to rescue this engaging pair from the dismay into which they fell at the fatal word. "No, no!" he conjured them. "*Not* commonplace. A judicious paragraph anticipative of your reappearance could be arranged, in which you could be hailed as the *normal* hero and heroine, and greeted as a grateful relief from the hackneyed freaks and deformities of the prevalent short story, or the impassioned paper-doll pattern of the mediæval men and maidens, or the spotted and battered figures of the studies in morbid analysis which pass for fiction in the magazines. We must get that luminous word *normal* before the reading public at once, and you will be rightly seen in its benign ray and recognized from the start—yes! in *advance* of the start—for what you are: types of the loveliness of our average life, the fairest blossoms of that faith in human nature which has flourished here into the most beautiful and glorious civilization of all times. With us the average life is enchanting, the normal is the exquisite. Have patience, have courage; your time is coming again!"

It seemed to him that the gentle shapes wavered in his vehement breath, and he could not realize that in their alien realm they could not have heard a word he uttered. They remained dreamily silent, as if he had not spoken, and then the heroine said: "Perhaps we shall have to wait for a new school of short-story writers before we can get back into the magazines. Some beginner *must* see in us what has always pleased: the likeness to himself or herself, the truth to nature, the loyalty to the American ideal of happiness. He will find that we easily and probably *end well,* and that we're a consolation and refuge for readers, who can take heart from our happy dénouements, when they see a family resemblance in us, and can reasonably hope that if they follow our examples they will share our blessings. Authors can't really enjoy themselves in the company of those degenerates, as *I* call them. They're mostly as young and right-principled and well-behaved as ourselves, and, if they could get to know us, we should be the best of friends. They would realize that there was plenty of harmless fun, as well as love, in the world, and that there was lots of good-luck."

"Like ours, now, with no work and no prospect of it?" he returned, in his refusal to be persuaded, yet ready to be comforted.

Having set out on that road, she would not turn back; she persisted, like any woman who is contraried, no matter how far she ends from her first position:

" Yes, like ours now. For this is probably the dark hour before the dawn. We must wait."

" And perish in the mean time?"

" Oh, we shall not perish," she responded, heroinical-ly. " It's not for nothing that we are immortal," and as she spoke she passed her translucent hand through his arm, and, rising, they drifted off together and left the emissary of the Easy Chair watching them till they mixed with the mists under the trees in the perspective of the Mall.

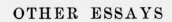

OTHER ESSAYS

I

AUTUMN IN THE COUNTRY AND CITY

In the morning the trees stood perfectly still: yellow, yellowish-green, crimson, russet. Not a pulse of air stirred their stricken foliage, but the leaves left the spray and dripped silently, vertically down, with a faint, ticking sound. They fell like the tears of a grief which is too inward for any other outward sign; an absent grief, almost self-forgetful. By-and-by, softly, very softly, as Nature does things when she emulates the best Art and shuns the showiness and noisiness of the second-best, the wind crept in from the leaden sea, which turned iron under it, corrugated iron. Then the trees began to bend, and writhe, and sigh, and moan; and their leaves flew through the air, and blew and scuttled over the grass, and in an hour all the boughs were bare. The summer, which had been living till then and dying, was now dead.

That was the reason why certain people who had been living with it, and seemed dying in it, were now in a manner dead with it, so that their ghosts were glad to get back to town, where the ghosts of thousands and hundreds of thousands of others were hustling in the streets and the trolleys and subways and elevateds, and shops and factories and offices, and making believe to be much more alive than they were in the country. Yet the town, the haunt of those harassed and hurried spectres, who are not without their illusory hilarity, their phantasmal happiness, has a charm which we of the Easy Chair always feel, on first returning to it in the autumn, and which the representative of the family we are imagining finds rather an impassioned pleasure in. He came on to New York, while the others lingered in a dim Bostonian limbo, and he amused himself very well, in a shadowy sort, looking at those other shades who had arrived in like sort, or different, and were there together with him in those fine days just preceding the election; after which the season broke in tears again, and the autumn advanced another step toward winter.

There is no moment of the New York year which is more characteristic of it than that mid-autumnal moment, which the summer and the winter are equally far from. Mid-May is very well, and the weather then is perfect, but that is a moment pierced with the unrest of going or getting ready to go away. The call of the eld in Europe, or the call of the wild in Newport, has already depopulated our streets of what is richest and naturally best in our city life; the shops, indeed, show a fevered activity in the near-richest and near-best who are providing for their summer wants at mountain or sea-shore; but the theatres are closing like fading flowers, and shedding their chorus-girls on every outward breeze; the tables d'hôte express a relaxed enterprise in the nonchalance of the management and service; the hotels yawn wearily from their hollow rooms; the greengroceries try to mask the barrenness of their windows in a show of tropic or semi-tropic fruits; the provision-men merely disgust with their retarded displays of butcher's meats and poultry.

But with what a difference the mid-autumn of the town welcomes its returners! Ghosts, we have called

BROADWAY AT NIGHT

them, mainly to humor a figure we began with, but they are ghosts rather in the meaning of *revenants,* which is a good meaning enough. They must be a very aged or very stupid sort of *revenants* if their palingenetic substance does not thrill at the first nightly vision of Broadway, of that fairy flare of electric lights, advertising whiskeys and actresses and beers, and luring the beholder into a hundred hotels and theatres and restaurants. It is now past the hour of roof-gardens with their songs and dances, but the vaudeville is in full bloom, and the play-houses are blossoming in the bills of their new comedies and operas and burlesques. The pavements are filled, but not yet crowded, with people going to dinner at the tables d'hôte; the shop windows glitter and shine, and promise a delight for the morrow which the morrow may or may not realize.

But as yet the town is not replete to choking, as it will be later, when those who fancy they constitute the town have got back to it from their Europes, their Newports, their Bar Harbors, their Lenoxes, their Tuxedos, weary of scorning delights and living laborious days in that round of intellectual and moral events duly celebrated in the society news of the Sunday papers. Fifth Avenue abounds in automobiles but does not yet superabound; you do not quite take your life in your hand in crossing the street at those corners where there is no policeman's hand to put it in. Everywhere are cars, carts, carriages; and the motorist whirs through the intersecting streets and round the corners, bent on suicide or homicide, and the kind old trolleys and hansoms that once seemed so threatening have almost become so many arks of safety from the furious machines replacing them. But a few short years ago the passer on the Avenue could pride himself on a count of twenty automobiles in his walk from Murray Hill to the Plaza;

now he can easily number hundreds, without an emotion of self-approval.

But their abundance is only provisional, a mere forecast of the superabundance to come. All things are provisional, all sights, all sounds, and this forms the peculiar charm of the hour, its haunting and winning charm. If you take the omnibus - top to be trundled whiningly up to one of the farther east-side entrances of the Park, and then dismount and walk back to the Plaza through it, you are even more keenly aware of the suspensive quality of the time. The summer, which you left for dead by mountain or sea-shore, stirs with lingering consciousness in the bland air of the great pleasance. Many leaves are yet green on the trees, and where they are not green and not there they are gay on the grass under the trees. There are birds, not, to be sure, singing, but cheerfully chirping; and there are occasional blazons of courageous flowers; the benches beside the walks, which the northern blasts will soon sweep bare, are still kept by the lovers and loafers who have frequented them ever since the spring, and by the nurses, who cumber the footway before them with their perambulators. The fat squirrels waddle over the asphalt, and cock the impudent eye of the sturdy beggar at the passer whom they suspect of latent peanuts; it is high carnival of the children with hoops and balls; it is the supreme moment of the saddle-donkeys in the by-paths, and the carriage-goats in the Mall, and of the rowboats on the ponds, which presently will be withdrawn for their secret hibernation, where no man can find them out. When the first snow flies, even while it is yet poising for flight in the dim pits of air, all these delights will have vanished, and the winter, which will claim the city for its own through a good four months, will be upon it.

Always come back, therefore, if you must come at all, about the beginning of November, and if you can manage to take in Election Day, and especially Election Night, it will not be a bad notion. New York has five saturnalia every year: New Year's Night, Decoration Day, Fourth of July, Election Night, and Thanksgiving, and not the least of these is Election Night. If it is a right first Tuesday of November, the daytime wind will be veering from west to south and back, sun and cloud will equally share the hours between them, and a not unnatural quiet, as of political passions hushed under the blanket of the Australian ballot, will prevail. The streets will be rather emptied than filled, and the litter of straw and scrap-paper, and the ordure and other filth of the great slattern town, will blow agreeably about under your feet and into your eyes and teeth. But with the falling of the night there will be a rise of the urban spirits; the sidewalks will thicken with citizens of all ages and sexes and nations; and if you will then seek some large centre for the cinemato-graphic dissemination of the election news, you will find yourself one of a multitude gloating on the scenes of comedy and tragedy thrown up on the canvas to stay your impatience for the returns. Along the curbstones are stationed wagons for the sale of the wind and string instruments, whose raw, harsh discords of whistling and twanging will begin with the sight of the vote from the first precinct. Meantime policemen, nervously fondling their clubs in their hands, hang upon the fringes of the crowd, which is yet so good-natured that it seems to have no impulse but to lift children on its shoulders and put pretty girls before it, and caress old women and cripples into favorable positions, so that they may see better. You will wish to leave it before the clubbing begins, and either go home to the slumbers which

the whistling and twanging will duly attend; or join
the diners going into or coming out of the restaurants,
or the throngs strolling down into the fairy realms of
Broadway, under the flare of the whiskeys and the actresses.

At such a time it is best to be young, but it is not so
very bad to be old, for the charm of the hour, the air,
and the place is such that even the heart of age must
rise a little at it. What the night may really be, if it
is not positively raining, you " do not know or need to
know." Those soft lamps overhead, which might alike
seem let garlanding down from the vault above or
flowering up from the gulfs below out of a still greater
pyrotechnic richness, supply the defect, if there is any,
of moon and stars. Only the air is actual, the air of the
New York night, which is as different from that of the
London night as from that of the Paris night, or, for
all we know, the St. Petersburg night. At times we
have fancied in its early autumnal tones something
Florentine, something Venetian, but, after all, it is
not quite either, even when the tones of these are crud-
est. It is the subtlest, the most penetrating expression
of the New York temperament; but what that is, who
shall say? That mystic air is haunted little from the
past, for properly speaking there never was a city so
unhistorical in temperament. A record of civic cor-
ruption, running back to the first servants of the Dutch
Companies, does not constitute municipal history, and
our part in national events from the time we felt the
stirrings of national consciousness has not been glorious,
as these have not been impressive. Of New York's
present at any given moment you wish to say in her
patient-impatient slang, " Forget it, forget it." There
remains only the future from which she can derive that
temperamental effect in her night air; but, again, what

ELECTION-NIGHT CROWDS

that is, who shall say? If any one were so daring, he might say it was confidence modified by anxiety; a rash expectation of luck derived from immunity for past transgression; the hopes of youth shot with youth's despairs: not sweet, innocent youth, but youth knowing and experienced, though not unwilling to shun evil because of the bad morrow it sometimes brings. No other city under the sun, we doubt, is so expressive of that youth: that modern youth, able, agile, eager, audacious; not the youth of the poets, but the youth of the true, the grim realists.

Something, a faint, faint consciousness of this, visits even the sad heart of age on any New York night when it is not raining too hard, and one thinks only of getting indoors, where all nights are alike. But mostly it comes when the autumn is dreaming toward winter in that interlude of the seasons which we call Indian Summer. It is a stretch of time which we have handsomely bestowed upon our aborigines, in compensation for the four seasons we have taken from them, like some of those Reservations which we have left them in lieu of the immeasurable lands we have alienated. It used to be longer than it is now; it used to be several weeks long; in the sense of childhood, it was almost months. It is still qualitatively the same, and it is more than any other time expressive of the New York temperament, perhaps because we have honored in the civic ideal the polity of our Indian predecessors, and in Tammany and its recurrently triumphant braves, have kept their memory green. But if this is not so, the spiritual fact remains, and under the sky of the Election Night you *feel* New York as you do in no other hour. The sense extends through the other autumn nights till that night, sure to come, when the pensive weather breaks in tears, and the next day it rains and rains, and the streets stream with the flood, and the dull air reeks with a sort of inner steam, hot, close, and sticky as a brother: a brother whose wants are many and whose resources are few. The morning after the storm, there will be a keen thrill in the air, keen but wholesome and bracing as a good resolution and not necessarily more lasting. The asphalt has been washed as clean as a renovated conscience, and the city presses forward again to the future in which alone it has its being, with the gay confidence of a sinner who has forgiven himself his sins and is no longer sorry for them.

After that interlude, when the streets of the Advanced Vaudeville, which we know as New York, begin again and continue till the Chasers come in late May, there will be many other sorts of weather, but none so characteristic of her. There will be the sort of weather toward the end of January, when really it seems as if nothing else could console him for the intolerable freezing and thawing, the snow upon snow, the rain upon rain, the winds that soak him and the winds that shrivel him, and the suns that mock him from a subtropic sky through subarctic air. We foresee him then settling into his arm-chair, while the wind whistles as naturally as the wind in the theatre around the angles of his lofty flat, and drives the snow of the shredded paper through the air or beats it in soft clots against the pane. He turns our page, and as he catches our vague drift, before yielding himself wholly to its allure, he questions, as readers like to do, whether the writer is altogether right in his contention that the mid-autumnal moment is the most characteristic moment of the New York year. Is not the mid-winter moment yet more characteristic? He conjures up, in the rich content of his indoor remoteness, the vision of the vile street below his flat, banked high with the garnered heaps of filthy snow, which alternately freeze and thaw, which the rain does not wash nor the wind blow away, and which the shredded - paper flakes are now drifting higher. He sees the foot-passers struggling under their umbrellas toward the avenues where the reluctant trolleys pause jarringly for them, and the elevated trains roar along the trestle overhead; where the saloon winks a wicked eye on every corner; where the signs of the whiskeys and actresses flare through the thickened night; and the cab tilts and rocks across the trolley rails, and the crowds of hotel-sojourners seek the shelter of the theatres, and all is bleak and wet and squalid. In more respectful vision he beholds the darkened mansions of the richest and best, who have already fled the scene of their brief winter revel and are forcing the spring in their Floridas, their Egypts, their Rivieras. He himself remains midway between the last fall and the next spring; and perhaps he decides against the writer, as the perverse reader sometimes will, and holds that this hour of suspense and misgiving is the supreme, the duodecimal hour of the metropolitan dial. He may be right; who knows? New York's hours are all characteristic; and the hour whose mystical quality we have been trying to intimate is already past, and we must wait another year before we can put it to the test again; wait till the trees once more stand perfectly still: yellow, yellowish - green, crimson, russet, and the wind comes up and blows them bare, and yet another summer is dead, and the mourners, the ghosts, the *revenants* have once more returned to town.

II

PERSONAL AND EPISTOLARY ADDRESSES

A CONSTANT reader of the Easy Chair has come to it with a difficulty which, at the generous Christmas-tide, we hope his fellow-readers will join us in helping solve: they may, if they like, regard it as a merry jest of the patron saint of the day, a sort of riddle thrown upon the table at the general feast for each to try his wits upon

"Across the walnuts and the wine."

"How," this puzzled spirit has asked, "shall I address a friend of mine who, besides being a person of civil condition, with a right to the respect that we like to show people of standing in directing our letters to them, has the distinction of being a doctor of philosophy, of letters, and of laws by the vote of several great universities? Shall I greet him as, say, Smythe Johnes, Esq., or Dr. Smythe Johnes, or Smythe Johnes, Ph.D., Litt.D., LL.D., or simply Mr. Smythe Johnes?"

Decidedly, we should answer, to begin with, *not* " Mr. Smythe Johnes " if you wish to keep the finest bloom on your friendship with any man who knows the world. He will much prefer being addressed simply " Smythe Johnes," with his street and number, for he feels himself classed by your " Mr. Smythe Johnes " with all those Mr. Smythe Johneses whom he loves and honors in their quality of tradesmen and working-men, but does not hold of quite the same social rank as himself. After our revolt in essentials from the English in the eighteenth century, we are now conforming more and more in the twentieth to their usages in non-essentials, and the English always write Smythe Johnes, Esq., or Dr. Smythe Johnes or the like, unless Mr. Smythe Johnes is in trade or below it. They, indeed, sometimes carry their scruple so far that they will address him as Mr. Smythe Johnes at his place of business, and Smythe Johnes, Esq., at his private residence.

The English, who like their taffy thick and slab, and who, if one of them happens to be the Earl of Tolloller, are not richly enough satisfied to be so accosted by letter, but exact some such address as The Right Honorable the Earl of Tolloller, all like distinctions in their taffy, and are offended if you give them a commoner sort than they think their due. But the Americans, who pretend to a manlier self-respect, had once pretty generally decided upon Mr. Smythe Johnes as the right direction for his letters. They argued that Esquire was the proper address for lawyers, apparently because lawyers are so commonly called Squire in the simpler life. In the disuse of the older form of Armiger they forgot that *inter arma silent leges,* and that Esquire was logically as unfit for lawyers as for civil doctors, divines, or mediciners. He of the Easy Chair, when an editor long ago, yielded to the prevalent American misrendering for a time, and indiscriminately addressed all his contributors as " Mr." One of them, the most liberal of them in principle, bore the ignominy for about a year, and then he protested. After that the young editor (he was then almost as young as any one now writing deathless fiction) indiscriminately addressed his contributors as Esq. Yet he had an abiding sense of the absurdity in directing letters to John G. Whittier, Esq., for if the poet was truly a Friend and an abhorrer of war, he could not be hailed Armiger without something like insult.

With doctors of divinity the question is not so vexing or vexed; but it is said that of late a lion is rising in the way of rightly addressing doctors of medicine. If you wish to be attended by a physician who pays all visits after nightfall in evening dress, it is said that you are now to write Smythe Johnes, M.D., Esq., and not Dr. Smythe Johnes, as formerly. In England, the source of all our ceremonial woes, you cannot call a surgeon "doctor" without offence; he is Mr. Smythe Johnes when spoken to, but whether he is Mr. Smythe Johnes through the post, Heaven knows.

It is a thousand pities that when we cut ourselves off from that troubled source politically, we did not dam it up in all the things of etiquette. We indeed struck for freedom and sense at the very highest point, and began at once to write George Washington, President, as we still write William H. Taft, President. The Chief Magistrate is offered no taffy in our nation, or perhaps the word President is held to be taffy enough and to spare; for only the Governor of Massachusetts is legally even so much as Excellency. Yet by usage you are expected to address all ambassadors and ministers as Excellencies, and all persons in public office from members of Congress and of the Cabinet down to the lowest legislative or judicial functionaries as Honorables. This simplifies the task of directing envelopes to them, and, if a man once holds military rank in any peace establishment, he makes life a little easier for his correspondents by remaining General, or Captain, or Admiral, or Commander. You cannot Mister him, and you cannot Esquire him, and there is, therefore, no question as to what you shall superscribe him.

A score of years ago two friends, now, alas! both doctors of philosophy, of letters, and of laws, agreed to superscribe their letters simply Smythe Johnes and Johnes Smythe respectively, without any vain prefix or affix. They kept up this good custom till in process of time they went to Europe for prolonged sojourns, and there corrupted their manners, so that when they came home they began addressing each other as Esq., and have done so ever since. Neither is any the better for the honors they exchange on the envelopes they do not look at, and doubtless if mankind could be brought to the renunciation of the vain prefixes and affixes which these friends once disused the race would be none the worse for it, but all the better. One prints Mr. Smythe Johnes on one's visiting-card because it passes through the hands of a menial who is not to be supposed for a moment to announce plain Smythe Johnes; but it is the United States post-office which delivers the letters of Smythe Johnes, and they can suffer no contamination from a service which conveys the letters of plain William H. Taft to him with merely the explanatory affix of President, lest they should go to some other William H. Taft.

Undoubtedly the address of a person by the name with which he was christened can convey no shadow of disrespect. The Society of Friends understood this from the beginning, and they felt that they were wanting in no essential civility when they refused name-honor as well as hat-honor to all and every. They remained covered in the highest presences, and addressed each by his Christian name, without conveying slight; so that a King and Queen of England, who had once questioned whether they could suffer themselves to be called Thy Majesty instead of Your Majesty by certain Quakers, found it no derogation of their dignity to be saluted as Friend George and Friend Charlotte. The signory of the proudest republic in the world held that their family names were of sufficiency to which titles could add nothing, and the Venetian who called himself Loredano, or Gradenigo, or Morosini, or Renier, or Rezzonico did not ask to be called differently. In our own day a lady of the ancient and splendid family of the Peruzzi in Florence denied that the title of count existed in it or need exist: " Ognuno può essere conte: Peruzzi, no." (" Any one may be a count; but not a Peruzzi.") In like manner such names as Lincoln and Franklin, and Washington and Grant, and Longfellow and Bryant could have gained nothing by Mr. before them or Esq. after them. Doctor Socrates or Doctor Seneca would not have descended to us in higher regard with the help of these titles; and Rear-Admiral Themistocles or Major-General Epaminondas could not have had greater glory from the survival of parchments so directed to them.

The Venetian nobles who disdained titles came in process of time to be saluted as Illustrissimo; but in process of time this address when used orally began to shed its syllables till Illustrissimo became Lustrissimo, and then Strissimo, and at last Striss, when perhaps the family name again sufficed. So with us, Doctor has familiarly become " Doc," and Captain, " Cap," until one might rather have no title at all. Mr. itself is a grotesque malformation of a better word, and Miss is a silly shortening of the fine form of Mistress. This, pronounced Misses, can hardly add dignity to the name of the lady addressed, though doubtless it cannot be disused till we are all of the Society of Friends. The popular necessity has resulted in the vulgar vocative use of Lady, but the same use of Gentleman has not even a vulgar success, though it is not unknown. You may say, with your hand on the bell-strap, " Step lively, lady," but you cannot say, " Step lively, gentleman," and the fine old vocative " Sir " is quite obsolete. We ourselves remember it on the tongues of two elderly men who greeted each other with " Sir!" and " Sir!" when they met; and " Step lively, sir," might convey the same delicate regard from the trolley conductor as " Step lively, lady." Sir might look very well on the back of a letter; Smythe Johnes, Sir, would on some accounts be preferable to Smythe Johnes, Esq., and, oddly enough, it would be less archaic.

Such of our readers as have dined with the late Queen or the present King of England will recall how much it eased the yoke of ceremony to say to the sovereign, " Yes, ma'am," or " Yes, sir," as the use is, instead of your Majesty. But to others you cannot say " Yes, ma'am," or " Yes, sir," unless you are in that station of life to which you would be very sorry it had pleased God to call you. Yet these forms seem undeniably fit when used by the young to their elders, if the difference of years is great enough.

The difficulty remains, however. You cannot as yet write on an envelope, Smythe Johnes, Sir, or Mary Johnes, Lady; and, in view of this fact, we find ourselves no nearer the solution of our constant reader's difficulty than we were at first. The Socialists, who wish to simplify themselves and others, would address Mr. Johnes as Comrade Smythe Johnes, but could they address Mrs. Johnes as Comradess? We fancy not; besides, Comrade suggests arms and bloodshed, which is hardly the meaning of the red flag of brotherhood, and at the best Comrade looks affected and sounds even more so. Friend would be better, but orally, on the lips of non - Quakers, it has an effect of patronage, though no one could rightly feel slight in a letter addressed to him as Friend Smythe Johnes.

It is wonderful to consider how the ancients apparently got on without the use of any sort of prefix or affix to their names on the roll of parchment or fold of papyrus addressed to them. For all we know, Cæsar was simply C. Julius Cæsar to his correspondents, and Pericles was yet more simply Pericles to the least of his fellow-citizens. These historical personages may have had the number of their houses inscribed on their letters; or Pericles might have had Son of Xanthippus added to his name for purposes of identification; but apparently he managed quite as well as our Presidents, without anything equivalent to Excellency or Hon. or Mr. or Esq. To be sure, with the decline of

> " The glory that was Greece
> And the grandeur that was Rome,"

name-honors crept in more and more. It was then not only politer but much safer to address your petition To the Divine Domitian, or To the Divine Nero, than to greet those emperors by the mere given names which were not yet Christian; probably it would not have been enough to add Cæsar to the last name, though Cæsar seems to have finally served the turn of Esq., for all the right that the emperors had to bear it. In the Eastern Empire, we are not ready to say what was the correct style for imperial dignitaries; but among the sovereigns who divided the Roman state and inherited its splendor, some rulers came to be sacred majesties, though this is still a sensible remove from divine.

However, our present difficulty is with that vast average who in common parlance are Mr. and Mrs. Smythe Johnes. How shall they be styled on the backs of their letters? How shall Mrs. Smythe Johnes especially, in signing herself Mary Johnes, indicate that she is not Miss Mary but Mrs. Smythe Johnes? When she is left a widow, how soon does she cease to be Mrs. Smythe Johnes and become Mrs. Mary? Is it requisite to write in the case of any literary doctorate, Smythe Johnes, LL.D., or Litt.D., or Ph.D., or is it sufficient to write Dr. before his name? In the case of a divine, do you put Rev. Dr. before the name, or Rev. before it and D.D. after it? These are important questions, or, if they are not important, they are at least interesting. Among the vast mass of unceremonied, or call it unmannered, Americans the receiver of a letter probably knows no better than the sender how it should be addressed; but in the rarer case in which he does know, his self-respect or his self-love is wounded if it is misaddressed. It is something like having your name misspelled, though of course not so bad as that, quite; and every one would be glad to avoid the chance of it.

The matter is very delicate and can hardly be managed by legislation, as it was on the point of our pen to suggest it should be. The first French Republic, one and indivisible, decreed a really charming form of address, which could be used without offence to the self-love or the self-respect of any one. Citoyen for all men and Citoyenne for all women was absolutely tasteful, modest, and dignified; but some things, though they are such kindred things, cannot be done as well as others. The same imaginative commonwealth invented a decimal chronology, and a new era, very handy and very clear; but the old week of seven days came back and replaced the week of ten days, and the Year of our Lord resumed the place of the Year of the Republic, as Monsieur and Madame returned victorious over Citoyen and Citoyenne. Yet the reform of weights and measures, when once established, continued, and spread from France to most other countries—to nearly all, indeed, less stupid than Great Britain and the United States—so that the whole civilized world now counts in grammes and metres. What can be the fine difference? Here is a pretty inquiry for the psychologist, who has an opportunity to prove himself practically useful. Is it that grammes and metres are less personal than week-days and addresses? That can hardly be, or else the Society of Friends could not have so absolutely substituted First Day and Second Day, etc., for the old heathen names of our week-days, and could not have successfully refused all name-honor whatsoever in addressing their fellow-mortals.

But titles have come back full-tide in the third French Republic, one and indivisible, so that anybody may wear them, though the oldest nobility are officially and legally known only by their Christian and family names, without any prefix. This is practically returning to Citoyen and Citoyenne, and it almost gives us the courage to suggest the experiment of Citizen and Citizenne as a proper address on the letters of American republicans. The matter might be referred to a Board, something like that of the Simplified Spelling Board, though we should not like to be included in a committee whose members must be prepared to take their lives in their hands, or, short of death, to suffer every manner of shame at the hands of our journalists and their correspondents. Short of the adoption of Citizen and Citizenne, we have no choice but to address one another by our given names and surnames merely, unless we prefer to remain in our present confusion of Mr. and Esq. In a very little while, we dare say, no lady or gentleman would mind being so addressed on his or her letters; but perhaps some men and women might. Now that we no longer use pets names so much, except among the very highest of our noblesse, where there are still Jimmies and Mamies, we believe, plain Gladys Smythe or Reginald Johnes would be the usual superscription. Such an address could bring no discomfort to the recipient (a beautiful word, very proper in this connection), and if it could once be generally adopted it would save a great deal of anxiety. The lady's condition could be indicated by the suffix Spinster, in the case of her being single; if married, the initials of her husband's given names could be added.

III

DRESSING FOR HOTEL DINNER

AMONG the high excitements of a recent winter in New York was one of such convulsive intensity that in the nature of things it could not last very long. It affected the feminine temperament of our public with hysterical violence, but left the community the calmer for its throes, and gently, if somewhat pensively, smiling in a permanent ignorance of the event. No outside observer would now be able to say, offhand, whether a certain eminent innkeeper had or had not had his way with his customers in the matter not only of what they should eat or drink, but what they should wear when dining in a place which has been described as " supplying exclusiveness to the lower classes." It is not even certain just how a crucial case was brought to the notice of this authority; what is certain is that his instant judgment was that no white male citizen frequenting his proud tavern should sit at dinner there unless clothed in a dress-coat, or at least in the smoking-jacket known to us as a Tuxedo; at breakfast or at luncheon, probably, the guest, the paying guest, could sufficiently shine in the reflected glory of the lustrous evening wear of the waiters. No sooner was the innkeeper's judgment rendered than a keen thrill of resentment, or at least amusement, ran through the general breast. From every quarter the reporters hastened to verify the fact at first-hand, and then to submit it to the keeper of every other eminent inn or eating-house in the city and learn his usage and opinion. These to a man disavowed any such hard-and-fast rule. Though their paying guests were ordinarily gentlemen of such polite habits as to be incapable of dining in anything but a dress-coat or a Tuxedo, yet their inns and eating-houses were not barred against those who chose to dine in a frock or cutaway or even a sacque. It is possible that the managers imagined themselves acquiring merit with that large body of our vulgar who demand exclusiveness by their avowal of a fine indifference or an enlightened tolerance in the matter. But at this distance of time no one can confidently say how the incident was closed with respect to the pre-eminent innkeeper and his proud tavern. Whether the wayfarer, forced by the conditions of travel upon the company of the exclusive vulgar, may now dine there in the public banqueting-hall in his daytime raiment, or must take his evening meal in his room, with a penalty in the form of an extra charge for service, nowise appears.

What is apparent from the whole affair is that the old ideal of one's inn, as a place where one shall take one's ease, has perished in the evolution of the magnificent American hotel which we have been maliciously seeking to minify in the image of its Old World germ. One may take one's ease in one's hotel only if one is dressed to the mind of the hotel-keeper, or perhaps finally the head waiter. But what is more important still is that probably the vast multitude of the moneyed vulgar whose exclusiveness is supplied to them in such a place dictate, tacitly at least, the Draconian policy of the management. No innkeeper or head waiter, no matter of how patrician an experience or prejudice, would imagine a measure of such hardship to wayfarers willing to pay for the simple comfort of their ancestors at the same rate as their commensals stiffly shining in the clothes of convention. The management might have its conception of what a hotel dining-room should look like, with an unbroken array of gentlemen in black dress-coats and ladies in white shoulders all feeding as superbly as if they were not paying for their dinners, or as if they had been severally asked for the pleasure of their company two weeks before; and the picture would doubtless be marred by figures of people in cutaways and high necks, to a degree intolerable to the artistic sense. But it is altogether impossible that the management would exact a conformity to the general effect which was not desired by the vast majority of its paying guests. What might well have seemed a break on the part of the pre-eminent innkeeper when he cited as a precedent for his decision the practice of the highest hotels in London was really no break, but a stroke of the finest juridical acumen. Nothing could have gone further with the vast majority of his paying guests than some such authority, for they could wish nothing so much, in the exclusiveness supplied them, as the example of the real characters in the social drama which they were impersonating. They had the stage and the scenery; they had spared no expense in their costuming; they had anxiously studied their parts, and for the space of their dinner-hour they had the right to the effect of aristocratic society, which they were seeking, unmarred by one discordant note. After that hour, let it be a cramped stall in the orchestra of another theatre, or let it be an early bed in a cell of their colossal columbary, yet they would have had their dinner-hour when they shone primarily just like the paying guests in the finest English hotel, and secondarily just like the non-paying guests at the innumerable dinners of the nobility and gentry in a thousand private houses in London.

Our aim is always high, and they would be right to aim at nothing lower than this in their amateur dramatics. But here we have a question which we have been holding back by main force from the beginning, and which now persists in precipitating itself in our peaceful page. It is a question which merits wider and closer study than we can give it, and it will, we hope, find an answer such as we cannot supply in the wisdom of the reader. It presented itself to the mind of Eugenio in a recent experience of his at a famous seaside resort which does not remit its charm even in the heart of winter, and which with the first tremor of the opening spring allures the dweller among the sky-scrapers and the subways with an irresistible appeal. We need not further specify the place, but it is necessary to add that it draws not only the jaded or sated New-Yorker, but the more eager and animated average of well-to-do people from every part of their country who have got bored out with their happy homes and want a few days' or a few weeks' change. One may not perhaps meet a single distinguished figure on its famous promenade, or at least more distinguished than one's own; with the best will in the world to find such figures, Eugenio could count but three or four: a tall, alert, correct man or two; an electly fashioned, perfectly set-up, dominant woman or so, whose bearing expressed the supremacy of a set in some unquestionable world. But there was obvious riches aplenty, and aplenty of the kind wholesomeness of the good, true, intelligent, and heaven-bound virtue of what we must begin to call our middle class, offensive as the necessity may be. Here and there the effect of champagne in the hair, which deceived no one but the wearer, was to be noted; here and there, high-rolling, a presence with the effect of something more than champagne in the face loomed in the perspective through the haze of a costly cigar. But by far, immensely far, the greater number of his fellow-frequenters of the charming promenade were simple, domestic, well-meaning Americans like Eugenio himself, of a varying simplicity indeed, but always of a simplicity. They were the stuff with which his fancy (he never presumed to call it his imagination) had hitherto delighted to play, fondly shaping out of the collective material those lineaments and expressions which he hoped contained a composite likeness of his American day and generation. The whole situation was most propitious, and yet he found himself moving through it without one of the impulses which had been almost lifelong with him. As if in some strange paralysis, some obsession by a demon of indifference unknown before, he was bereft of the will to realize these familiar protagonists of his plain dramas. He knew them, of course; he knew them all too well; but he had not the wish to fit the likest of them with phrases, to costume them for their several parts, to fit them into the places in the unambitious action where they had so often contributed to the modest but inevitable catastrophe.

The experience repeated itself till he began to take himself by the collar and shake himself in the dismay of a wild conjecture. What had befallen him? Had he gone along, young, eager, interested, delighted with his kind for half a century of æsthetic consciousness, and now had he suddenly lapsed into the weariness and apathy of old age? It is always, short of ninety, too soon for that, and Eugenio was not yet quite ninety. Was his mind, then, prematurely affected? But was not this question itself proof that his mind was still

importunately active? If that was so, why did not he
still wish to make his phrases about his like, to repro-
duce their effect in composite portraiture? Eugenio
fell into a state so low that nothing but the confession
of his perplexity could help him out; and the friend to
whom he owned his mystifying, his all but appalling,
experience did not fail him in his extremity. "No,"
he wrote back, "it is not that you have seen all these
people, and that they offer no novel types for observation, but even more that they illustrate the great fact
that, in the course of the last twenty years, society in
America has reached its goal, has 'arrived,' and is
creating no new types. On the contrary, it is obliterat-
ing some of the best which were clearly marked, and
is becoming more and more one rich, dead level of medi-
ocrity, broken here and there by solitary eminences,
some of which are genuine, some only false peaks without solid rock foundations."

Such a view of his case must be immediately and
immensely consoling, but it was even more precious to
Eugenio for the suggestion from which his fancy—never
imagination—began to play forward with the vivacity
of that of a youth of sixty, instead of a middle-aged
man of eighty-five. If all this were true—and its truth
shone the more distinctly from a ground of potential
dissent—was not there the stuff in the actual conditions
from which a finer artist than he could ever hope to
be, now that the first glow of his prime was past, might
fashion an image of our decadence, or our arrest, so
grandly, so perfectly dull and uninteresting, that it
would fix all the after-ages with the sovereign authority
of a masterpiece? Here, he tremblingly glowed to realize, was opportunity, not for him, indeed, but for some
more modern, more divinely inspired lover of the mediocre, to eternize our typelessness and establish himself

among the many-millioned heirs of fame. It had been easy—how easy it had been!—to catch the likeness of those formative times in which he had lived and wrought; but the triumph and the reward of the new artist would be in proportion to the difficulty of seizing the rich, self - satisfied, ambitionless, sordid commonplace of a society wishing to be shut up in a steam-heated, electric-lighted palace and fed fat in its exclusiveness with the inexhaustible inventions of an overpaid chef. True, the strong, simple days of the young republic, when men forgot themselves in the struggle with the wild continent, were past; true, the years were gone when the tremendous adventure of tearing from her heart the iron and the gold which were to bind her in lasting subjection gave to fiction industrial heroes fierce and bold as those of classic fable or mediæval romance. But there remained the days of the years which shall apparently have no end, but shall abound forever in an inexhaustible wealth of the sort wishing not so much to rise itself as to keep down and out all suggestion of the life from which it sprang.

The sort of type which would represent this condition would be vainly sought in any exceptionally opulent citizen of that world. He would have, if nothing else, the distinction of his unmeasured millions, which would form a poetry, however sordid; the note of the world we mean is indistinction, and the protagonist of the fiction seeking to portray its fads and characters must not have more than two or three millions at the most. He, or better she, were better perhaps with only a million, or a million and a half, or enough to live handsomely in eminent inns, either at home or abroad, with that sort of insolent half-knowledge to which culture is contemptible; which can feel the theatre, but not literature; which has passed from the horse to the automobile; which has its moral and material yacht, cruising all social coasts and making port in none where there is not a hotel or cottage life as empty and exclusive as its own. Even in trying to understate the sort, one overstates it. Nothing could be more untrue to its reality than the accentuation of traits which in the arrivals of society elsewhere and elsewhen have marked the ultimation of the bourgeois spirit. Say that the Puritan, the Pilgrim, the Cavalier, and the Merchant Adventurer have come and gone; say that the Revolutionist Patriot, the Pioneer and the Backwoodsman and the Noble Savage have come and gone; say that the Slaveholder and the Slave and the Abolitionist and the Civil Warrior have come and gone; say that the Miner, the Rancher, the Cowboy, and the sardonically humorous Frontiersman have come and gone; say that the simple-hearted, hard-working, modest, genial Homemakers have come and gone; say that the Captain of Industry has come and gone, and the world-wide Financier is going: what remains for actuality-loving art to mould into shapes of perdurable beauty? Obviously, only the immeasurable mass of a prosperity sunken in a self-satisfaction unstirred by conscience and unmoved by desire. But is that a reason why art should despair? Rather it is a reason why it should rejoice in an opportunity occurring not more than once in the ages to seize the likeness and express the significance of Arrival, the arrival of a whole civilization. To do this, art must refine and re-refine upon itself; it must use methods of unapproached delicacy, of unimagined subtlety and celerity. It is easy enough to catch the look of the patrician in the upper air, of the plebeian underfoot, but to render the image of a world-bourgeoisie, compacted in characters of undeniable verisimilitude, that will be difficult, but it will be possible,

and the success will be of an effulgence such as has
never yet taken the eyes of wonder.

We should not be disposed to deny the artist, dedicated to this high achievement by his love of the material not less than by his peculiar gift, the range of a
liberal idealism. We would not have him bound by any
procedent or any self-imposed law of literality. If he
should see his work as a mighty historical picture, or
series of such pictures, we should not gainsay him his
conception or bind him rather to any *genre* result. We
ourselves have been evolving here the notion of some
large allegory which should bear the relation to all
other allegories that Bartholdi's colossus of Liberty
bears to all other statues, and which should carry forward the story and the hero, or the heroine, to some
such supreme moment as that when, amid the approving
emotion of an immense hotel dining-room, all in *décol-
letée* and *frac paré,* the old, simple-lived American,
wearing a sack-coat and a colored shirt, shall be led out
between the eminent innkeeper and the head waiter and
delivered over to the police to be conducted in ignominy
to the nearest Italian table d'hôte. The national character, on the broad level of equality which fiction once
delighted to paint, no longer exists, but if a deeper, a
richer, a more enduring monotony replaces it, we have
no fear but some genius will arrive and impart the effect of the society which has arrived.

IV

THE COUNSEL OF LITERARY AGE TO LITERARY YOUTH

As Eugenio—we will call him Eugenio: a fine impersonal name—grew older, and became, rightfully or wrongfully, more and more widely known for his writings, he found himself increasingly the subject of appeal from young writers who wished in their turn to become, rightfully or wrongfully, more and more widely known. This is not, indeed, stating the case with the precision which we like. His correspondents were young enough already, but they were sometimes not yet writers; they had only the ambition to be writers. Our loose formulation of the fact, however, will cover all its meaning, and we will let it go that they were young writers, for, whether they were or not, they all wished to know one thing: namely, how he did it.

What, they asked in varying turns, was his secret, his recipe for making the kind of literature which had made him famous: they did stint their phrase, and they said famous. That always caused Eugenio to blush, at first with shame and then with pleasure; whatever one's modesty, one likes to be called famous, and Eugenio's pleasure in their flatteries was so much greater than his shame that he thought only how to return them the pleasure unmixed with the shame. His heart went out to those generous youths, who sometimes confessed themselves still in their teens, and often of the sex

which is commonly most effective with the fancy while
still in its teens. It seemed such a very little thing
to show them the way to do what he had done, and,
while disclaiming any merit for it, to say why it was
the best possible way. If they had grouped him with
other widely known writers in their admiration, he
never imagined directing his correspondents to those
others' methods; he said to himself that he did not
understand them, and at bottom he felt that it would
have been better taste in the generous youths to have
left them out of the question.

In the end he never answered his correspondents in
the handsome way he had fancied. Generally he did
not answer them at all, or, if he did, he put them off
with some such cheap excuse as advising them to be sure
they had something to say, and then to say it as simply
and clearly as they could. He knew very well that this
was begging the question; that the question was how
to be artistic, graceful, charming, and whatever else
they said he himself was. If he was aware of not
being all that, he was aware also of having tried to
be it; of having sought from the beginning to captivate
the reader's fancy as well as convince his reason. He
had never been satisfied with being plain and direct;
he had constantly wished to amuse as well as edify, and
following the line of beauty, as that of the least re-
sistance, had been his practice if not his precept. If
he counselled his correspondents otherwise, he would
be uncandid, and when he had imagined putting them
off in that fashion he was more ashamed than he had
been with their praise.

Yet, upon reflection, he perceived that what they
asked was impossible. If ever he had a formula he
had lost it; he was no longer in his own secret, if ever
he had been. All that he could have said with perfect

honesty would have been that he had never found any
royal road to literature; that to his experience there
was not even a common highway; that there were only
byways; private paths over other people's grounds; ease-
ments beaten out by feet that had passed before, and
giving by a subsequent overgrowth of turf or brambles
a deceitful sense of discovery to the latest-comer.

His correspondents would not have liked that. He
knew that what they wanted was his measure of the
old success in some new way, which they could feel
their own after it had been shown them. But the only
secret that he was still in was the very open one of
working hard at whatever he had in hand, and this he
suspected they would have scorned sharing with him.
He could have said that if you want to keep three or
five balls in the air at once you must learn how by
practising; but they knew that as well as he; what they
asked was being enabled to do it themselves from *his*
having practised.

The perception of this fact made Eugenio very sad,
and he asked himself if the willingness to arrive only
after you had got there had gone out of the world and
left nothing but the ambition to be at this point or that
without the trouble of having reached it. He smiled
as he recalled the stock criticism of the connoisseur in
The Vicar of Wakefield, that the picture would have
been better if the painter had taken more pains; but
he did not smile gayly: there seemed to him a sum of
pathetic wisdom in the saying which might well weigh
down the blithest spirit. It had occurred to him in
connection with an old essay of Hazlitt's, which he had
been reading, on the comparative methods of English
and French painters in their work. The essayist held,
almost literally, that the French pictures were better
because the French painters had taken more pains, and

taken especial pains in the least interesting parts of their pictures. He was dealing more specifically with copying, but his words applied to the respective schools in their highest work, and he could only save his patriotic pride, so far as he might, by saying: " Courage is pure will without regard to consequences, and this the English have in perfection. Poetry is our element, for the essence of poetry is will and passion. The English fail as a people in the fine arts, namely, because the end with them absorbs the means."

Eugenio knew nothing practically and very little theoretically of painting; but it appeared to him that what Hazlitt said was of equal force with respect to the fine art of literature; and that in his own American field the English race failed, as far as it had failed, for the same reason as that given by Hazlitt for its failure in painting. In his mind he went further than Hazlitt, or came short of him, in refusing the consolation of our race's superiority in poetry because it was will and passion. As far as they had excelled in that, it was because they had tried hard and not neglected the means for the end. Where they had excelled most, it was quite imaginable that the poem would still have been better if the poet had taken more pains. In the case of prose, he thought we failed of the end because we were impatient of the means, and as elderly men will, he accused the present of being more hasty and indifferent to form than the past. He recalled the time when he was apprentice in the art in which he could not yet call himself a master workman, and thought how he tried to make what he did beautiful, and fashioned his work with tireless pains after some high model. Perhaps the young writers of this time were striving as earnestly; but he could not see it, or thought he could not. He fancied their eyes dazzled

286

by the images of easy success, instead of taken with the glory of a thing beautifully done. He remembered, with fond emotion, how once his soul had glowed over some " cunning'st pattern of excelling nature," and had been filled with longing to learn from it the art of surprising some other mood or aspect of nature and making that loveliness or grandeur his own. He had talked with other youths who were trying at the same time to do good work, and he remembered that they too were trying in the same way; and now, long after, he fancied that their difference from the youth of the present day was in their willingness to strive for perfection in the means and to let the end take care of itself. The end could no more justify bad means in æsthetics than in ethics; in fact, without the carefully studied means there could be no artistic result. If it was true that the young writers of the present expected a high result from hurried or neglected processes, they could have only the results that Eugenio saw around him. If they admired these, and were coming to him for the secret of achieving them, they were coming to the wrong shop.

Yet he did not harshly blame them. He remembered how he, too, when he had been impatient of the means, had once fancied postponing them to the end. That was in the days which were mainly filled for him with the business of writing fiction, and when the climax of his story seemed always threatening to hide itself from him or to elude his grasp. There were times when it changed to some other end or took a different significance from that it had primarily had. Then he had said to himself that if he could only write the end first, or boldly block it out as it first presented itself, and afterward go back and write in the events and characters leading up to it, he would have an effect glorified by all the fervor of his primal inspiration. But he never did that, or even tried to do it. Perhaps, when he came to consider it more carefully, it appeared impossible; perhaps it approved itself ridiculous without experiment. His work of art, such as it was, was a growth from all his thinking and feeling about it; and without that it could no more eventuate in a climax than a tree could ripen fruit without the preliminaries of striking its roots into the ground, coming of the age to bear, and then some springtime budding, putting out leaves, breaking into blossom, and setting its young apples, or whatever else it was going to bear. The fruit it bore would be according to its kind, and he might have been mistakenly expecting to grow peaches from an apple stock when he was surprised to find apples on it, or the end of his novel turning out other than he had forecast it.

In literature the reader's affair is with results, but the author's with processes. Eugenio had realized this more and more distinctly, and, as he now reflected on the appeals of those fond young correspondents of his, it occurred to him that their confusion as to literary methods and manners lay in their being still readers so largely and so little authors as yet. They were dealing with the end, in their mistaken minds, and not with the means, as they supposed. The successes which dazzled them might very well have been written backward in some such fashion as he had once imagined, for the end was the main thing with them, and was the end of the story as well as the end of the book. But the true story never ends. The close of the book is simply the point at which the author has stopped, and, if he has stopped wisely, the reader takes up the tale and goes on with it in his own mind.

As for the variance of the close from the forecast of it, Eugenio was less and less dismayed by that, when in the course of time he looked more closely at his own life and the lives of other men. Only on some spiritual terms was there the fulfilment of forecast in them, and the more art resembled life the less responsive it was to any hard-and-fast design. He perceived that to find the result changing from the purpose might very well be a proof of vitality in it, an evidence of unconscious insight, the sort of inspiration that comes to crown faithful work with unimagined beauty. He looked round at the great works of literary art, and he believed that he saw in them the escape from implicit obedience to a first intention. Only in the inferior things, the mechanical things, could he discern obedience. In something supreme, like *Hamlet,* say, there was everything to make him think that the processes had educated Shakespeare as to the true nature of his sublime endeavor and had fixed the terms of its close. Probably the playwright started with the notion of making Hamlet promptly kill his stepfather, rescue Ophelia from the attempt to climb out over the stream on a willow branch, forgive his erring mother as more sinned against than sinning, welcome Laertes back to Denmark, and with the Ghost of his father blessing the whole group, and Polonius with his arm in a sling, severely but not fatally wounded, form the sort of stage picture, as the curtain went down, that has sent audiences home, dissolved in happy tears, from so many theatres. But Shakespeare, being a dramatist as well as a playwright, learned from Hamlet himself that Hamlet could not end as he had meant him to end. Hamlet, in fact, could not really end at all, and, in the sort of anticlimax in which the tragedy closes, he must rise from death, another and a truer ghost than the buried majesty of Denmark, and walk the world forever.

Could Eugenio, however, advise his youthful correspondents to work so reckless of their original conceptions as Shakespeare had probably done? The question was serious; it put him upon his conscience, and he decided that at the most he could not do more than urge them, with all the earnestness of his nature, to write their *Hamlets* from the beginning forward, and never from the ending backward, even in their own minds. He saw that if he were to answer them collectively (and he certainly did not intend to answer them severally) he must say that their only hope of producing an effective whole was through indefatigable work upon every part. Make each smallest detail beautiful, and despise none because it seemed to perform a poor and lowly office in the assemblage of the parts. Let these youths be sure that they could not know the meaning of any design from imagining it, but only from expressing it, and that the true result could come only from the process. They could not hope to outdo Shakespeare and foreknow their respective *Hamlets;* they must slowly make their *Hamlets'* acquaintance by living with them.

If Eugenio's correspondents were dashed by this hard saying, he thought he might raise their spirits by adding that they would find compensation for their slow, arduous toil in particulars from a fact which he had noted in his own case. A thing well done looks always very much better in the retrospect than could have been hoped. A good piece of work would smile radiantly upon them when it was accomplished. Besides, after a certain experience in doing, they would learn that the greatest happiness which could come to them from their work would be through the perfecting of details. This would make their performance a succession of little victories which alone could constitute the great ultimate triumph.

"But style, but style!" they might return. "What about style? That was one of the miracles we asked you the sleight of, and are you going to say nothing about that? Or did you mean style, in your talk about perfecting details? Do you want us to take infinite pains in acquiring a style?"

"By no means," Eugenio was prepared to declare in the event of this come-back. "Do not think about style. If you do your work well, patiently, faithfully, truly, style will infallibly be added unto you. That is the one thing you must *not* try for. If you try for style, you will be like a man thinking about his clothes or his manners. You will be self-conscious, which is the fatal opposite of being yourself. You will be yourself when you are lost in your work, and then you will come into the only style that is proper to you: the beauty and the grace that any sort of workman has in the exercise of his craft. You will then have, without seeking it, your own swing of phrase, your own turn of expression, your own diction, and these will be your style by which every reader will know you. But if you have a manner which you have borrowed or imitated, people will see that it is second-hand and no better than something shop-worn or cast off. Besides, style is a thing that has been grossly overvalued in the general appraisal of literary qualities. The stylists are not the greatest artists, the supreme artists. Who would think of Shakespeare as a stylist, or Tolstoy, or Dante?"

Eugenio thought he could count upon a vanity in his correspondents so dense as not to be pierced by any irony. In fact, it could not be said that, though he felt the pathos of their appeals, he greatly respected the motives which actuated them in writing to him. They themselves respected their motives because they did not know them as he did, but probably they did not pity themselves so much as he pitied them. He realized that they turned to him from a literary remoteness which they did not realize, and it was very natural that they should turn for help outside their circumstance; but Eugenio had not lived to his age without learning that many natural impulses are mistaken if not wrong. He reflected sadly that those far-off solitaries could alone burst their circumstance and find their way out of it. He perceived that they could do this only by their own devout and constant toil in the line of their aspiration. But would it avail to tell them so?

One of the knowledges of a period of life which we will call the riper maturity is that we need all the accumulated vigilance of the past to secure us from the ever-besetting dangers of the present: the dangers of indolence, of slovenly performance, of indistinct vision, of weakening conscience in our work. We need every atom of force, every particle of the stored electricity of youth, to keep us going in later years. While we are still young we are aware of an environing and pervading censure, coming from the rivalry, the envy, the generous emulation, the approval, the disapproval, the love, the hate of all those who witness our endeavor. No smallest slip, no slightest defect will be lost upon this censure, equally useful whether sympathetic or antipathetic. But as we grow old we are sensible of a relaxing, a lifting, a withdrawal of the environing and pervading censure. We have become the objects of a compassionate toleration or a contemptuous indifference; it no longer matters greatly to the world whether we do our work well or ill. But if we love our work as we ought till we die, it should matter more than ever to us whether we do it well or ill. We have come to the most perilous days of our years when we are tempted not so much to slight our work as to spare our nerves, in which the stored electricity is lower and scanter than it was, and to let a present feeble performance blight the fame of strenuous achievements in the past. We may then make our choice of two things — stop working; stop going, cease to move, to exist — or gather at each successive effort whatever remains of habit, of conscience, of native force, and put it into effect till our work, which we have not dropped, drops us.

Should Eugenio address these hard sayings to his appealing, his palpitating correspondents? He found himself on the point of telling them that of all the accumulated energies which could avail them when they came of his age, or were coming of it, there was none that would count for so much as the force of habit; and what could be more banal than that? It would not save it from banality if he explained that he meant the habit of loving the very best one can do, and doing that and not something less. It would still be banal to say that now in their youth was the only time they would have to form the habit of tirelessly doing their best at every point, and that they could not buy or beg or borrow such a habit for the simple reason that nobody who had it could sell or give or lend it.

Besides, as Eugenio very well perceived, his correspondents were not only young now, but were always intending to be so. He remembered how it used to be with himself, and that was how it used to be. He saw abundance of old, or older, people about him, but he himself instinctively expected to live on and on, without getting older, and to hive up honey from experience without the beeswax which alone they seemed to have stored from the opening flowers of the past. Yet, in due course of time, he found himself an old or older man simply through living on and on and not dying earlier. Upon the whole, he liked it and would not have gone back and died earlier if he could. But he felt that it would be useless trying to convince his youthful correspondents that, whether they liked it or not, they too would grow old, or older, if they lived. How, then, teach them by precept, if they would not learn by universal example, that unless they were to be very miserable old men, and even miserable old women, they must have the habit of work? How instruct them further that unless they had the habit of good work, patient, faithful, fine work, the habit which no one can buy, beg, or borrow, because no one can sell, give, or lend it, they were worse than idle, cumberers of the earth, with no excuse for being above it?

If he had set out to do that, they might have retorted upon him that he was making a petty personal matter of art, which was not only so much longer than life, but so much wider, deeper, and higher. In this event he saw that he would have nothing for it but to confirm his correspondents in their disappointment with him by declaring that art *was* a personal matter, and that though longer, it was not wider, deeper, or higher than life, and could not be. It might be mysterious in being personal, but it was not necessarily petty. It would be great if the artist was so, but not otherwise; it could be fine on no other terms. There was a theory and an appearance that it existed somehow apart from the artist and that it made him. But the fact was he made it, partly wittingly, partly unwittingly; and it had no being except in his achievement. The power of imagining a work of art was the gift of nature, as being long or short, dark or fair was. The concern of him it was given to was how, after he found it out, to make the most of his gift. It had no power to make much or little of him. If he cherished it and served

it, when he had made sure of it, by fulfilling the law
that its possession imposed, then it would rise up in
something he had done and call him master.

But how could Eugenio make such things—so true
and yet so self-contradictory, so mutually repellent—
clear to these simple-hearted young correspondents of
his? The more he thought of the matter, the more he
resolved to do nothing about it.

V

THE UNSATISFACTORINESS OF UNFRIENDLY CRITICISM

IT was the experience of Eugenio that the criticisms of his books, when they were unfriendly, presented a varying offence, rather than a cumulative offence, as the years wore on. The criticisms of one's books are always hard to bear if they are unfavorable, but he thought that displeasure for displeasure the earlier refusal to allow him certain merits was less displeasing than the later consent to take these merits for granted. To be taken for granted in any wise is to be limited. It is tantamount to having it said of one that, yes, one has those virtues, but one has no others. It comes also to saying that one has, of course, the defects of one's virtues; though Eugenio noted that, when certain defects of his were taken for granted, it did not so distinctly and immediately follow that he was supposed to have the virtues of these.

Now, Eugenio's theory of himself was that he was not limited, and that, if he modestly stopped short of infinity, it was because he chose. He had a feeling of always breaking new ground; and he did not like being told that he was tilling the old glebe and harvesting the same crops, or that in the little garden-ground where he let his fancy play he was culling flowers of such familiar tint and scent that they seemed to be the very flowers he had picked thirty or forty years before.

What made it harder to endure suggestion of this sort was that in his feeling of always breaking new ground there was an inner sense, or fear, or doubt, that perhaps it was not really virgin soil he was turning up, but merely the sod of fields which had lain fallow a year or two or had possibly been cropped the season before.

The misgiving was forced upon him by certain appearances in the work of other veteran authors. When he took up the last book of some lifelong favorite, no matter how great a master he knew him still to be, he could not help seeing that the poor old master was repeating himself, though he would not have phrased the case in such brutal terms. Then the chill wonder how long he could hope to escape the like fate pierced him, and for a moment he could not silence the question whether it might not have already befallen him. In another moment he knew better, and was justly aggrieved with the next reviewer who took things in him for granted, quite as offensively if they were merits as if they were defects. It was vital to him to be always breaking new ground, and, if at times it seemed to him that he had turned this or that furrow before, he said to himself that it was merely one of those intimations of pre-existence which are always teasing us here with the sense of experience in circumstances absolutely novel; and he hoped that no one else would notice the coincidence.

He was, indeed, tolerably safe from the chance, for it is one of the conditions of literary criticism that the reviewers shall be nearly always young persons. They, if they alone are capable of the cruelties they sometimes practise, are alone capable of the enthusiasms which supply publishers with quotable passages for their advertisements, and which lift authors' hearts in pride and joy. It is to their advantage that they generally bring to the present work of a veteran author an ignorance of all that he has done before, and have the zest for it which the performance of a novice inspires. They know he is not a novice, of course, and they recognize his book as that of a veteran, but they necessarily treat it as representative of his authorship. Of course, if it is his twentieth or thirtieth book, or his fortieth or fiftieth, it is merely one of a long series which fully represents him. Even these collectively represent him inadequately as long as he is adding to them, if he has the habit, like Eugenio, of always breaking new ground. The reviewer, however, is probably much newer than the ground which the established author breaks in his last book, and, coming to it in his generous ignorance, which he has to conceal under a mask of smiling omniscience, he condemns or praises it without reference to the work which has gone before it and which it is merely part of, though of course it has entirety enough of a sort to stand alone. If the author has broken ground in the direction of a new type of heroine, the reviewer, by the conditions of his calling, is all but obliged to say that here is one of those enchanting girls whom the author in question has endeared to generations of readers; or one of those tedious prudes for whom his name is a synonyme. If, after many psychological romances, the author has stepped down to the level of actual life, he is praised or blamed for the vital or servile naturalism of his work; or if the contrary is the case, he has to read of himself as doing something habitual and entirely characteristic of him. In vain, so far as that acute young critic is concerned, has he broken new ground. But if he has with much compunction consciously turned his furrows in a field tilled before, he stands a fair chance of being hailed at the outset of a new career.

He cannot openly complain, and if he could the critic cannot help being what he is. If the critic were older and more versed in the veteran author, he might not like him so well, and he could not, at any rate, bring the fresh interest to his work which the young reviewer brings. What Eugenio would really wish would be to have each successive book of his given for review to some lifelong admirer, some dear and faithful friend, all the better for not being an acquaintance, who had liked him from the beginning and was intimately versed in all his work. Such a critic would know that Eugenio was always breaking new ground, and that he was never more true to this inherent tendency than when he seemed to be ploughing the same old furrows in the same old fields. Such a critic would be alert to detect those fine differences of situation which distinguish a later from an earlier predicament. He would note with unfailing perspicacity the shades of variance which constitute Florindo an essentially novel character when presented under the name of Lindoro, or Floribella a fresh delight when she reappears as Doralinda. Even when he could not deny that these persons were in themselves one and the same, he would be able to make the reader observe that the new light thrown upon them by the author's ever-renascent art revealed in familiar creations traits of mind and charms of spirit unimagined before. He would insist that, if not new, they were newer, because being more fully ascertained they were truer. He would boldly recur to the personages in Eugenio's former books whom they reminded one of, and, studying them in contrast, would convince the reader that the increasing purpose of the author in the treatment of the well-known types had been to reveal the infinite variety of character which lay hid in each and every human type.

Some such reviewer, Eugenio thought, all journals pretending to literary authority ought to keep on their staff for the comfort of veteran authors and for the dispensation of that more delicate and sympathetic justice which their case required. It might be well enough to use a pair of ordinary steelyards, or even hay-scales, in weighing out the rewards and punishments of younger authors, but some such sensitive balance as only the sympathetic nerves of equal years, and, if possible, equal intelligence, could adjust ought to be used in ascertaining the merits of a veteran author.

In his frankest self-consciousness, Eugenio did not say a veteran author like himself, and he did not insist exclusively upon a veteran critic for his behoof. There were times when he thought that a young critic, coming in the glow of adolescence and the freshness of knowledge won from the recent study of all his works, might be better fitted to appreciate the qualities of the latest. He quite rejected the notion, when it came to business, with which he had sometimes played, of an author reviewing his own books, and this apart from his sense of its immodesty. In the course of his experience he had known of but one really great author who had done this, and then had done it upon the invitation of an editor of rare if somewhat wilful perspicacity, who invited the author to do it on the ground that no one else could do it so well. But though he would not have liked to be his own reviewer, because it was not seemly, he chiefly feared that if put upon his honor, as he would be in such a case, he must deal with his work so damagingly as to leave little or nothing of it. He might make the reputation of a great critic, but in doing execution upon his own shortcomings he might be the means of destroying himself as a great author.

After all, authors are not the self-satisfied generation

they must often seem to the public which has tried to spoil them with praise. There is much in doing a thing which makes a man modest in regard to the way he has done it. Even if he knows that he has done it well, if the testimony of all his faculties is to that effect, there is somehow the lurking sense that it was not he who really did it, but that there is a power, to turn Matthew Arnold's phrase to our use, " not ourselves, that works for " beauty as well as righteousness, and that it was this mystical force which wrought through him to the exquisite result. If you come to the second-best results, to the gold so alloyed that you may confidently stamp it your own, do you wish to proclaim it the precious metal without alloy? Do you wish to declare that it is to all intents and purposes quite as good as pure gold, or even better? Do you hold yourself quit of the duty of saying that it is second-best, that it is something mixed with copper or nickel, and of the value of oroide, say? You cannot bring yourself to this extreme of candor, and what right, then, have you to recognize that something else is fine gold when it is really so? Ought not you to feign that it is only about thirteen carats when it is actually eighteen?

Considerations like these always stayed Eugenio when it came to the point of deciding whether he would care to be his own reviewer, but the desire to be adequately reviewed still remained with him, a fond longing amid repeated disappointments. An author often feels that he has got too much praise, though he never has got all he wants. " Why don't they clap?" Doctor Holmes once whimsically demanded, speaking of his audiences in those simple early days when he went about lecturing like Emerson and Alcott and other saints and sages of New England. " Do they think I can't stand it? Why don't they give me three times

three? I can stand it very well." An author may
sometimes think he is fulsomely praised and may even
feel a sort of disgust for the slab adulation trowelled
upon him, but his admirer need not fear being accused
of insincerity. He may confidently count upon being
regarded as a fine fellow who has at worst gone wrong
in the right direction. It ought, therefore, to be a very
simple matter to content a veteran author in the article
of criticism, but somehow it is not.

Perhaps the trouble is in the nature of criticism,
which, unwillingly enough, no doubt, assumes to be and
to do more than it can. Its convention is that it is an
examination of a book and a report upon its qualities.
But it is not such a report, and it cannot be in the
limits assigned it, which are the only tolerable limits
with the reader. The author would not mind if the
critic's report were physically commensurate with his
book; but, of course, the reader could not stand that;
and, generous as they are, other authors might complain. Sometimes, as it is, they think that any one of
their number who gets something like a good report
from a critic is getting more than his deserts. Yet authors, though a difficult, are not an impossible generation. Few of them would allow that they are even unreasonable with regard to criticism, and they would
probably hail any improvement in its theories and methods with gratitude.

As criticism cannot be an adequate report upon the
qualities of a book, even a book which has not been
examined, why should it assume to do more than talk
about it and talk all the better for being merely tentative and altogether unfinal? Nobody can really be au-
thoritative concerning anything, for there is no one
whose wisdom will not be disputed by others of the
wise. The best way, then, might be for a reviewer to

go round collecting sentiment and opinion about the book he means to talk of, and then to give as many qualifying varieties of impression as the general un-handsomeness of human nature will allow him to give when they differ from his own impression. On the terms of the old and still accepted convention of criti-cism, Eugenio had himself done a vast deal of review-ing, an amount of it, in fact, that he could not consider without amaze, and in all this reviewing he had not once satisfied himself with his work. Never once had he written a criticism which seemed to him adequate, or more than an approximation to justice, even when he had most carefully, almost prayerfully, examined the work he reported upon. He was aware of writing from this mood or that, of feeling hampered by editorial conditions, of becoming impatient or jaded, and finally employing the hay-scales when he ought to have used the delicate balances with which one weighs out life-giving elixirs or deadly poisons. But he used to im-agine that if he could have put himself in the attitude of easy discussion or light comment, instead of the judicial pose he felt obliged to take, he could have ad-ministered a far finer and more generous measure of justice. In these moments he used to wonder whether something stated and organized in the way of intelli-gent talk about books might not be substituted for the conventional verdicts and sentences of the courts of criticism.

In this notion he proceeded upon a principle evolved from his own experience in fields far from the flinty and sterile ranges of criticism. He had not only done much reviewing in those days, but he had already writ-ten much in the kinds which he could not, in his modesty, bring himself to call " creative," though he did not mind others calling it so. Whatever had been the shortcomings of the conventional reports upon his work, it was his glad experience that nothing he said or meant, not the slightest intention or airiest intimation in his books, was ever wholly lost. Somewhere, some one, somehow had caught it, liked it, remembered it, and had by a happy inspiration written him of it, it might be diffident, it might be confident, of his pleasure in the recognition.

Such recognition was always more precious than the reports of the conventional critics, though if these were favorable the author was glad of them, as of any good that the gods gave. But what struck Eugenio was that such recognition was the real, the very, the vital criticism, and that if it could be evoked in behalf of others, in its sincerity, it might be helpful to the cause of literature far beyond anything that the courts of criticism could do or effect in its behalf. After all, as he said to himself, an author wrote for his readers and not for his critics, for pleasure and not for judgment; and if he could be assured publicly, as he sometimes was assured privately, that nothing he did was lost, he might be encouraged to keep on doing his best. Why, indeed, should not there be a critical journal embodying in a species of fragrant bouquet the flowers of thought and emotion springing up in the brains and bosoms of readers responsive to the influence of a new book? Such readers would have only to suppose themselves addressing the author direct, and the thing could be done. It might be done in another way by the authors contributing the praises privately sent him. In a time when personal letters to authors are constantly quoted in advertisements, this might not seem so immodest as in some earlier literary condition.

In the mean time the question of what shall be done for veteran authors who are always breaking new

304

ground still remains, and it is complicated by a fact of psychological import for the reader as well as the author. What first gives an author his hold upon the reader is not the novelty of his theme, but a pleasing, it may be a painfully pleasing, quality which in its peculiar variation must be called his personal quality. It is the sense of this in each of his successive books which deepens his hold upon the reader, and not the style, or the characters, or the intrigue. As long as this personal quality delights, he is new whether he breaks new ground or not, or he is newly welcome. With his own generation, with the readers who began young with him and have grown old with him, he is always safe. But there is danger for him with the readers who begin young with him after he has grown old. It is they who find his tales twice told and himself hackneyed, unless they have been trained to like his personal quality by their elders. This might be difficult, but it is not impossible, and ought not it to be the glad, the grateful care of such elders?

VI

THE FICKLENESS OF AGE

ALL forms of literature probably hold a great deal more meaning than people commonly get out of them; but prose may be likened to a cup which one can easily see to the bottom of, though it is often deeper and fuller than it looks; while verse is the fount through which thought and feeling continually bubble from the heart of things. The sources that underlie all life may be finding vent in a rhyme where the poet imagined he was breathing some little, superficial vein of his own; but in the reader he may unawares have reached the wells of inmost passion and given them release. The reader may himself live with a certain verse and be aware of it now and then merely as a teasing iterance that

> "From some odd corner of the mind
> Beats time to nothing in the brain."

But suddenly some experience, or perhaps the exfoliation of the outer self through the falling away of the withered years, shall open to him its vital and cosmical significance. He shall know then that it is not an idle whisper of song, but a message to his soul from the senate where the immortals gather in secular counsel and muse the wisdom of all the centuries since humanity came to its earliest consciousness. The bearer of the message may not have known it in the translation which it wears to the receiver; each must read it in his own tongue and read meaning into it; perhaps it always takes two to make a poet, and singer and listener are the twin spheres that form one star.

A valued correspondent of ours, one of those whose letters are oftener than we should like to own fraught with the suggestion of our most fortunate inspirations, believes himself to have been recently the confidant of the inner sense of certain lines in a familiar poem of Longfellow's. Its refrain had, from the first reading, chanted in the outer chamber of his ear, but suddenly, the other day, it sang to his soul with a newly realized purport in the words,

> " A boy's will is the wind's will,
>   And the thoughts of youth are long, long thoughts."

The words are, as the poet promptly declares, the burden of a Lapland song, which " is haunting his memory still," which " murmurs and whispers still," which " is singing and saying still," which " is mournful " and " sweet " and " fitful " and " fatal " and " strange " and " beautiful." Yet he seems not to have known, as our friend now thinks he himself knows, that they express a difference, unrecognized hitherto, between youth and age, and rightfully attribute to the young a steadfastness and persistence in objects and ideals formerly supposed the distinguishing qualities of the old. In other words, they have precipitated into his consciousness a truth unwittingly held in solution by both the poets in their verse. Or, if it was conveyed to him by their sensible connivance, he is the first who has been made its repositary. Or, if he cannot claim an exclusive property in the revelation, it is now his, in his turn, by that sad right of seniority whose advantages are not ours till there are few or none left to contest them with

us. One has not been promoted to them because of any
merit or achievement; one has simply lived into them;
and how much of one has died in the process of survival! The lines speak to our friend's age a language
which his youth could not have understood, and it is
because he is no longer young that he perceives how
long the thoughts of youth were and how brief the
thoughts of age.

He had always fancied that his later years should be
a time of repose in the faiths, loves, and joys through
which he realized himself. But nothing apparently
was farther from the fact. Such length of thoughts
as he had, such abiding pleasures, such persistent
hopes, were from his youth; and the later sort were
as the leaves of the tree to the tree itself. He put
them forth at the beginning of an epoch, a season, and
they dropped from him at the close. In as great bit-
terness as is consonant with his temperament he has
asked us why youth should ever have been deemed fickle
and age constant when so precisely the contrary is true.
Youth, he owns, is indeed full of vain endeavors and of
enterprises that come to nothing, but it is far more fixed
than age in its aspirations. His aspirations change now
with such rapidity that they seem different not only
from year to year, but from month to month, from
day to day. He has not merely discarded his old ideals,
he loathes them. He used to like going out to dinner,
above all things; and he was fond of lunches, even of
afternoon teas; but in a day, in an hour, such delights
became wearinesses and vexations of spirit. Formerly
he enjoyed travel with all its necessary concomitants.
It amused him to check his baggage and depart from
stations, to arrive at hotels and settle himself in new
rooms; the very domiciliation in sleeping-cars or the
domestication in diners had a charm which was appar-

ently perennial; a trip in a river-boat was rapture; an ocean voyage was ecstasy. The succession of strange faces, new minds, was an unfailing interest, and there was no occurrence, in or out of the ordinary, which did not give him release from self and form a true recreation. The theatre does not amuse him now, though the time has been, and lately, for the curtain, when it rose on a play, new or old, to lift his spirit with it and to hold him entranced till its fall. As for the circus, he once rejoiced in all its feats; performing elephants could not bore him, nor acts of horsemanship stale its infinite variety. But the time has come abruptly when the smell of the sawdust, or the odor of the trodden weed, mixed with the aroma of ice-cold lemonade, is a stench in his nostrils.

These changes of ideal have occurred, not through the failure of any powers that he can note in himself, but as part of the great change from youth to age, which he thinks is far greater morally than physically. He is still fairly strong; he has not lost his appetite or the teeth to gratify it; he can walk his miles, always rather two than ten, and rest refreshed from them; except that he does not like to kill things, he could trudge the whole day through fields and woods with his gun on his shoulder; though he does not golf, and cannot know whether or no it would bore him, he likes to wield the axe and the scythe in the groves and meadows of his summer place. When he stretches himself on the breast of the mother alike of flesh and grass, it is with a delicious sense of her restorative powers and no fear of rheumatism. If he rests a little longer than he once used, he is much more rested when he rises from his repose.

His body rejoices still in its experiences, but not his soul: it is not interested; it does not care to have known

its experiences or wish to repeat them.   For this reason
he thinks that it is his spirit which is superannuated,
while its " muddy vesture of decay " is in very tolerable
repair.   His natural man is still comparatively young,
and lives on in the long, long thoughts of youth; but
his supernatural man has aged, with certain moral effects which alarm his doubts of the pleasures he once
predicated of eternity.   " If it is going to be like *this*
with me!" he says to himself, and shrinks from supplying the responsive clause of his conditional.

But mainly his mind turns upon itself in contemplation of its earthly metamorphoses, in which it hardly
knows itself for the mind of the same man.   Its ap-
prehensions are for the time when, having exhausted
all the differences, it shall care for none; but meanwhile it is interested in noting the absurdity of that
conventional view of age as the period of fixed ideals.
It may be the period of fixed habits, of those helpless
iterances which imply no intentions or purposes; but it
is not the period in which the mind continues in this
or that desire and strives for its fulfilment.   The same
poet who sang at second hand those words of the Lapland song,

> " The thoughts of youth are long, long thoughts,"

erred, to our friend's sense, in singing of

> " The young heart hot and restless,
> And the old subdued and slow."

He believes the reverse would rightly characterize the
heart of youth and the heart of age.   Age is not slow
in its mental motions; it is hurried and anxious, with
that awful mystical apprehension of the swift-coming
moment when time shall be no more and nothing but
eternity shall be left.   It is not subdued; its heart is

hot with rebellion against the inevitable. But for youth there is no inevitable; there is no conclusion, no catastrophe, which it may not hope to escape; and, so it is patient of chances, it is glad of them. Its heart is not restless; it is quite at peace in the bosom which is secure of all the time there is.

Our friend believes that a variety of popular superstitions will fall at the recognition of the truth in this matter, and none more finally than that which attributes to the junior partner the unhappiness of those marriages in which youth and crabbed age try to live together. In such hazardous unions the junior partner is, for some unexplained reason, of the sex which has the repute of a generic fickleness as well as the supposed volatility of its fewer years. Probably repute wrongs it as much in one respect as in the other, but our friend contends only for greater justice to it in the last. In the light that he has come into, he holds that where such unions are unhappy, though they may have been formed with a fair appearance of affection, it is the senior partner who is to blame if blame may ever be attached to involuntary change. It is the senior partner who has wearied first of the companionship and wished for release with the impatience natural to age. This is intolerant of the annoyances which seem inherent in every union of the kind, and impatient of those differences of temperament which tell far more than any disparities of age, and which exist even where there are no such disparities. The intolerance, the impatience, is not more characteristic of the husband where he is the elder than of the wife in the much fewer instances of her seniority. In the unions where two old people join their faltering destinies, the risks of unhappiness are, logically, doubled; and our friend holds it a grotesque folly to expect anything else of marriages in which two lovers, disappointed of each other in their youth, attempt to repair the loss in their age. Where any such survive into later life, with the passion of earlier life still rife in their hearts, he argues that they had much better remain as they are, for in such a belated union as they aspire to the chances are overwhelmingly against them.

Very probably, like other discoverers, he is too much impressed with the value of his divination. It is something that, at any rate, can appeal for recognition only to the aged or the aging. With these we could imagine it bringing a certain consolation, a relief from vain regret, an acquittal from self-accusation. If one has suddenly changed for no apparent reason, one must be glad to find a reason in the constitution of things, and to attribute one's fickleness to one's time of life. Youth's errors have possibly been too much condoned upon grounds where age could more justly base its defence. It may be more reckless than age, but it is not nearly so rash. It keeps thinking its long, long thoughts and questioning the conclusions to which age eagerly hobbles or hurls itself from its crutches. Youth is deliberate, for it has plenty of time, while, as our friend notes, age has little but eternity before it. Not youth, but age, leaps from life's trolley while it is still in motion, or, after mismeasuring the time and space, limps impatiently before it and is rolled under its fender. You may see physical proof of this difference, our friend insists, in the behavior of two people, one young and one old, at any street-crossing; and why should so many old ladies fall on the stairs, but that they are apt to precipitate themselves wildly from landings where young girls linger to dream yet one dream more before they glide slowly down to greet the young men who would willingly wait years for them?

The distrust of eternity at which our friend hints is perhaps the painfulest of his newly discovered differences between youth and age. Resting so serenely as it does in practically unlimited time, with ideals and desires which scarcely vary from year to year, youth has no fears of infinity. It is not afraid but it shall have abundant occupation in the æons before it, or that its emotions or volitions shall first be exhausted. Its blithe notion of immortality is that it is immortal youth. It has no conception of age, and could not imagine an eternity of accomplished facts. It is, perhaps, for this reason that doubt of immortality never really comes to youth. One of the few things which our friend still believes is that every sceptic who deals honestly with his only history must be aware of an hour, almost a moment, of waning youth, when the vague potentiality of disbelief became a living doubt, thenceforward to abide with him till death resolve it. Endless not-being is unthinkable before that time, as after it endless being is unthinkable. Yet this unthinkable endless being is all that is left to age, and it is in the notion of it alone that age can get back to the long, long thoughts in which is surcease from unrest. Our old friend may accuse us of proposing the most impossible of paradoxes when we invite him to take refuge from his whirling ideals, not in an unavailing endeavor to renew the conditions of youth in time, but in the forecast of youth in eternity. We think that the error of his impatience, his despair with the state he has come to here, is largely if not wholly through his failure to realize that he is not going to wake up old in some other being, but young, and that the capacity of long, long thoughts will be renewed in him with the renewal of his life. The restlessness of age, its fickleness, its volatility, is the expression of immense fatigue.

It tosses from side to side and tries for this and that like a sick man from sheer weakness; or, rather, if the reader prefers another image, it is like some hapless wild thing caught by rising floods on a height of land which they must soon submerge, and running incessantly hither and thither as the water more narrowly hems it in.

Undoubtedly the mutability of age in its ideals has been increased of late by the restriction of human hope to the years which remain, few and brief to the longest earthly life, by the sciences which provisionally darken counsel. When these shall have penetrated to a point where they can discern the light, they will " pour the day " on the dim orbs of age and illumine the future with new hope. Then doubting age can enter into the rest now forbidden it and take its repose between illimitable horizons in the long, long thoughts of eternal youth. We speak here in behalf of the sceptic, the agnostic few. For the many who have not lost their hope because they have never lost their faith, doubtless all the trouble of change which disquiets our friend will seem something temperamental merely, and not something essential or inseparable from human nature. Their thoughts have remained long, their ideals steadfast, because they have not lost the most precious jewel of their youth—the star of trust and hope which

" Flames in the forehead of the morning sky."

These are the most enviable of their kind, and there are signs that their turn may be coming once more in the primacy to which their numbers have always entitled them. Only the other day we were reading a paper by a man of that science which deals with life on strictly physical lines, and drawing from it an immense consolation because it reaffirmed that the soul has not

only its old excuse for being in the unthinkability of
an automatic universe and the necessity of an intentional first cause, but with Evolution, in the regard of
some scientists, tottering on its throne, and Natural
Selection entering the twilight into which the elder
pagan deities have vanished, is newly warranted in
claiming existence as that indestructible life-property
or organizing power which characterizes kind through
kind from everlasting to everlasting. In this consolation we seemed well on our way back to the encounter
of a human spirit such as used to be rapt to heaven or
cast into hell for very disproportionate merits or de-
merits; but we were supported for the meeting by the
probability that in the fortunate event the spirit would
be found issuing from all the clouds of superstition,
and when it was reconstituted in the universal belief,
that the time, with eternity in its train, would have
returned for fitly hailing it in the apostrophe of the
Addisonian Cato:

"But thou shalt flourish in immortal youth,
Unhurt amidst the war of elements,
The wreck of matter, and the crush of worlds."

VII

THE RENEWAL OF INSPIRATION

There comes a time in the experience of perhaps every stated purveyor of intellectual food when the stock he has long been drawing upon seems finally exhausted. There is not a grain left in the barns where he had garnered up the harvests of the past; there is not a head of wheat to be found in the fields where he had always been able to glean something; if he shakes the tree of knowledge in the hope of a nut to crack or a frozen-thaw to munch, nothing comes down but a shower of withered leaves. His condition is what, in the parlance of his vocation, he calls being out of a subject, and it is what may happen to him equally whether he is preaching twice a Sunday from the pulpit, or writing leaders every day for a prominent journal, or merely contributing a monthly essay to a magazine. As the day or hour or moment approaches when he must give forth something from his destitution, he envies the hungriest of his auditors or readers who do not yet know that there is nothing in him to appease their famine. There is only the barren will to give which only a miracle can transform into a vitalizing bounty.

Yet is not this miracle always wrought? When did a pulpit ever fail of a sermon, or a journal of a leading article, or a magazine of its stated essay? The fact might argue the very contrary of the appearance and convince the desperate purveyor that what he mistook for hopeless need was choice which mocked him with a myriad alternatives. From cover to cover the Scripture is full of texts; every day brings forth its increase of incident; the moral and social and æsthetical world is open on every side to polite inquiry and teems with inspiring suggestion. If ever the preacher or editor or essayist fancies he has exhausted these resources, he may well pause and ask whether it is not himself that he has exhausted. There may be wanting the eye to see the riches which lie near or far, rather than the riches which are always inviting the eye.

A curious trait of the psychology of this matter is that it is oftener the young eye than the old which lacks the visual force. When Eugenio was beginning author and used to talk with other adolescent immortals of the joyful and sorrowful mysteries of their high calling, the dearth of subjects was the cause of much misgiving and even despair among them. Upon a certain occasion one of that divine company, so much diviner than any of the sort now, made bold to affirm: "I feel that I have got my technique perfect. I believe that my poetic art will stand the test of any experiment in the handling of verse, and now all that I want is a subject." It seemed a great hardship to the others, and they felt it the more keenly because every one of them was more or less in the same case. They might have none of them so frankly owned their fitness for their work as the one who had spoken, but they were all as deeply aware of it; and if any subject had appeared above the horizon there could have been no question among them except as to which should first mount his winged steed and ride it down. It did not occur to any of them that the want of a subject was the defect of their art, and that until they were equipped with the eye that never fails to see occasion for song all round the heavens they were not yet the champions of poetry which they fancied themselves. He who had uttered their common belief sufficiently proved afterward, in the range of things he did, that he had ultimately come into possession of the highest of the poetic gifts, the poetic vision of life, and that he had completed his art at a point where it had been most imperfect before, when he supposed it so perfect. As soon as he ceased looking for subjects, which were mainly the conventional themes of verse, the real and vital subjects began looking for him.

Eugenio himself, on his lower level, had something of the same experience. When he first began those inventions in prose which long seemed to him worthy of the best that his kindest friends said of them, he had great trouble in contriving facts sufficiently wonderful for the characters who were to deal with them, and characters high and noble enough to deal with the great and exalted facts. On one hand or the other his scheme was always giving out. The mirage of fancy which painted itself so alluringly before him faded on his advance and left him planted heavy-footed in the desert sands. In other words, he was always getting out of a subject. In the intervals between his last fiction and his next, when his friends supposed he was purposely letting his mind lie fallow (and perhaps willingly acquiesced in the rest they were sharing with him), he was really in an anguish of inquiry for something on which to employ his powers; he was in a state of excruciating activity of which the incessant agitation of the atoms in the physical world is but a faint image; his repose was the mask of violent vibrations, of volcanic emotions, which required months to clear them-

selves in the realization of some ideal altogether dis-
proportioned to the expenditure of energy which had
been tacitly taking place. At these periods it seemed
to him that his lot had been cast in a world where he
was himself about the only interesting fact, and from
which every attractive subject had been removed before
he came into it.

He could never tell just how or when all this changed,
and a little ray, very faint and thin at first, stole in
upon his darkness and broadened to an effulgence which
showed his narrow circle a boundless universe thronged
with the most available passions, interests, motives,
situations, catastrophes and dénouements, and characters eagerly fitting themselves with the most appropriate
circumstances. As nearly as he could make out, his
liberation to this delightful cosmos took place through
his gradual perception that human nature was of a
vast equality in the important things, and had its difference only in trifles. He had but to take other men
in the same liberal spirit that he took himself to find
them all heroes; he had but to take women at their own
estimate to find them all heroines, if not divinely beautiful, then interesting, fascinating, irresistibly better
than beautiful. The situation was something like this;
it will not do to give away his whole secret; but the reader needs only a hint in order to understand how in his
new mind Eugenio was overwhelmed with subjects.

After this illumination of his the only anxiety he
had was concerning his ability to produce all the masterpieces he felt himself capable of in the short time al-
lotted to the longest-lived writer. He was aware of a
duty to the material he had discovered, and this indeed
sometimes weighed upon him. However, he took courage from the hope that others would seize his point of
view and be able to carry on the work of producing

masterpieces indefinitely. They could never use up all the subjects, any more than men can exhaust the elements of the aluminium which abound in every piece of the common earth; but, in their constant reliance upon every-day life as the true and only source of surprise and delight in art, they could never be in the terrible despair which had afflicted him from time to time before his illumination.

Doubtless there is an overruling Providence in this matter which we may not distrust without accusing the order which has not yet failed in the due succession of the seasons and the days and nights. While we are saying it is never going to rain, it rains; or when it seems as if nature were finally frozen up, a thaw begins; when we feel that the dark will not end, the dawn is already streaking the east. If the preacher thinks that the old texts are no longer applicable to life, there is suddenly reported an outbreak of vice in the city which puts him in mind of Sodom and Gomorrah; or the opportune flight of a defaulter furnishes material for a homily which searches the consciences of half the congregation with the words of the commandment against stealing. The journalist wakes in heavy-eyed despair, but he finds from the papers on his breakfast-table that there has been a revolution in South America, or that the Socialists have been doing something in Belgium almost too bad even for Socialists as the capitalists imagine them, and his heart rises again. Even the poor magazine essayist, who has lived through the long month in dread of the hour when his copy shall be due, is not forbidden his reprieve. He may not have anything to say, but he certainly has something to say it about. The world is always as interesting to-day as it was yesterday, and probably to-morrow will not be so dull as it promises.

One reason for the disability of the essayist, as distinguished from the preacher or the journalist, is that he does not give himself range enough. Expecting to keep scrupulously to one subject, he cannot put his hand on a theme which he is sure will hold out under him to the end. Once it was not so. The essayists of antiquity were the most vagariously garrulous people imaginable. There was not one of them who, to our small acquaintance with them, kept to his proposition or ended anywhere in sight of it. Aristotle, Epictetus, Marcus Aurelius, Plutarch, they talk of anything but the matter in hand, after mentioning it; and when you come down to the moderns, for instance, to such a modern as Montaigne, you find him wandering all over the place. He has no sooner stated his subject than he begins to talk about something else; it reminds him (like Lincoln) of a story which has nothing to do with it; and that story reminds him of another, and so on, till the original thesis is left flapping in the breeze somewhere at the vanishing-point in the tortuous perspective and vainly signalling the essayist back. It was the same, or nearly the same, with the English essayists quite down to the beginning of the last century, when they began to cease being. The writers in the *Spectator,* the *Guardian,* the *Tatler,* the *Rambler,* and the rest, contrived to keep a loose allegiance to the stated topic, because they treated it so very briefly, and were explicitly off to something else in the next page or two with a fresh text. But if we come to such delightful masters of the art as Lamb and Leigh Hunt and De Quincey and Hazlitt, it will not be easy, opening at any chance point, to make out what they are talking about. They are apparently talking about everything else in the world but the business they started with. But they are always talking delightfully, and that is the great matter with any sort of talker.

When the reviewers began to supplant the essayists, they were even more contemptuously indifferent to the obligations of constancy. Their text was nominally some book, but almost as soon as they had named it they shut it and went off on the subject of it, perhaps, or perhaps not. It was for the most part lucky for the author that they did so, for their main affair with the author was to cuff him soundly for his ignorance and impudence, and then leave him and not return to him except for a few supplementary cuffs at the close, just to show that they had not forgotten him. Macaulay was a notorious offender in this sort; though why do we say offender? Was not he always delightful? He was and he is, though we no longer think him a fine critic; and he meant to be just, or as just as any one could be with a man whom one differed from in the early Victorian period.

But Macaulay certainly did not keep harking back to his text, if ever he returned to it at all. His instinct was that a preacher's concern was with his text, but not an essayist's or a reviewer's, and he was right enough. The essayist certainly has no such obligation or necessity. His reader can leave him at any moment, unless he is very interesting, and it does not matter where they part company. In fact, it might be argued that the modern fidelity to its subject is one of the chief evidences or causes of the essay's decay. The essayist tries to make a mechanical conscience perform the duty of that fine spiritual freedom in which the essay once had its highest effect with the reader, and in his dull loyalty to the stated thesis he is superficial as well as tiresome.

The true subject is not one subject only, but many. It is like that pungent bulb whose odorous energy increases with exfoliation, and remains a potent fragrance in the air after the bulb has substantially ceased to be under the fingers. The error of the modern essayist is to suppose that he can ever have a single subject in hand; he has a score, he has a hundred, as his elders and betters all know; and what he mistakes for his destitution is really his superfluity. If he will be honest (as he may with difficulty be), must not he recognize that what seems a search for one theme is a hesitation between many pressing forward for his choice? If he will make this admission we believe he will be nearer the fact, and he will be a much more respectable figure than he could feel himself in blindly fumbling about for a single thesis. Life is never, and in nothing, the famine, perhaps, that we imagine it. Much more probably it is a surfeit, and what we suppose are the pangs of hunger are really the miseries of repletion. More people are suffering from too much than from too little. Especially are the good things here in a demoralizing profusion. Ask any large employer of labor, and he will tell you that what ails the working-classes is an excess of pianos and buggies and opera-boxes. Ask any workman what ails his employer, and he will say that it is the ownership of the earth, with a mortgage on planetary space. Both are probably right, or at least one is as right as the other.

When we have with difficulty made our selection from the divine redundancy of the ideal world, and so far as we could have reduced ourselves to the penury of a sole possession, why do not we turn our eyes to the example of Nature in not only bringing forth a hundred or a thousand fold of the kind of seed planted, but in accompanying its growth with that of an endless variety of other plants, all coming to bear in a like profusion? Observe that wise husbandwoman (this is not the contradiction in terms it seems), how when her business is apparently a hay harvest, she mingles myriads of daisies and milkweed and wild carrot and redtop with the grass, and lets her fancy riot all round the meadow in a broidery of blackberries and asters and dogroses and goldenrod. She never works without playing; and she plays even while man is working—plays so graciously and winningly that it takes the heart with joy. Who has ever looked upon an old-world wheat-field, where poppies and vetches are frolicking among the ears, and begrudged Nature her pastime? No one, we will venture, but the owner of the field, who is perhaps also too much of a philosopher to grieve over it. In the ideal world it is much the same. There, too, art having chosen a kind brings it to bear with all the other kinds which have been lurking in the unconscious soil of the mind and only waiting tilth for any purpose before springing up in company with the selected seed. This is what makes the poets and novelists and dramatists so much more profitable reading than the moralists. From whom, indeed, has the vital wisdom of the race been garnered? Not from those hard, ethical masters who have sought to narrow culture to the business of growing precepts, but from the genial teachers who have inculcated amusement and breathed into the unwary mind some inspiration which escaped as unconsciously from themselves. Which philosopher or sage of them all has instructed mankind a hundredth part as much as Shakespeare, who supposed himself to be merely providing diversion for the patrons of the Globe Theatre?

It follows, if not directly, then a long way about, from what we have been saying, that the real artist is never at a loss for a subject. His trouble is too many themes, not too few; and, having chosen among them, his error will be in an iron sequence rather than in a desultory progression. He is to arrive, if at all, laden with the spoil of the wayside, and bringing with him the odor of the wild flowers carpeting or roofing the by-paths; if he is a little bothered by the flowering brambles which have affectionately caught at him in his course, that does not greatly matter; or, at least, it is better than coming back to his starting-point in boots covered with the mud of the high-road or coat powdered with its dust. The sauntering ease, the excursive delays, will be natural to the poet or the novelist, who is born to them; but the essayist must in a manner make them his own, if he would be an artist and survive among the masters, which there has been some doubt of his doing. It should be his care to shun every appearance of continuity; only in the practice of the fitful, the capricious, the desultory, can he hope to emulate the effects of the creative. With any other ideal he cannot hope to be fit company for the high minds who have furnished mankind with quotations. But for the prevalence of the qualities which we have been urging the essayist to cultivate, in the essays of Bacon, it is not probable that any one would ever have fancied that Bacon wrote Shakespeare.

VIII

THE SUMMER SOJOURN OF FLORINDO AND LINDORA

At the moment of this writing, everybody is hurrying into the country, eager to escape the horrors of summer in the city; at the moment when it becomes that reading we hope for, everybody will be hurrying into the city, eager to escape the horrors of summer in the country. At either moment the experiences of Florindo and Lindora should have a certain interest.

Florindo and Lindora are a married pair, still comparatively happy after forty years of wedded life, who have spent the part or the whole of each hot season out of town, sometimes in the hills, sometimes by the sea, sometimes in Europe. Their acquaintance with either form of sojourn, if not exhaustive, is so comprehensive that it might be cited as encyclopædic.

The first season or so they did not think of shutting up their house in the city, or doing more than taking, the latter part of August, a trip to Niagara or Saratoga or Cape May or Lake George, or some of those simple, old-fashioned resorts whose mere mention brings a sense of pre-existence, with a thrill of fond regret, to the age which can no longer be described as middle and is perhaps flattered by the epithet of three-quartering. No doubt people go to those places yet, but Florindo and Lindora have not been to any of them for so many summers that they can hardly realize them as still open:

for them they were closed in the earliest of the eighteen-seventies.

After that, say the third summer of their marriage, it appeared to Lindora essential to take board somewhere for the whole summer, at such an easy distance that Florindo could run up or down or out every Saturday afternoon and stay Sunday with her and the children; for there had now begun to be children, who could not teethe in town, and for whom the abundance of pure milk, small fruits, and fresh vegetables promised with the shade and safety of the farm was really requisite. She kept the house in town still open, as before, or rather half-open, for she left only the cook in it to care for her husband, and do the family wash, sent to and fro by express, while she took the second girl with her as maid. In the first days of September, when the most enterprising of the fresh vegetables were beginning to appear on the table, and the mosquitoes were going, and the smell of old potatoes in the cellar and rats in the walls was airing out, and she was getting used to the peculiar undulations of her bed, she took the little teethers back to town with her; and when she found her husband in the comfortable dimensions of their own house, with melons and berries and tender steak, and rich cream (such as never comes on " pure milk "), and hot and cold baths, and no flies, she could not help feeling that he had been very selfish. Now she understood, at least, why he never failed on Monday morning to wake in time for the stage to carry him to the station, and she said, No more farm-board for her if she knew it.

In those idyllic days, while they were making their way, and counting the cost of every step as if it were the proverbial first step, the next step for Lindora was a large boarding-house for the summer. She tried it first in the country, and she tried it next at the seaside, with the same number of feet of piazza in both cases, and with no distinct difference except in the price. It was always dearer at the seaside, but if it had been better she should not have thought it so dear. Yet, as it was dearer, she could not help thinking it was better; and there was the beach for the teethers to dig in, and there was an effect of superior fashion in the gossipers on the piazza, one to every three of the three hundred feet of the piazza, rocking and talking, and guessing at the yachts in the offing, and then bathing and coming out to lie on the sand and dry their hair.

At the farm she had paid seven dollars a week for herself, and half-price for the children; at the country boarding-house she had paid ten for herself, and again half-price for the children; at the seaside boarding-house the rate for her was fourteen dollars, and nine for the children and the maid. Everybody on the piazza said it was very cheap, but to Lindora it was so dear that she decided for Florindo that they could not go on keeping the house open and the cook in it just for him, as the expressage on the wash took away all the saving in that. If she allowed him to sleep in the house, he could pick up his meals for much less than they now cost. They must not burn their candle at both ends; he must put out his end. There was reason in this, because now Florindo was sometimes kept so late at business that he could not get the last train Saturday night for the beach, and he missed the Sunday with his family on which she counted so much. Thinking these things over during the ensuing winter, she began to divine, toward spring, that the only thing for the teethers, and the true way for Florindo, was for her to get away from the city to a good distance, where there would be a real change of air, and that a moderate hotel in the White Mountains or the Adirondacks was the only hopeful guess at their problem. If Florindo could not come for Sunday when they were off only an hour or two, it would be no worse for them to be seven or eight hours off. Florindo agreed the more easily because he had now joined a club, where he got his meals as comfortably as at home and quite as economically, counting in the cook. He could get a room also at the club, and if they shut the house altogether, and had it wired by the burglar-insurance company, they would be cutting off a frightful drain.

It was, therefore, in the interest of clearly ascertained economy that Lindora took her brood with her to a White Mountain hotel, where she made a merit of getting board for seventeen dollars and a half a week, when so many were paying twenty and twenty-five. Florindo came up twice during the summer, and stayed a fortnight each time, and fished, and said that it had been a complete rest. On the way back to town Lindora stopped for October in one of those nice spring-and-fall places where you put in the half-season which is so unwholesome in the city after a long summer in the country, and afterward she always did this. Fortunately, Florindo was prospering, and he could afford the increased cost of this method of saving. The system was practised with great success for four or five years, and then, suddenly, it failed.

Lindora was tired of always going to the same place, sick and tired; and, as far as she could see, all those mountain-places were the same places. She could get no good of the air if she bored herself; the nice people did not go to hotels so much now, anyway, and the children were dreadful, no fit associates for the teethers, who had long ceased to teethe but needed a summer outing as much as ever. A series of seasons followed when the married pair did not know where to go, in the person of the partner who represented them, and they had each spring a controversy vividly resembling a quarrel, but which was really not a quarrel, because the Dear knew that if it were not for the children Lindora would only be too glad never to leave their own house winter or summer, but just to stick there, year out and year in. Then, at least, she could look a little after Florindo, who had lived so much at the club that he had fairly forgotten he *had* a wife and children. The trouble was all with Florindo, anyway; he cared more for his business than his family, much; if he did not, he could have managed somehow to spend the summers with them. Other men did it, and ran down once a month, or once a fortnight, to put things in shape, and then came back.

Sleeping on a midnight view of her hard case, Lindora woke one morning with an inspiration; it might not be too much to call it a revelation. She wondered at herself, she was ashamed of herself, for not having thought of it before. Europe, of course, was the only solution. Once in Europe, you need not worry about where to go, for you could go anywhere. Europe was everywhere, and you had your choice of the Swiss mountains, where every breath made another person of you, or the Italian lakes with their glorious scenery, or the English lakes with their literary associations, or Scheveningen and all Holland, or Étretât, or Ostend, or any of those thousands of German baths where you could get over whatever you had, and the children could pick up languages with tutors, and the life was so amusing. Going to Europe was excuse enough in itself for Florindo to leave his business, and, if he could not be gone more than one summer, he could place her and the children out there till their health and education were completed, and they could all return home when it was time for the girls to think of coming out and the boys of going to college.

Florindo, as she expected, had not a reasonable word to say against a scheme that must commend itself to any reasonable man. In fact, he scarcely opposed it. He said he had begun to feel a little run down, and he had just been going to propose Europe himself as the true solution. She gladly gave him credit for the idea, and said he had the most inventive mind she ever heard of. She agreed without a murmur to the particular German baths which the doctor said would be best for him, because she just knew that the waters would be good for all of them; and when he had taken his cure the family made his after-cure with him, and they had the greatest fun, after the after-cure, in travelling about Germany. They got as far down as the Italian lakes in the early autumn, and by the time Florindo had to go back the rest were comfortably settled in Paris for the winter.

As a solution Europe was perfect, but it was not perpetual. After three years the bottom seemed to fall out, as Florindo phrased it, and the family came home to face the old fearful problem of where to spend the summer. Lindora knew where not to spend it, but her wisdom ended there, and when a friend who was going to Europe offered them her furnished cottage at a merely nominal rent, Lindora took it because she could not think of anything else. They all found it so charming that after that summer she never would think again of hotels or any manner of boarding. They hired cottages, at rents not so nominal as at first, but not so very extravagant if you had not to keep the city rent going, too; and it finally seemed best to buy a cottage, and stop the leak of the rent, however small it was.

Lindora did not count the interest on the purchase-money, or the taxes, or the repairs, or the winter caretaking.

She was now living, and is still living, as most of her contemporaries and social equals are living, not quite free of care, but free of tiresome associations, cramped rooms, bad beds, and bad food, with an environment which you can perfectly control if you are willing to pay the price. The situation is ideal to those without, and, if not ideal to those within, it is nevertheless the best way of spending the hot season known to competitive civilization. What is most interesting to the student of that civilization is the surprisingly short time in which it has been evolved. Half a century ago it was known only to some of the richest people. A few very old and opulent families in New York had country-places on the Hudson; in Boston the same class had summer houses at Nahant or in Pepperell. The wealthy planters of the South came North to the hotels of Saratoga, Lake George, and Niagara, whither the vast majority of the fashionable Northern people also resorted. In the West it was the custom to leave home for a summer trip up the lakes or down the St. Lawrence. But this was the custom only for the very sophisticated, and even now in the West people do not summer outside of their winter homes to at all the same extent as in the East.

The experience of Florindo and Lindora is easily parallelable in that of innumerable other married pairs of American race, who were the primitive joke of the paragrapher and the caricaturist when the day of farm-boarding began. Though the sun of that day has long set for Florindo and Lindora, it seems to be still at the zenith for most young couples beginning life on their forgotten terms, and the joke holds in its pristine freshness with the lowlier satirists, who hunt the city boarder in the country and the seaside boarding-houses. The Florindos and the Lindoras of a little greater age and better fortune abound in the summer hotels at the beaches and in the mountains, though at the more worldly watering-places the cottagers have killed off the hotels, as the graphic parlance has it. The hotels nowhere, perhaps, flourish in their old vigor; except for a brief six weeks, when they are fairly full, they languish along the rivers, among the hills, and even by the shores of the mournful and misty Atlantic.

The summer cottage, in fine, is what Florindo and Lindora have typically come to in so many cases that it may be regarded as the typical experience of the easily circumstanced American of the East, if not of the West. The slightest relaxation of the pressure of narrow domestic things seems to indicate it, and the reader would probably be astonished to find what great numbers of people, who are comparatively poor, have summer cottages, though the cottage in most cases is perhaps as much below the dignity of a real cottage as the sumptuous villas of Newport are above it. Summer cottages with the great average of those who have them began in the slightest and simplest of shanties, progressing toward those simulacra of houses aptly called shells, and gradually arriving at picturesque structures, prettily decorated, with all the modern conveniences, in which one may spend two-thirds of the year and more of one's income than one has a quiet conscience in.

It would not be so bad, if one could live in them simply, as Lindora proposed doing when she made Florindo buy hers for her, but the graces of life cannot be had for nothing, or anything like nothing, and when you have a charming cottage, and are living on city terms in it, you have the wish to have people see you doing it. This ambition leads to endless and rather aimless hospitality, so that some Lindoras have been known, after keeping a private hotel in their cottages for a series of summers, to shut them or let them, and go abroad for a much-needed rest, leaving their Florindos to their clubs as in the days of their youth, or even allowing them to live in their own houses with their cooks.

Nothing in this world, it seems, is quite what we want it to be; we ourselves are not all that we could wish; and, whatever shape our summering takes, the crumpled rose-leaf is there to disturb our repose. The only people who have no crumpled rose-leaves under them are those who have no repose, but stay striving on amid the heat of the city while the prey of the crumpled rose-leaf is suffering among the hills or by the sea. Those home - keeping Sybarites, composing seven-eighths of our urban populations, immune from the anguish of the rose-leaf, form themselves the pang of its victims in certain extreme cases; the thought of them poisons the pure air, and hums about the sleepless rest-seeker in the resorts where there are no mosquitoes. There are Florindos, there are Lindoras, so sensitively conscienced that, in the most picturesque, the most prettily appointed and thoroughly convenienced cottages, they cannot forget their fellow-mortals in the summer hotels, in the boarding-houses by sea or shore, in the farms where they have small fruits, fresh vegetables, and abundance of milk and eggs; yes, they even remember those distant relations who toil and swelter in the offices, the shops, the streets, the sewers; and they are not without an unavailing shame for their own good-fortune.

But is it really their good-fortune? They would not exchange it for the better fortune of the homekeepers, and yet it seems worse than that of people less voluntarily circumstanced. There is nothing left for Florindo and Lindora to try, except spending the summer on a yacht, which they see many other Florindos and Lindoras doing. Even these gay voyagers, or gay anchorers (for they seem most of the time to be moored in safe harbors), do not appear altogether to like their lot, or to be so constantly contented with it but that they are always coming off in boats to dine at the neighboring hotels. Doubtless a yacht has a crumpled rose-leaf under it, and possibly the keelless hull of the houseboat feels the irk of a folded petal somewhere.

Florindo and Lindora are not spoiled, she is sure of that in her own case, for she has never been unreasonably exacting of circumstance. She has always tried to be more comfortable than she found herself, but that is the condition of progress, and it is from the perpetual endeavor for the amelioration of circumstance that civilization springs. The fault may be with Florindo, in some way that she cannot see, but it is certainly not with her, and, if it is not with him, then it is with the summer, which is a season so unreasonable that it will not allow itself to be satisfactorily disposed of. In town it is intolerable; in the mountains it is sultry by day and all but freezing by night; at the seaside it is cold and wet or dry and cold; there are flies and mosquitoes everywhere but in Europe, and, with the bottom once out of Europe, you cannot go there without dropping through. In Lindora's experience the summer has had the deceitful effect of owning its riddle read at each new conjecture, but, having exhausted all her practical guesses, she finds the summer still the mute, inexorable sphinx for which neither farm-board, boardinghouses, hotels, European sojourn, nor cottaging is the true answer.

Sometimes Florindo or Lindora is out of all patience with the summer, and in a despair which she is careful to share with Florindo, as far as she can make him a partner of it. But as it is his business to provide the means of each new condition, and hers to prove it impossible, he is not apt to give way so fully as she. He tells her that their trouble is that they have always endeavored to escape an ordeal which if frankly borne might not have been so bad, and he has tried to make her believe that some of the best times he has had in summer have been when he was too busy to think about it. She retorts that she is busy, too, from morning till night, without finding the least relief from the summer ordeal or forgetting it a single moment.

The other day he came home from the club with a beaming face, and told her that he had just heard of a place where the summer was properly disposed of, and she said that they would go there at once, she did not care where it was.

"Well, I don't know," he answered. "There would have to be two opinions, I believe."

"Why?" she demanded, sharply. "Where is it?"

"In the other world. Fanshawe, the Swedenborgian, was telling me about it. In one of the celestial heavens —there seem to be seven of them—it appears that all the four seasons are absorbed into one, as all the different ages are absorbed into a sort of second youth. This sole season is neither hot nor cold, but has the quality of a perpetual springtime. How would you like that?"

Lindora was too vexed with him to make any answer, and he was sorry. He, too, felt the trouble of the summer more than he would allow, and he would willingly have got away from it if he could. Lindora's impatience with it amused him, but it is doubtful if in the moment of his greatest amusement with her impatience he had any glimpse of that law of the universal life by which no human creature is permitted to escape a due share of the responsibilities and burdens of the common lot, or realized that to seek escape from them is a species of immorality which is unfailingly punished like any other sin, in and from itself.

IX

TO HAVE THE HONOR OF MEETING

As the winter deepens and darkens, the people who have time and money to waste, and who are always seeking opportunities for squandering both, find none so gracious and graceful as giving dinners to other people who have time and money to waste. The prime condition of such dinners is that neither host nor guest shall need them. The presence of a person who actually wanted meat and drink would imply certain insuperable disqualifications. The guest must have the habit of dining, with the accumulated indifference to dinners and the inveterate inability to deal peptically with them which result from the habit of them. Your true diner must be well on in middle life, for though the young may eat and drink together and apparently dine, it is of the gray head difficultly bowed over the successive courses, and the full form of third youth straining its silken calyx and bursting all too richly out above it, that the vision presents itself when one thinks of dinners and diners.

After all the exclusions are made, dinner is still a theme so large that one poor Easy Chair paper could not compass it, or do more than attach itself here and there to its expanse. In fact, it was only one kind of dinner we had in mind at the beginning, and that was the larger or smaller public dinner. There the process

of exclusion is carried yet a step further, and the guests
are all men, and for the most part elderly men. The
exceptional public dinners where women are asked need
not be counted; and at other public dinners they do not
seem eager to throng the galleries, where they are
handsomely privileged to sit, looking down, among the
sculptured and frescoed arabesques, on the sea of bald
heads and shirt-fronts that surge about the tables below, and showing like dim, décolleté angels to the
bleared vision raised to them from the floor. As they
are not expected to appear till the smoking and speaking have begun, they grow fainter and fainter through
the clouds of tobacco and oratory, and it is never known
to the diners whether they abuse the chary hospitality
of coffee and ices offered them in their skyey height,
where from time to time the sympathetic ear may hear
them softly gasping, gently coughing.

It is a pity that none of these witnesses of a large
public dinner has recorded her bird's-eye impression of
it at the interesting moment when their presence is
suffered or desired. All those gray or bald heads, and
all those bulging shirt-fronts, must look alike at the
first glance, and it can be only to carefuler scrutiny
that certain distinctions of projecting whiskers and
mustaches pronounce themselves. The various figures,
lax or stiff in their repletion, must more or less repeat one another, and the pudgy hands, resting heavily
on the tables' edges or planted on their owners' thighs,
must seem of a very characterless monotony. The poor
old fellows ranked in serried sameness at the tables
slanted or curved from the dais where the chairman
and the speakers sit must have one effect of wishing
themselves at home in bed.

What do they really think of it, those angels, leaning
over and looking down on it? Does it strike them with

envy, with admiration? Does it seem one of the last
effects of a high and noble civilization? To their
"finer female sense," what is the appeal of that evanes-
cing spectacle, as the noise of the cheering and the
laughing and the clapping of hands rises to them at
some more rocket-like explosion of oratory? Is the
oratory mainly of the same quality to those supernal
intelligences as the fading spectacle? None of them
has said, and we may have still the hope that the whole
affair may have seemed to them the splendid and graceful ceremonial which it appears in the illustrations of
the next day's papers.

The speaking is perhaps not always so good as it
seems to the mellowed tolerance of the listener, when it
begins after all those courses of meat and drink, but
not perhaps always so bad as he thinks it when, the
morning following, he wakes "high sorrowful and
cloyed," and has not yet read the reports of it. In
confidence, however, it may be owned that it is apt
rather to be bad than good. If what has led up to it
has softened the critical edge of the listener, it has not
sharpened the critical edge of the speaker, and they
meet on the common ground where any platitude passes,
where a farrago of funny stories serves the purpose of
coherent humor, where any feeble flash of wit lights up
the obscurity as with an electric radiance, where any
slightest trickle or rinsing of sentiment refreshes "the
burning forehead and the parching tongue" like a gush
of genuine poetry. The mere reputation of the speaker
goes a great way, almost the whole way; and, especially
if he is a comic speaker, he might rise up and sit down
without a word and yet leave his hearers the sense of
having been richly amused. If he does more, if he
really says something droll, no matter how much below
the average of the give and take of common talk, the

listener's gratitude is frantic. It is so eager, it so out-
runs utterance, that it is not strange the after-dinner
speech should be the favorite field of the fake-humorist,
who reaps a full and ever-ripened harvest in it, and
prospers on to a celebrity for brilliancy which there is
little danger of his ever forfeiting so long as he keeps
there.

The fake-humorous speaker has an easier career than
even the fake-eloquent speaker. Yet at any given dinner the orator who passes out mere elocution to his
hearers has a success almost as instant and splendid
as his clowning brother. It is amazing what things
people will applaud when they have the courage of
one another's ineptitude. They will listen, after dinner, to anything but reason. They prefer also the old
speakers to new ones; they like the familiar taps of
humor, of eloquence; if they have tasted the brew before, they know what they are going to get. The note
of their mood is tolerance, but tolerance of the accustomed, the expected; not tolerance of the novel, the surprising. They wish to be at rest, and what taxes their
minds molests their intellectual repose. They do not
wish to climb any great heights to reach the level of
the orator. Perhaps, after all, they are difficult in their
torpidity.

The oratory seems to vary less throughout any given
dinner than from dinner to dinner, and it seems better
or worse according as the dinner is occasional or personal. The occasional dinner is in observance of some
notable event, as the Landing of the Pilgrims, or the
Surrender of Cornwallis, or the Invention of Gunpowder, or the Discovery of America. Its nature in-
vites the orator to a great range of talk; he may browse
at large in all the fields of verbiage without seeming to
break bounds. It rests with him, of course, to decide

whether he will talk too long, for the danger that he may do so cannot be guarded from the outside. The only good after-dinner speaker is the man who likes to speak, and the man who likes to speak is always apt to speak too much. The hapless wretch whom the chairman drags to his feet in a cold perspiration of despair, and who blunders through half a dozen mismated sentences, leaving out whatever he meant to say, is not to be feared; he is to be pitied from the bottom of one's soul. But the man whose words come actively to the support of his thoughts, and whose last word suggests to him another thought, he is the speaker to be feared, and yet not feared the worst of all. There is another speaker more dreadful still, who thinks as little standing as sitting, and whose words come reluctantly, but who keeps on and on in the vain hope of being able to say something before he stops, and so cannot stop.

The speaking at the occasional dinner, however, is much more in the control of the chairman than the speaking at the personal dinner. The old fashion of toasts is pretty well past, but the chairman still appoints, more or less, the subject of the speaker he calls up. He may say, if the dinner is in honor of the Invention of Gunpowder, "We have with us to-night a distinguished soldier who has burned a good deal of gunpowder in his time; and I am sure we should all like to hear from General Jones something of his experience with the new smokeless explosives." Or if it is the Discovery of America they are commemorating, he may call to his feet some representatively venerable citizen, with a well-earned compliment to his antiquity, and the humorous suggestion that he was personally knowing to the landing of Columbus. Then General Jones, or the venerable citizen, will treat at his pleasure of any subject under heaven, after having made his

manners to that given him by the chairman and professed his unfitness to handle it.

At the personal dinner, the speaker must in decency
stick for a while at least to his text, which is always
the high achievement of the honored guest, in law,
letters, medicine, arms, drainage, dry-goods, poultry-
farming, or whatever. He must not, at once, turn his
back on the honored guest and talk of other things;
and when sometimes he does so it seems rude.

The menu laid before the diner at this sort of dinner
may report a variety of food for the others, but for the
honored guest the sole course is taffy, with plenty of
drawn butter in a lordly dish. The honored guest is
put up beside the chairman, with his mouth propped
open for the taffy, and before the end he is streaming
drawn butter from every limb. The chairman has
poured it over him with a generous ladle in his opening
speech, and each speaker bathes him with it anew from
the lordly dish. The several speakers try to surpass
one another in the application, searching out some corner or crevice of his personality which has escaped
the previous orators, and filling it up to overflowing.
The listeners exult with them in their discoveries, and
roar at each triumph of the sort: it is apparently a
proof of brilliant intuition when a speaker seizes upon
some forgotten point in the honored guest's character
or career and drenches it with drawn butter.

To what good end do men so flatter and befool one
of their harmless fellows? What is there in the nature
of literary or agricultural achievement which justifies
the outrage of his modest sense of inadequacy? It is a
preposterous performance, but it does not reach the
climax of its absurdity till the honored guest rises,
with his mouth filled with taffy, and, dripping drawn
butter all over the place, proceeds to ladle out from the

lordly dish, restored to its place before the chairman, a portion for each of the preceding speakers. He may not feel quite like doing it. In their fierce rivalry of adulation, some of them, in order to give fresh flavor to the taffy, may have mingled a little vinegar with it. One may have said that the bantams of the honored guest were not perhaps as small as some other bantams, but that the colossal size of his shanghais was beyond parallel. Another may have hinted, for the purpose of superiorly praising his masterly treatment of the pip, that the diet of his hens was not such as to impart to their eggs the last exquisite flavor demanded by the pampered palate of the epicure. Another yet may have admitted that the honored guest had not successfully grappled with the great question of how to make hens lay every working-day of the year, and he may have done this in order to heighten his grand climax that the man who teaches a hen to lay an egg with two yolks where she laid eggs of but one yolk before is a greater benefactor to the human race than all the inventors of all the missiles of modern warfare. Such a poultry-farmer, he may have declared, preparatory to taking his seat amid thunders of applause, is to other poultry-farmers what the poet who makes the songs of a people is to the boss who makes their laws. This sentiment may have been met with a furore of acceptance, all the other guests leaning forward to look at the honored guest and concentrate their applause upon him, as they clapped and cheered, and one fine fellow springing to his feet and shouting, " Here's to the man who made two-yolk eggs grow where one-yolk eggs grew before."

Yet these artfully studied qualifications of the cloying sweet may have been all of the taste of wormwood to the honored guest, who cared nothing for his easy triumph with shanghais and the pip and these two-yolk

344

eggs, but prided himself on his bantams and his hen-food, and was clinging to the hope that his discoveries in the higher education would teach hens to observe the legal holidays if they could not be taught to lay on every working-day, and was trusting to keep his measure of failure a secret from the world. It would not do, however, to betray anything of his vexation. That would be ungracious and ungrateful, and so he must render back taffy for taffy, drawn butter for drawn butter, till the whole place sticks and reeks with it.

Of course, the reader—especially if he has never been asked to a personal dinner of this sort—will be saying that the fault is not with the solemnity or its nature, but with the taste of those who conduct the ceremony. He will no doubt be thinking that if he were ever made the object of such a solemnity, or the chairman, or the least of the speakers, he would manage differently. Very likely he will allege the example of the Greeks, as we have it recorded in the accounts of the banquet offered to Themistocles after the battle of Salamis, and the supper given to Æschylus on the hundredth performance of the *Œdipus* of Sophocles.

The supper has always been considered rather a refinement upon the banquet, in taste, as it was offered to the venerable poet not upon the occasion of any achievement of his own, but in recognition of the prolonged triumph of his brother dramatist, in which it was assumed that he would feel a generous interest. The banquet to Themistocles was more in the nature of a public rejoicing, for it celebrated a victory due as much to the valor of all the Greeks as to the genius of the admiral; and it could, therefore, be made more directly a compliment to him. Even under these circumstances, however, the guest of the evening occupied an inconspicuous place at the reporters' table, while he

was represented on the chairman's right by the bust of
Poseidon, hastily modelled for the occasion by Prax-
iteles, and dedicated to Themistocles, who was a plain
man, but whose portrait, even if he had been handsome,
it was thought would not have looked well in such a
position at a time when portrait-statuary was unknown.
The only direct allusion to him was in the opening toast,
"The Dewey of Our Day," which was drunk sitting,
the guests rising from their recumbent postures in honor
of it. The chairman's opening address was almost
wholly a plea for the enlargement of the Athenian
navy : the implication that the republic had been saved,
in spite of its inefficient armament, was accepted as the
finest possible compliment to the guest of the evening.
The note of all the other speeches was their exquisite
impersonality. They got further and further from the
occasion of the evening, until the effort of Demosthenes
closed the speaking with a scathing denunciation of the
machine politicians who had involved the Athenians in
a war with Persia to further the interests of Sparta.
It was held that this was the noblest tribute which
could be paid to the genius of the man who had brought
them safely out of it. As the company broke up, Di-
ogenes with his lantern approached Themistocles, who
was giving the reporters copies of the speech he had
not been asked to deliver, and, after examining his
countenance with a sigh of disappointment, accom-
panied him home as far as his own tub; Athens at
that time being imperfectly lighted, and the reform
government having not yet replaced the street names
wantonly obliterated under the régime of the Thirty
Tyrants.

At the supper to Æschylus the tablets of the menu
were inscribed with verses from the elder poet ingen-
iously chosen for their imaginable reference to the mas-

terpiece of the younger, whose modesty was delicately spared at every point. It was a question whether the committee managing the affair had not perhaps gone too far in giving the supper while Sophocles was away from Athens staging the piece at Corinth; but there was no division of opinion as to the taste with which some of the details had been studied. It was considered a stroke of inspiration to have on the speaker's left, where Sophocles would have sat if he had been present at a supper given to Æschylus, the sitting figure of Melpomene, crowned with rosemary for remembrance. No allusion was made to Æschylus during the evening, after his health had been proposed by the chairman and drunk in silence, but a great and exquisite surprise was reserved for him in the matter of the speeches that followed. By prior agreement among the speakers they were all ostensibly devoted to the examination of the *Œdipus* and the other dramas of Sophocles, which in his absence were very frankly dealt with. But the unsparing criticism of their defects was made implicitly to take the character of appreciation of the Æschylus tragedies, whose good points were all turned to the light without open mention of them. This afforded the aged poet an opportunity of magnanimously defending his younger *confrère*, and he rose to the occasion, beaming, as some one said, from head to foot and oozing self-satisfaction at every pore. He could not put from him the compliments not ostensibly directed at him, but he could and did take up the criticisms of the Sophoclean drama, point by point, and refute them in the interest of literature, with a masterly elimination of himself and his own part in it. A Roman gentleman present remarked that he had seen nothing like it, for sincere deprecation, since Cæsar had refused the thrice-offered crown on the Lupercal; and

the effect was that intended throughout—the supreme
honor of Æschylus in the guise of a tribute to Sophocles. The note of the whole affair was struck by the
comic poet Aristophanes, whom the chairman called
upon to make the closing speech of the evening, and
who merely sat up long enough to quote the old Attic
proverb, "Gentlemen, there are many ways to kill a
dog besides choking him to death with butter," and then
lay down again amid shrieks of merriment from the
whole company.

There is, perhaps, a middle course between the American and Athenian ways of recognizing achievement in
the arts or interests, or of commemorating great public events. This would probably derive from each certain advantages, or at least the ancient might temper
the modern world to a little more restraint than it now
practises in the celebration of private worth, especially.
The public events may be more safely allowed to take
care of themselves, though it is to be questioned whether
it is well for any people to make overmuch of themselves. They cannot do it without making themselves
ridiculous, and perhaps making themselves sick of what
little real glory there is in any given affair; they will
have got that so inextricably mixed up with the vainglory that they will have to reject the one to free themselves from the humiliating memory of the other.

There is nothing that so certainly turns to shame in
the retrospect as vainglory, and this is what the personal dinner is chiefly supposed to inspire in the victim
of it. If he is at all honest with himself, and he probably is before he can have done anything worthy of
notice, he knows perfectly well that he has not merited
all if any of the fond flatteries with which he is heaped,
as he sits helpless with meat and drink, and suffers
under them with the fatuous smile which we all have

seen and which some of us have worn. But as the flatterers keep coming on and on, each with his garland of tuberoses or sunflowers, he begins to think that there must be some fire where there is so much smoke, and to feel the glow of the flame which he is not able exactly to locate. He burns in sympathy with his ardent votaries, he becomes inevitably a partner in his own apotheosis. It is the office of the sad, cold morrow, and the sadder and colder after-morrows, to undo this illusion, to compress his head to the measure of his hat, to remove the drawn butter from his soul.

They may never wholly succeed, but this is not probable, and it is not against a permanent *folie des grandeurs* that we need seek to guard the victim of a personal dinner. We have, indeed, so much faith in the ultimate discretion of the race that we should be quite willing to intrust the remarkable man himself with the office of giving himself a public dinner when he felt that his work merited signal recognition. In this way the whole affair could be kept within bounds. He could strike the note, he could set the pace, in his opening address; and, having appointed the speakers, with a full knowledge of their honesty and subordination, he could trust the speeches to be sane and temperate. In calling the speakers successively up, he could protest against anything that seemed excessive eulogy in the words already spoken, and could invite a more modest estimate of his qualities and achievements in the speeches to follow.

X

A DAY AT BRONX PARK

In the beginning of the season which is called Silly in the world of journalism, because the outer vacuity then responds to the inner, and the empty brain vainly interrogates the empty environment for something to write of, two friends of the Easy Chair offered to spend a holiday in search of material for a paper. The only conditions they made were that the Easy Chair should not exact material of weight or importance, but should gratefully accept whatever they brought back to it, and make the most of it. On these terms they set out on their labor of love.

By the time the sun had quitted the face of the vast apartment-house on which the day habitually broke, and had gone about its business of lighting and heating the city roofs and streets, the holiday companions were well on their way up the Third Avenue Elevated toward that region of the Bronx which, in all their New York years, they had never yet visited. They exulted at each stop and start of the train in the long succession of streets which followed so fast upon one another that the guards gave up trying to call them out as a hundred-and-so-many, and simply said Fifty-fifth, and Sixty-sixth, and Seventy-seventh Street. This slight of their duty to the public comported agreeably with the slip-

shod effectiveness of the whole apparatus of the New
York life: the rows and rows of shops, the rows and
rows of flats, the rows and rows of back yards with
miles of wash flying in the soft May wind, which, probably, the people in the open car ahead felt almost a
gale.

When the train got as far as the composite ugliness
of the ships and tugs and drawbridges of Harlem River,
the companions accepted the ensemble as picturesqueness, and did not require beauty of it. Once they did
get beauty in a certain civic building which fronted the
track and let fall a double stairway from its level in
a way to recall the Spanish Steps and to get itself
likened to the Trinità de' Monti at Rome.

It was, of course, like that only in their fond remembrance, but this was not the only Roman quality
in their cup of pleasure that day; and they did not care
to inquire whether it was merely the flavoring extract
of fancy, or was a genuine infusion from the Italian
sky overhead, the classic architectural forms, the loosely
straggling grass, the flowering woods, the rapture of the
birds, the stretches of the river, the tumbling rapids,
which so delicately intoxicated them. There was a
certain fountain gave a peculiar authenticity to their
pleasure, as of some assurance blown in the bottle from
which their joy-draught was poured. Nowhere else but
in Rome could they have imagined such a group of
bronze men and maidens and web-footed horses struggling so bravely, so aimlessly (except to show their figures), in a shallow bowl from which the water spilled
so unstintedly over white marble brims beginning to
paint themselves palely green.

At the end of their glad day this fountain came last
of the things that made Bronx Park such a paradise
for eight hours; though it might have been their first

delight if they had taken one way about instead of another in their tour of the large, easy pleasance. But
suddenly at half - past eleven they found themselves
ravenously hungry, and demanded to be driven to the
best restaurant by the shortest way that the mild youth
whom they fell to at once inside the park gate could
find.

He had the very horse he ought to have had—old,
weary, infirm, decently hiding its disabilities under a
blanket, and, when this was stripped away, confessing
them in a start so reluctant that they had to be explained as the stiffness natural to any young, strong,
and fresh horse from resting too long. It did, in fact,
become more animated as time went on, and perhaps it
began to take an interest in the landscape left so charmingly wild wherever it could be. It apparently liked
being alive there with its fares, kindred spirits, who
could appreciate the privacy of a bland Monday after
the popular outing of the day before. Almost nobody
else was in the park. For a time they noted only a
young fellow with a shut book in his hand taking his
way up a woody slope and fading into a green shadow;
but presently they came to a grassy point running down
to the road, where, under a tree, there was a young
mother sitting with an open book in her lap, and, a
little way from her outstretched little foot, her baby
asleep in the smallest of go-carts—the collapsible sort
that you can fold and carry in the cars and then unfold
for use when you come to the right place. The baby
had a white sunbonnet, and a thick fringe of her straw-
colored hair came out over her forehead under it, and
when the companions smiled together at the baby, and
the horse intelligently faltered, the young mother flut-
tered the idle leaves of her book with her hand and
smiled back at them, and took the credit of the little

ZOÖLOGICAL GARDENS, BRONX PARK.

one, not unkindly, yet proudly. They said it was all
as nice as it could be, and they were still so content in
her and her baby that, when they had to drive out of the
park to cross a street to the section where the restaurant
and the menagerie were, they waited deferentially for a
long, long funeral to get by. They felt pity for the
bereaved, and then admiration for people who could
afford to have so many carriages; and they made their
driver ask the mounted policeman whose funeral it
was. He addressed the policeman by name, and the
companions felt included in the circle of an acquaintance where a good deal of domesticity seemed to prevail. The policeman would not join in the conjecture
that it was some distinguished person; he did not give
his reasons; and the pair began to fret at their delay,
and mentally to hurry that poor unknown underground
—so short is our patience with the dead! When at last
their driver went up round the endless queue of hacks,
it suddenly came to an end, and they were again in
the park and among the cages and pens and ranges
of the animals, in the midst of which their own restaurant appeared. An Italian band of mandolins
and guitars was already at noonday softly murmuring and whimpering in the corner of the veranda
where the tables were set; and they got an amiable
old waiter, whose fault it was not if spring-lamb ma-
tures so early in the summer of its brief term as to
seem last-fall-lamb. There is no good reason either to
suppose he did not really believe in the pease. But
why will pease that know they have been the whole
winter in the can pretend to be just out of the pod?
Doubtless it is for every implication that all vegeta-
tion is of one ichor with humanity; but the waiter
was honester than the pease. He telephoned for two
wheeled chairs, and then said he had countermanded

them because they would be half an hour coming; but again he telephoned, for by this time the pair had learned that they might drive into the zoological grounds, but not drive round them; and they saw from the window the sun smoking hot on the asphalt paths their feet must press.

While the chairs lingered on the way, they went to get what comfort they could from the bears, whose house was near at hand. They might well have learned patience here from a bear trying to cope with a mocking cask in a pool. He pushed it under the water with his paw and held it hard down; when he turned away as if *that* cask were done for, there it was bobbing about on the surface, and he had to down it again and hold it under till life seemed extinct. At last he gave it up and left it floating in triumph, but one could infer with what perseverance he would renew the struggle presently.

There might have been too many bears; but this was the fault of all their fellow-captives except perhaps the elephants. One cannot really have enough of elephants; and one would have liked a whole herd of giraffes, and a whole troop of gnus would not have glutted one's pleasure in their goat-faces, cow-heads, horse-tails, and pig-feet. But why so many snakes of a kind? Why such a multiplicity of crocodiles? Why even more than one of that special pattern of Mexican iguana which looked as if cut out of zinc and painted a dull Paris green? Why, above all, so many small mammals?

Small mammals was the favorite phrase of the friendly colored chair-man, who by this time had appeared with an old-soldier comrade and was pushing the companions about from house to house and cage to cage. Small mammals, he warned them, were of an offensive odor, and he was right; but he was proud of them and of such scientific knowledge of them as he had. The old soldier did not pretend to have any such knowledge. He fell into a natural subordination, and let his colored superior lead the way mostly, though he asserted the principle that this is a white man's country by pushing first to the lions' house instead of going to the flying-cage, as his dark comrade instructed him.

It was his sole revolt. "But what," we hear the reader asking, "is the flying-cage?" We have not come to that yet; we are lingering still at the lions' house, where two of the most amiable lions in the world smilingly illustrate the effect of civilization in such of their savage species as are born in the genial captivity of Bronx Park. We are staying a moment in the cool stone stable of the elephants and the rhinoceroses and the hippopotamuses; we are fondly clinging to the wires of the cages where the hermit-thrushes, snatched from their loved solitude and mixed with an indiscriminate company of bolder birds, tune their angelic notes only in a tentative staccato; we are standing rapt before the awful bell-bird ringing his sharp, unchanging, unceasing peal, as unconscious of us as if he had us in the heart of his tropical forest; we are waiting for the mighty blue Brazilian macaw to catch our names and syllable them to the shrieking, shrilling, snarling society of parrots trapezing and acrobating about him; we are even stopping to see the white peahen wearing her heart out and her tail out against her imprisoning wires; we are delaying to let the flying-cage burst upon us in the unrivalled immensity promised. That is, we are doing all this in the personalities of those holiday companions, who generously found the cage as wide and high as their chair-men wished, and gratefully gloated upon its pelicans and storks and cranes and

swans and wild geese and wood-ducks and curlews and
sea-pigeons, and gulls, and whatever other water-fowl
soars and swims. It was well, they felt, to have had
this kept for the last, with its great lesson of a com-
munistic captivity in which all nations of men might
be cooped together in amity and equality, instead of
being, as now, shut up each in his own cell of need and
fear.

Not having come in an automobile, the companions
were forced by an invidious regulation to find their
carriage outside the gate of the Concourse; but neither
the horse nor the driver seemed to feel the slight of
the discrimination. They started off to complete the
round of the park with all their morning cheerfulness
and more; for they had now added several dollars to
their tariff of charges by the delay of their fares, and
they might well be gayer. Their fares did not refuse
to share their mood, and when they crossed the Bronx
and came into the region of the walks and drives they
were even gayer than their horse and man. These were
more used to the smooth level of the river where it
stretched itself out between its meadowy shores and
mirrored the blue heaven, rough with dusky white
clouds, in its bosom; they could not feel, as their fares
did, the novelty in the beauty of that hollow, that wide
grassy cup by which they drove, bathed in the flowery
and blossomy sweetness that filled it to its wood-bor-
dered brim.

But what is the use of counting one by one the joys
of a day so richly jewelled with delight? Rather let us
heap them at once in the reader's lap and not try to
part the recurrence of the level-branched dogwoods in
bloom; the sunny and the shadowy reaches of the woods
still in the silken filminess of their fresh young leaves;
the grass springing slenderly, tenderly on the unmown

slopes of the roadsides, or giving up its life in spicy sweetness from the scythe; the gardeners pausing from their leisurely employ, and once in the person of their foreman touching their hats to the companions; the wistaria-garlanded cottage of the keeper of the estate now ceded to the city; the Gothic stable of the former proprietor looking like a Gothic chapel in its dell; the stone mansion on its height opening to curiosity a vague collection of minerals, and recalling with its dim, hard-wood interior the ineffectual state of a time already further outdated than any colonial prime; the old snuff-mill of the founders, hard by; the dam breaking into foam in the valley below; the rustic bridge crossing from shore to shore, with steel-engraving figures leaning on its parapet and other steel-engraving presences by the water's brink.

The supreme charm is that you are so free to all things in that generous park; that you may touch them and test them by every sense; that you may stray among the trees, and lie down upon the grass, and possess yourself indiscriminately of them quite as if they were your own.

They are indeed yours in the nobler sense of public proprietorship which will one day, no doubt, supersede all private ownership. You have your share of the lands and waters, the birds in the cages and the beasts, from the lions and elephants in their palaces, and the giraffes freely browsing and grazing in their paddock, down to the smallest of the small mammals giving their odor in their pens. You have as much right as another to the sculptures (all hand-carved, as your colored chair-man will repeatedly tell you) on the mansions of the lordlier brutes, and there is none to dispute your just portion of the Paris-green zinc iguana, for you have helped pay for them all.

The key-word of this reflection makes you anxious to find whether your driver will make you pay him too much, but when you tot up the hours by his tariff, and timidly suggest that it will be so many dollars and offer him a bill for the same, he surprises you by saying, No, he owes you fifty cents on that; and paying it back.

Such at least was the endearing experience of the companions at the end of their day's pleasure. Not that it was really the end, for there was the airy swoop homeward in the Elevated train, through all that ugly picturesqueness of bridges and boats and blocks of buildings, with the added interest of seeing the back-flying streets below now full of children let loose from school for the afternoon, and possessing the roadways and sidewalks as if these, too, were common property like the park. It seemed to the companions that the children increased toward the shabbier waterside, and decreased wherever the houses looked better, through that mystical law of population by which poverty is richer than prosperity is in children. They could see them yelling and screaming at their games, though they could not hear them, and they yelled and screamed the louder to the eye because they were visibly for the greatest part boys. If they were the offspring of alien parents, they might be a proof of American decay; but, on the other hand, the preponderance of boys was in repair of that disproportion of the sexes which in the east of these States is such a crying evil.

Perhaps it was the behavior of the child in the opposite seat which made the companions think of girls as a crying evil; the mental operations are so devious and capricious; but this child was really a girl. She was a pretty child and prettily dressed, with a little face full of a petulant and wilful charm, which might well have been too much for her weak, meek young mother. She wanted to be leaning more than half out of the window and looking both ways at once, and she fought away the feebly restraining hands with sharp, bird-like shrieks, so that the companions expected every moment to see her succeed in dashing herself to death, and suffered many things from their fear. When it seemed as if nothing could save them, the guard came in and told the weak, meek mother that the child must not lean out of the window. Instantly, such is the force of all constituted authority among us, the child sat down quietly in her mother's lap, and for the rest of the journey remained an example to angels, so that the companions could rejoice as much in her goodness as in her loveliness. She became, indeed, the crown of their happy day, a day so happy that now in the faint air of August it is hard to believe it even of May.

THE END

Date Due

	PRINTED	IN U. S. A.	